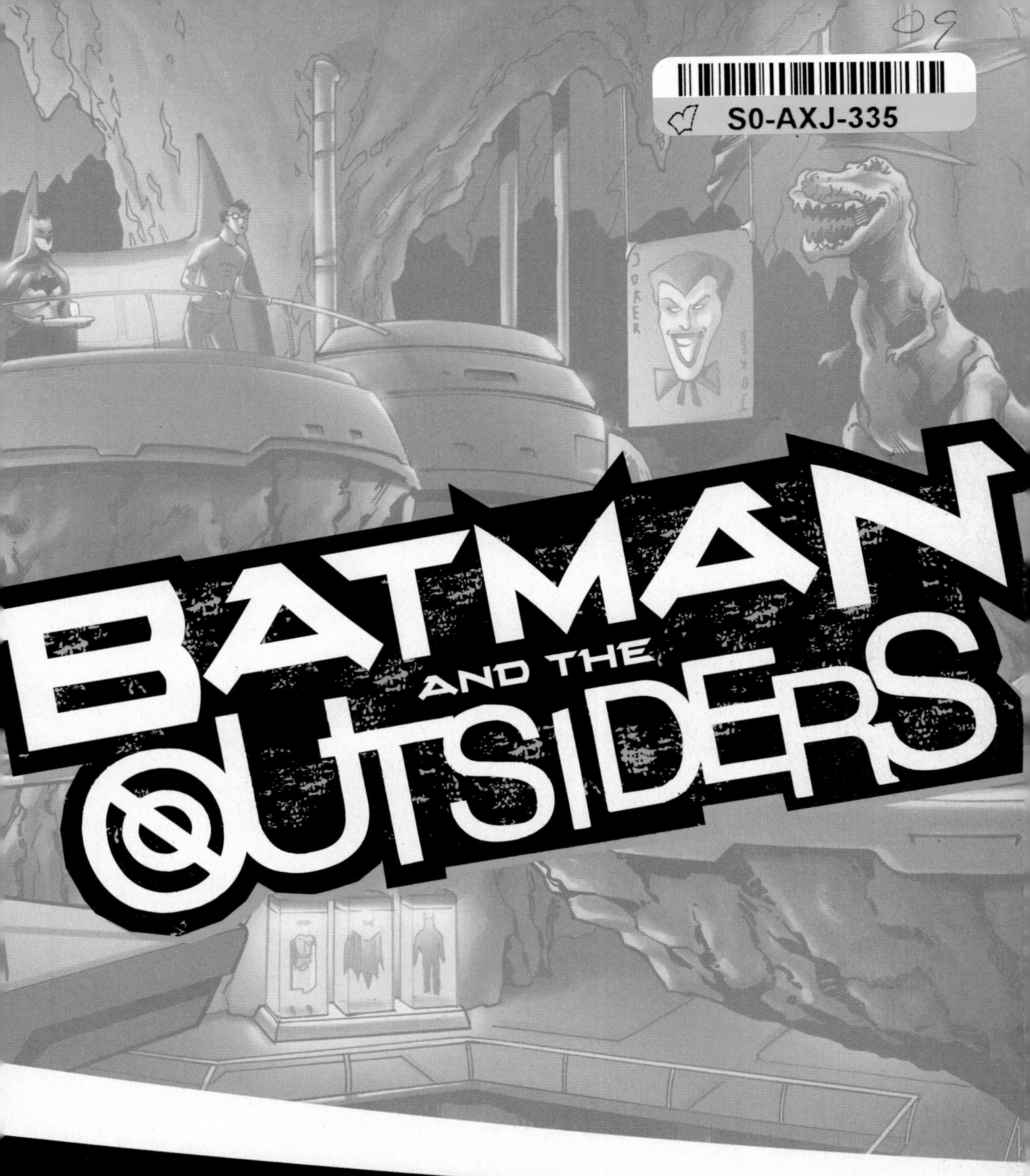

# BATMAN AND THE OUTSIDERS

## The SNARE

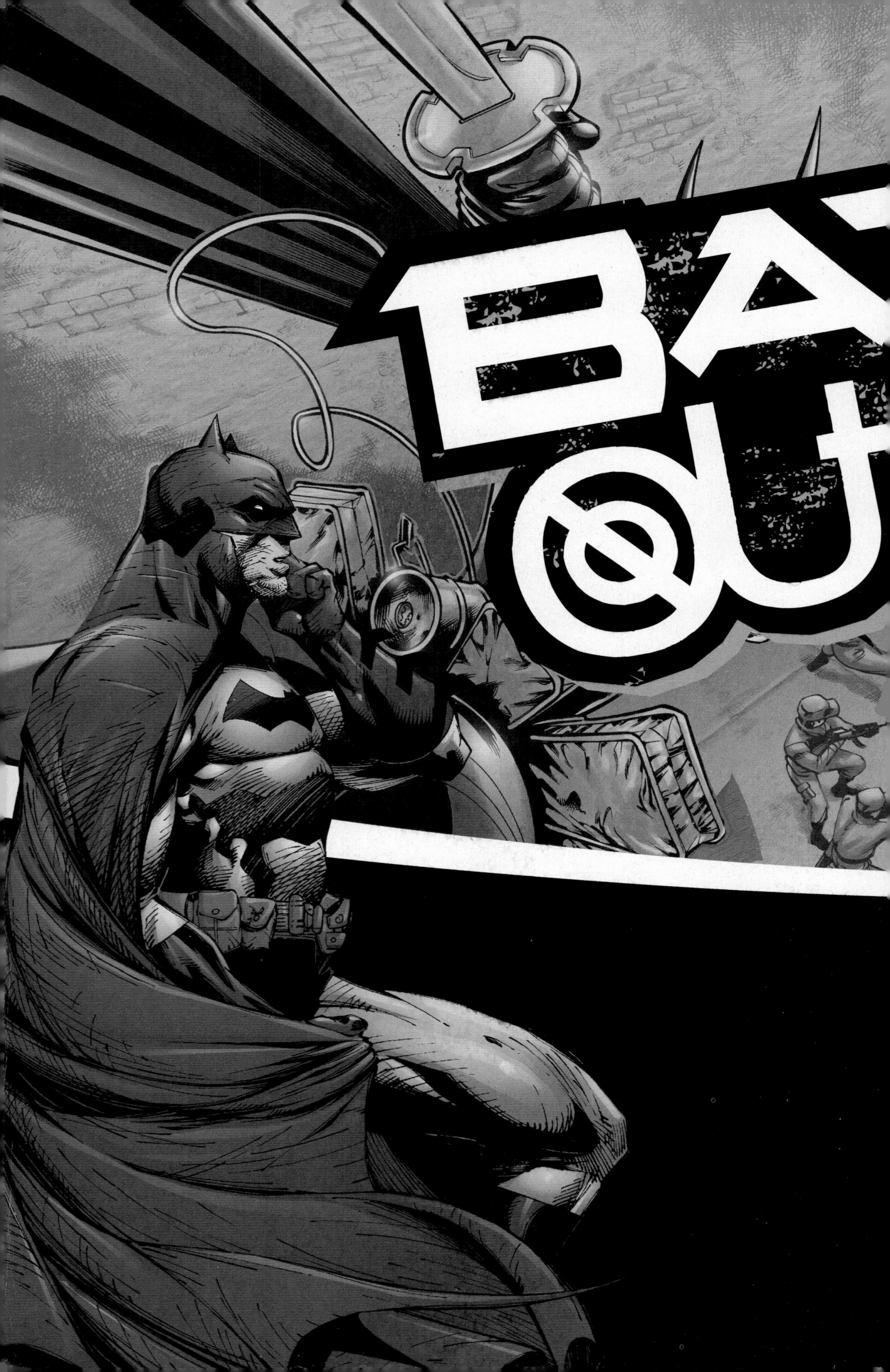
BA

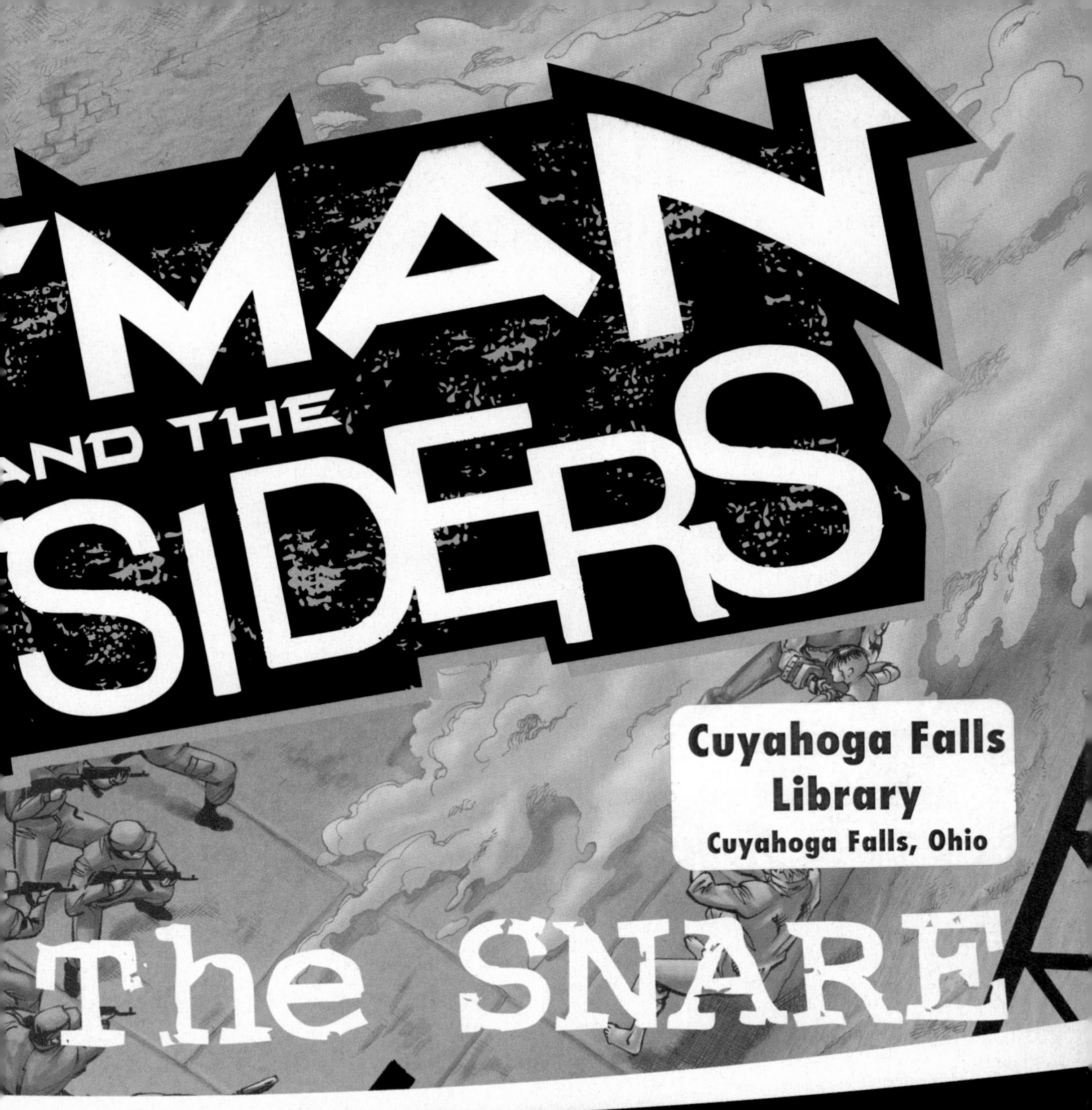
MAN
AND THE
SIDERS
The SNARE



WRITTEN BY
**CHUCK DIXON**

PENCILS BY
**CARLOS RODRIGUEZ**
**JULIAN LOPEZ**
**RYAN BENJAMIN**

INKS BY
**BIT**
**SALEEM CRAWFORD**

COLORS BY
**MARTA MARTINEZ**
**TOM CHU**

LETTERED BY
**SAL CIPRIANO**
**STEVE WANDS**
**TRAVIS LANHAM**

ORIGINAL SERIES COVERS BY
**DOUG BRAITHWAITE**
**J. CALAFIORE**
**MARK MCKENNA**

**BATMAN CREATED BY BOB KANE**

**DAN DIDIO** Senior VP-Executive Editor
**MIKE MARTS** Editor-original series
**JEANINE SCHAEFER** Associate Editor-original series
**SCOTT NYBAKKEN** Editor-collected edition
**ROBBIN BROSTERMAN** Senior Art Director
**PAUL LEVITZ** President & Publisher
**GEORG BREWER** VP-Design & DC Direct Creative
**RICHARD BRUNING** Senior VP-Creative Director
**PATRICK CALDON** Executive VP-Finance & Operations
**CHRIS CARAMALIS** VP-Finance
**JOHN CUNNINGHAM** VP-Marketing
**TERRI CUNNINGHAM** VP-Managing Editor
**AMY GENKINS** Senior VP-Business & Legal Affairs
**ALISON GILL** VP-Manufacturing
**DAVID HYDE** VP-Publicity
**HANK KANALZ** VP-General Manager, WildStorm
**JIM LEE** Editorial Director-WildStorm
**GREGORY NOVECK** Senior VP-Creative Affairs
**SUE POHJA** VP-Book Trade Sales
**STEVE ROTTERDAM** Senior VP-Sales & Marketing
**CHERYL RUBIN** Senior VP-Brand Management
**ALYSSE SOLL** VP-Advertising & Custom Publishing
**JEFF TROJAN** VP-Business Development, DC Direct
**BOB WAYNE** VP-Sales

Cover art by Doug Braithwaite.
Cover color by Brian Reber.
Publication design by Joseph DiStefano.

**BATMAN AND THE OUTSIDERS: THE SNARE**



DC Comics, 1700 Broadway, New York, NY 10019
A Warner Bros. Entertainment Company
Printed in Canada. First Printing.
ISBN: 978-1-4012-2199-7

SFI CERTIFIED SOURCING
Fiber used in this product line meets the sourcing requirements of the SFI program.
www.sfiprogram.org
PWC-SFICOC-260

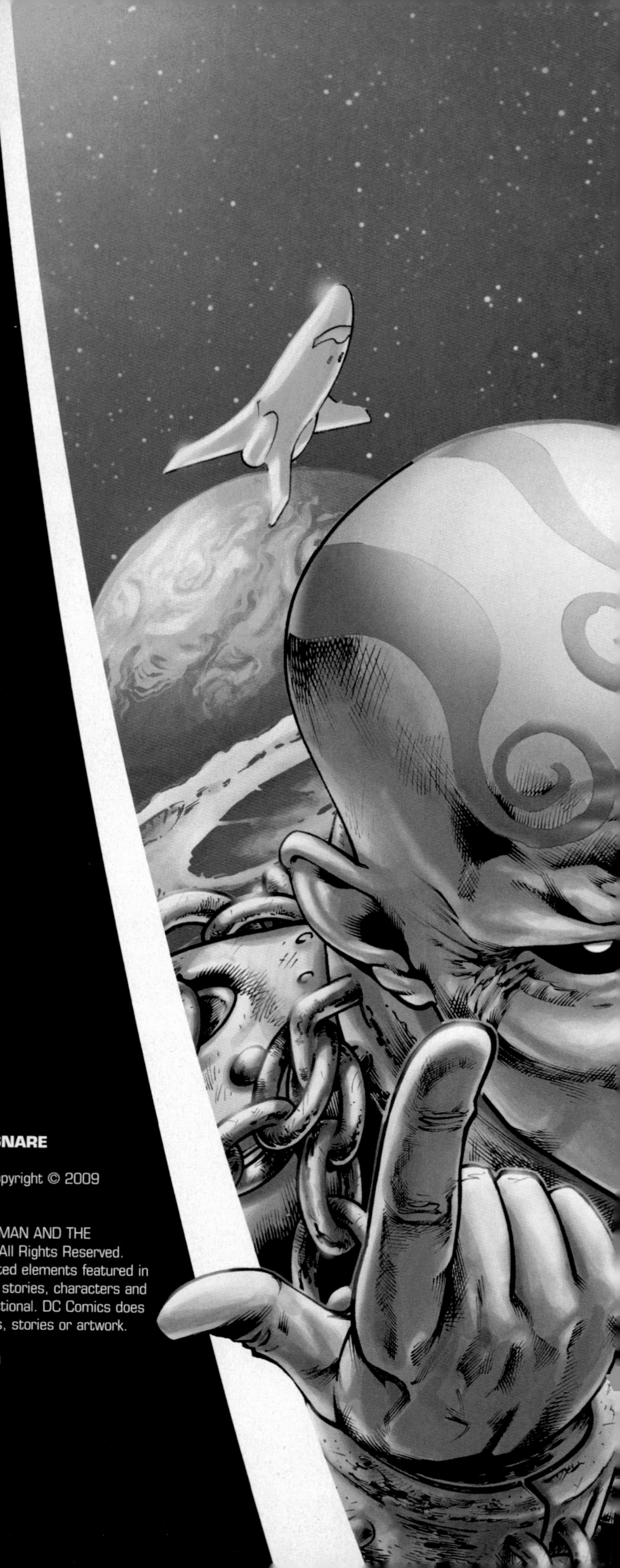

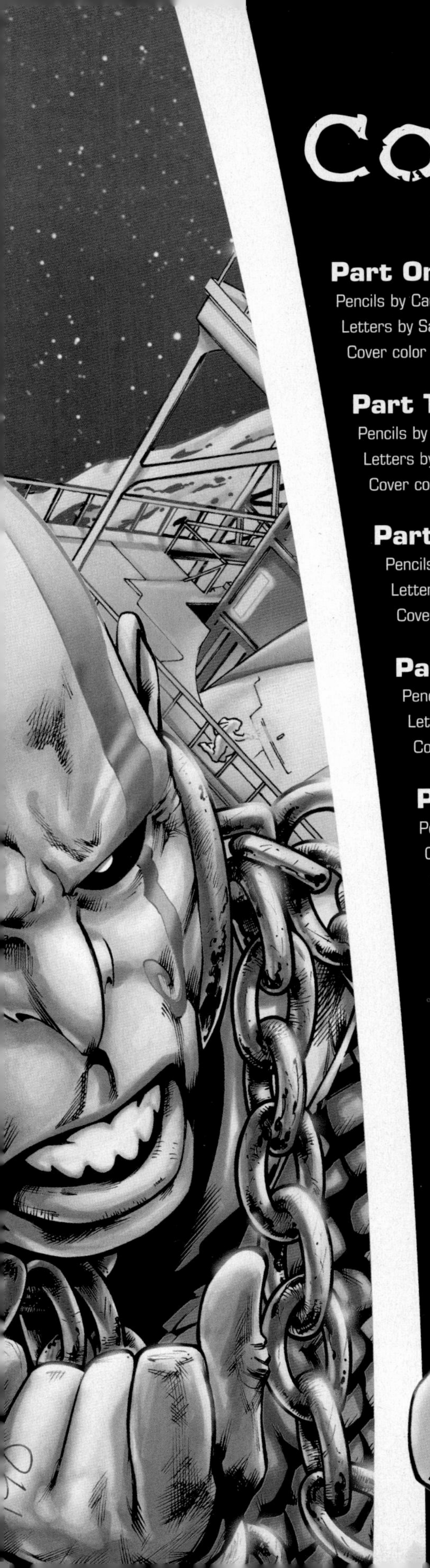

# Contents



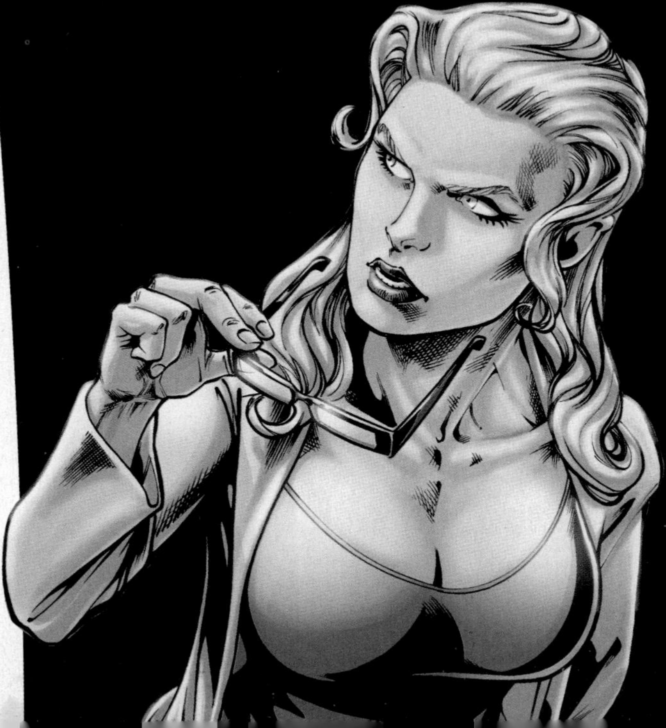

# BATMAN AND THE OUTSIDERS

## The SNARE

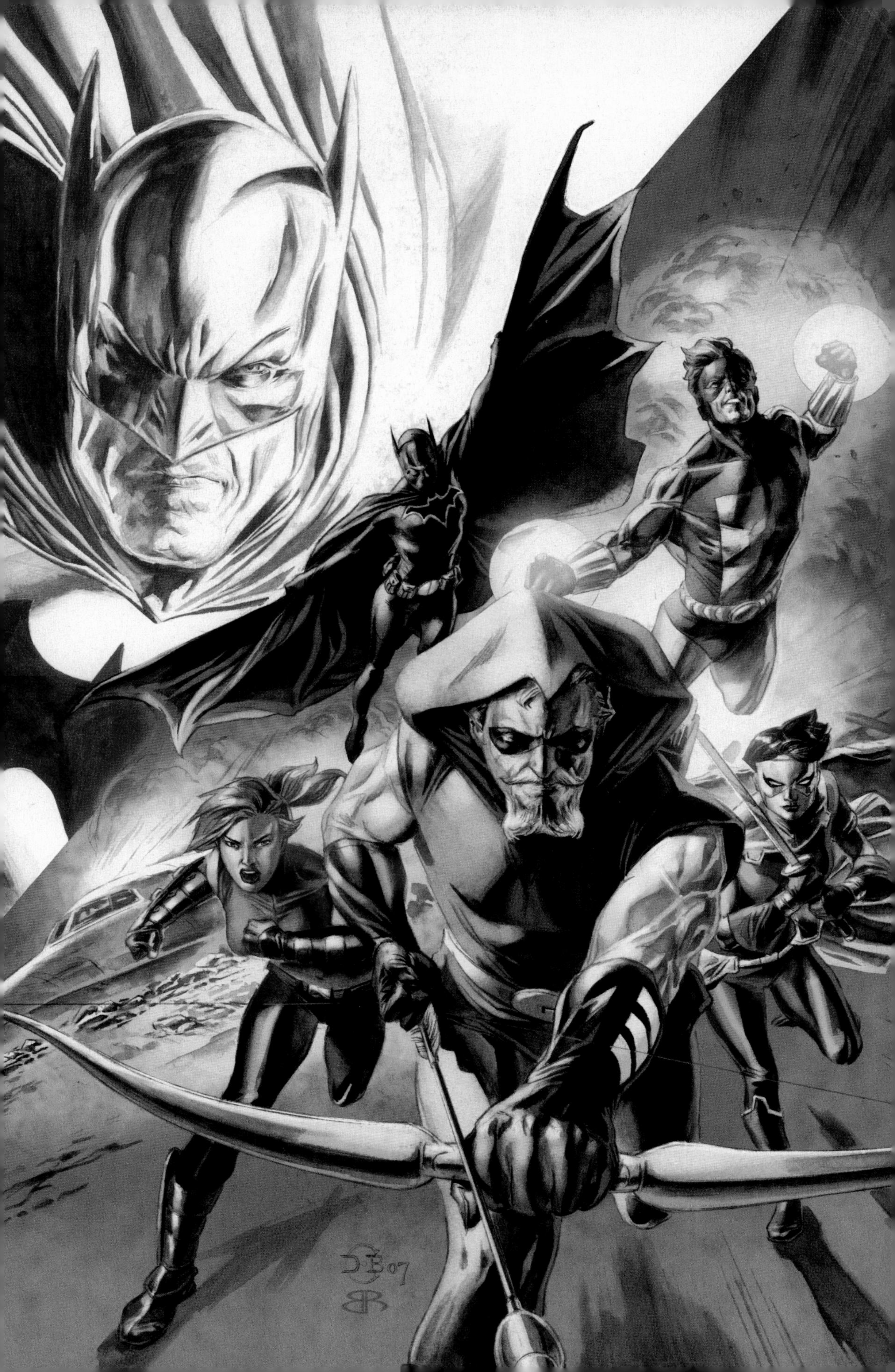

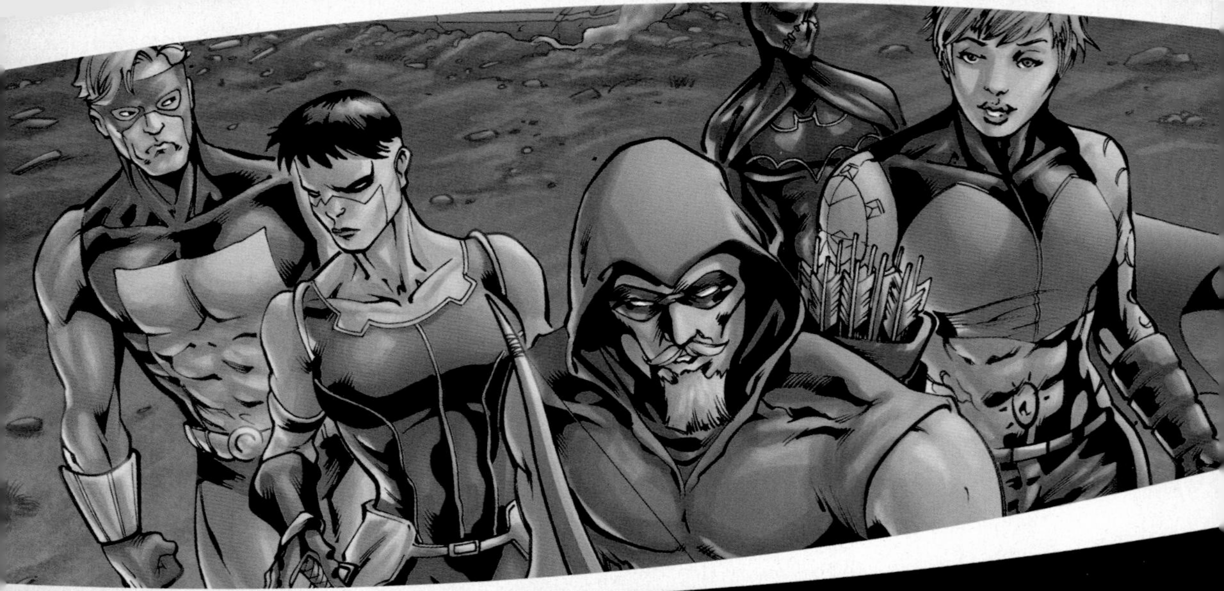

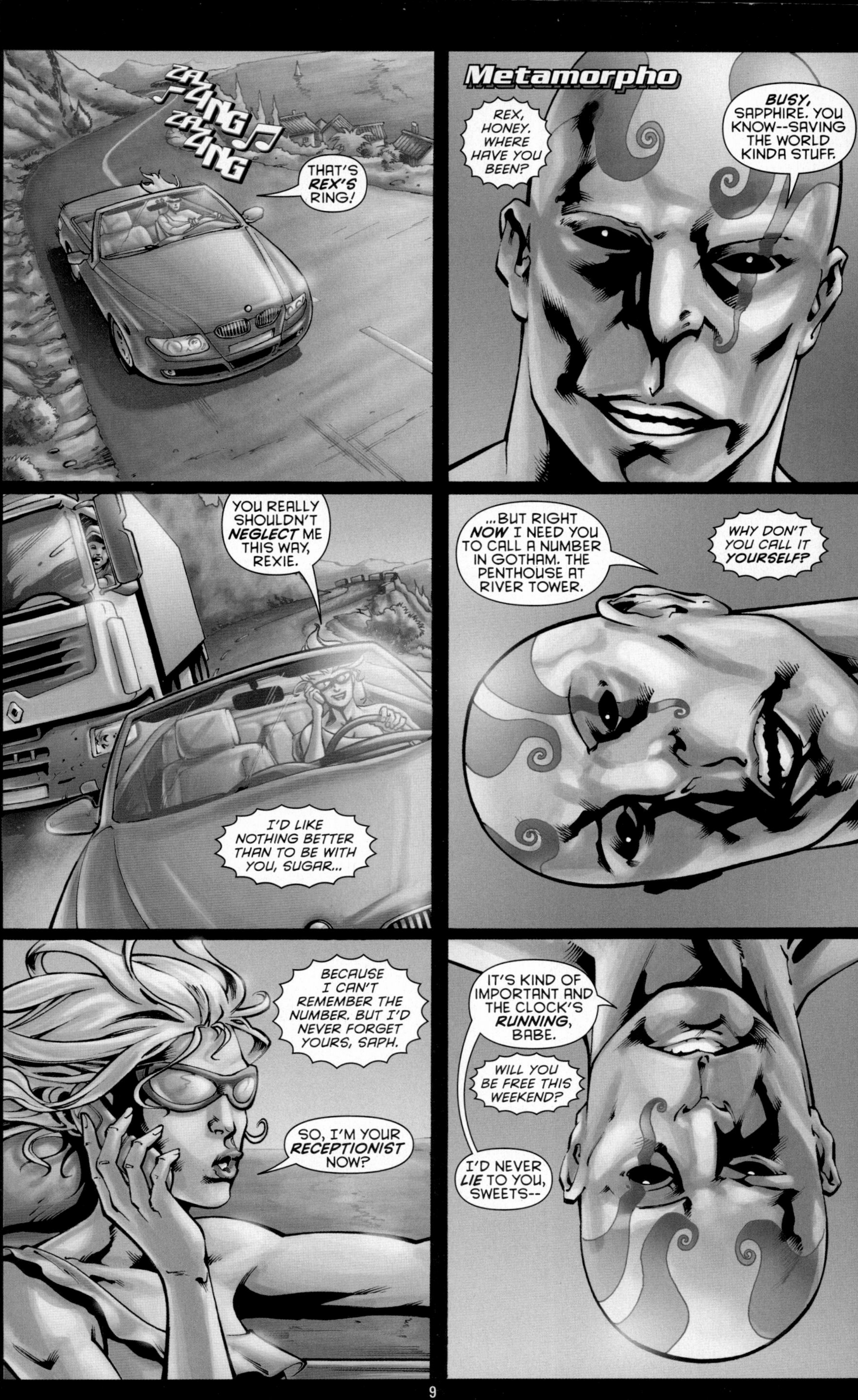

ZAZING ZAZING
THAT'S REX'S RING!
Metamorpho
REX, HONEY. WHERE HAVE YOU BEEN?
BUSY, SAPPHIRE. YOU KNOW--SAVING THE WORLD KINDA STUFF.
YOU REALLY SHOULDN'T NEGLECT ME THIS WAY, REXIE.
I'D LIKE NOTHING BETTER THAN TO BE WITH YOU, SUGAR...
...BUT RIGHT NOW I NEED YOU TO CALL A NUMBER IN GOTHAM. THE PENTHOUSE AT RIVER TOWER.
WHY DON'T YOU CALL IT YOURSELF?
BECAUSE I CAN'T REMEMBER THE NUMBER. BUT I'D NEVER FORGET YOURS, SAPH.
SO, I'M YOUR RECEPTIONIST NOW?
IT'S KIND OF IMPORTANT AND THE CLOCK'S RUNNING, BABE.
WILL YOU BE FREE THIS WEEKEND?
I'D NEVER LIE TO YOU, SWEETS--

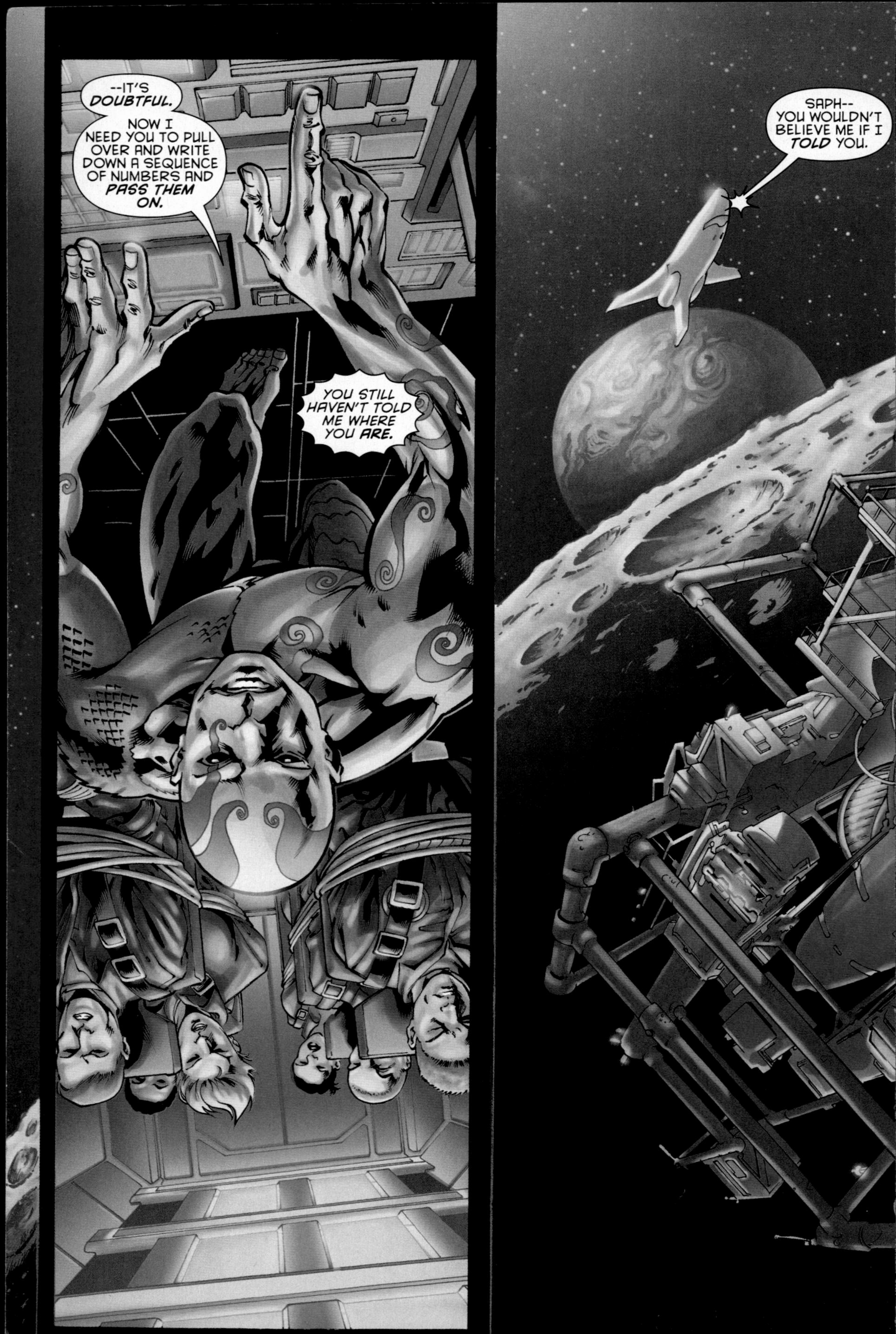
--IT'S DOUBTFUL.
NOW I NEED YOU TO PULL OVER AND WRITE DOWN A SEQUENCE OF NUMBERS AND PASS THEM ON.
YOU STILL HAVEN'T TOLD ME WHERE YOU ARE.
SAPH-- YOU WOULDN'T BELIEVE ME IF I TOLD YOU.

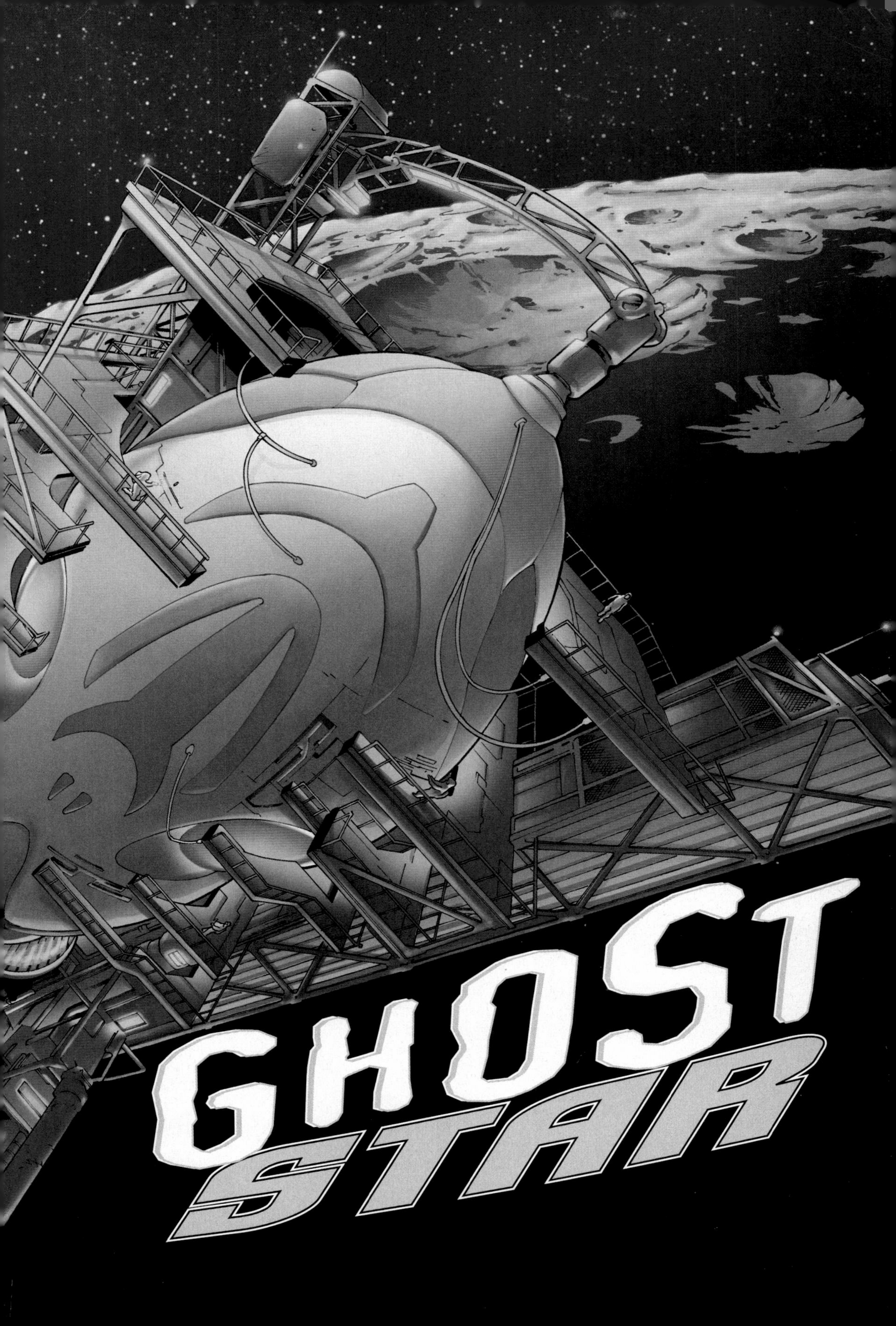
GHOST
STAR

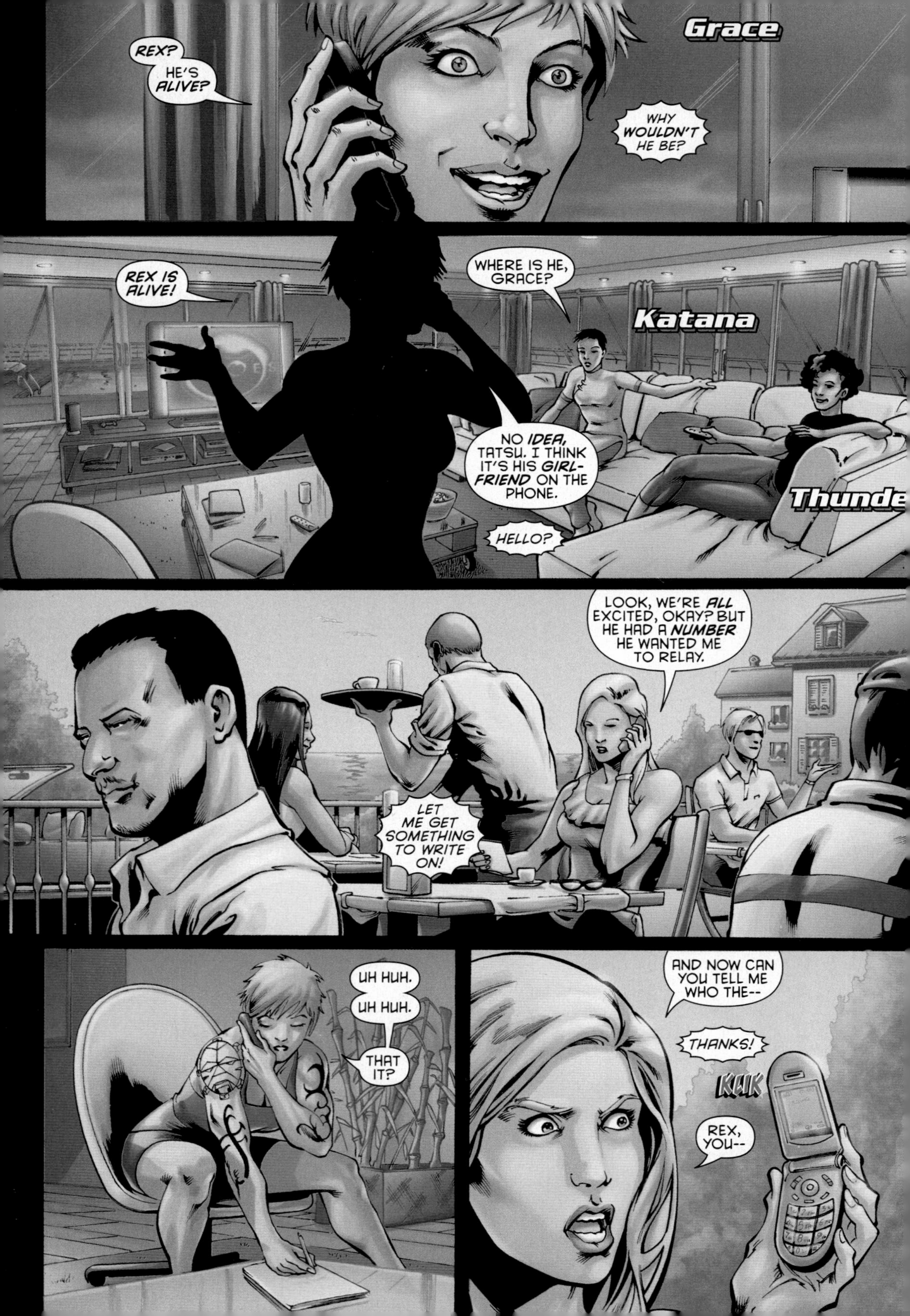
Grace
REX?
HE'S ALIVE?
WHY WOULDN'T HE BE?
REX IS ALIVE!
WHERE IS HE, GRACE?
Katana
NO IDEA, TATSU. I THINK IT'S HIS GIRL-FRIEND ON THE PHONE.
Thunde
HELLO?
LOOK, WE'RE ALL EXCITED, OKAY? BUT HE HAD A NUMBER HE WANTED ME TO RELAY.
LET ME GET SOMETHING TO WRITE ON!
UH HUH.
UH HUH.
THAT IT?
AND NOW CAN YOU TELL ME WHO THE--
THANKS!
KLIK
REX, YOU--

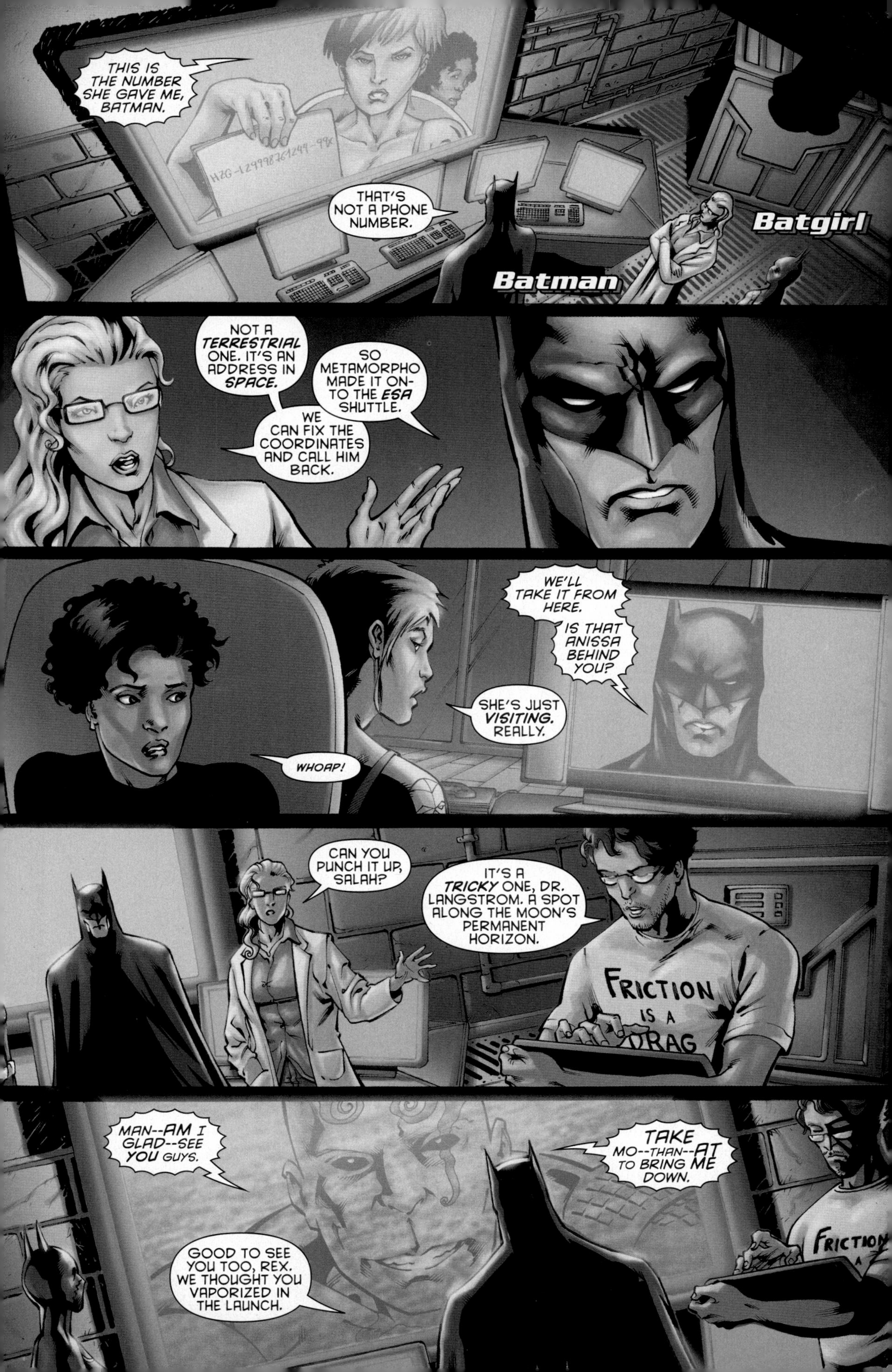
THIS IS THE NUMBER SHE GAVE ME, BATMAN.
THAT'S NOT A PHONE NUMBER.
Batgirl
Batman
NOT A TERRESTRIAL ONE. IT'S AN ADDRESS IN SPACE.
SO METAMORPHO MADE IT ON-TO THE ESA SHUTTLE.
WE CAN FIX THE COORDINATES AND CALL HIM BACK.
WE'LL TAKE IT FROM HERE.
IS THAT ANISSA BEHIND YOU?
SHE'S JUST VISITING. REALLY.
WHOAP!
CAN YOU PUNCH IT UP, SALAH?
IT'S A TRICKY ONE, DR. LANGSTROM. A SPOT ALONG THE MOON'S PERMANENT HORIZON.
FRICTION IS A DRAG
MAN--AM I GLAD--SEE YOU GUYS.
TAKE MO--THAN--AT TO BRING ME DOWN.
GOOD TO SEE YOU TOO, REX. WE THOUGHT YOU VAPORIZED IN THE LAUNCH.

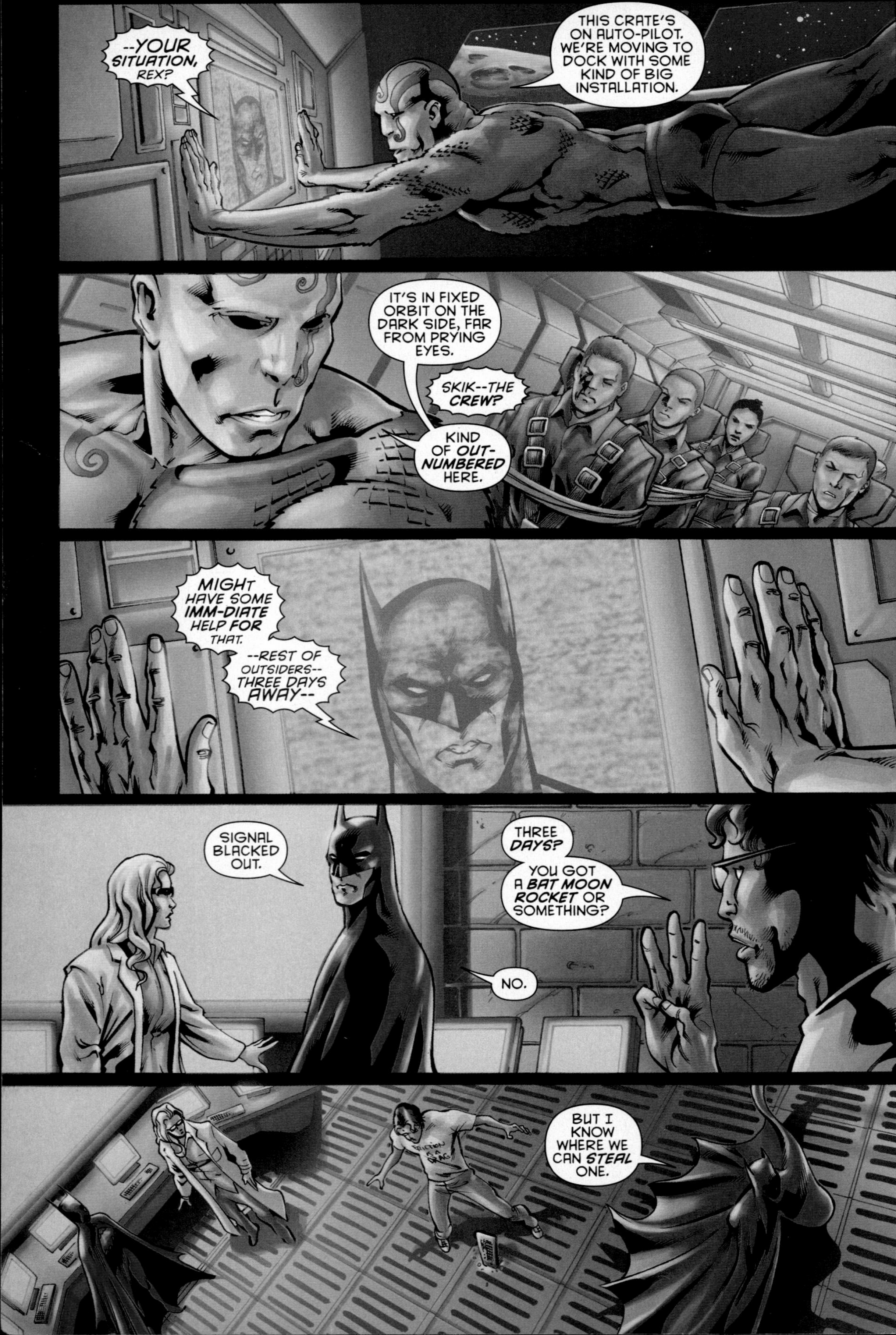
--YOUR SITUATION, REX?
THIS CRATE'S ON AUTO-PILOT. WE'RE MOVING TO DOCK WITH SOME KIND OF BIG INSTALLATION.
IT'S IN FIXED ORBIT ON THE DARK SIDE, FAR FROM PRYING EYES.
SKIK--THE CREW?
KIND OF OUT-NUMBERED HERE.
MIGHT HAVE SOME IMM-DIATE HELP FOR THAT.
--REST OF OUTSIDERS-- THREE DAYS AWAY--
SIGNAL BLACKED OUT.
THREE DAYS?
YOU GOT A BAT MOON ROCKET OR SOMETHING?
NO.
BUT I KNOW WHERE WE CAN STEAL ONE.

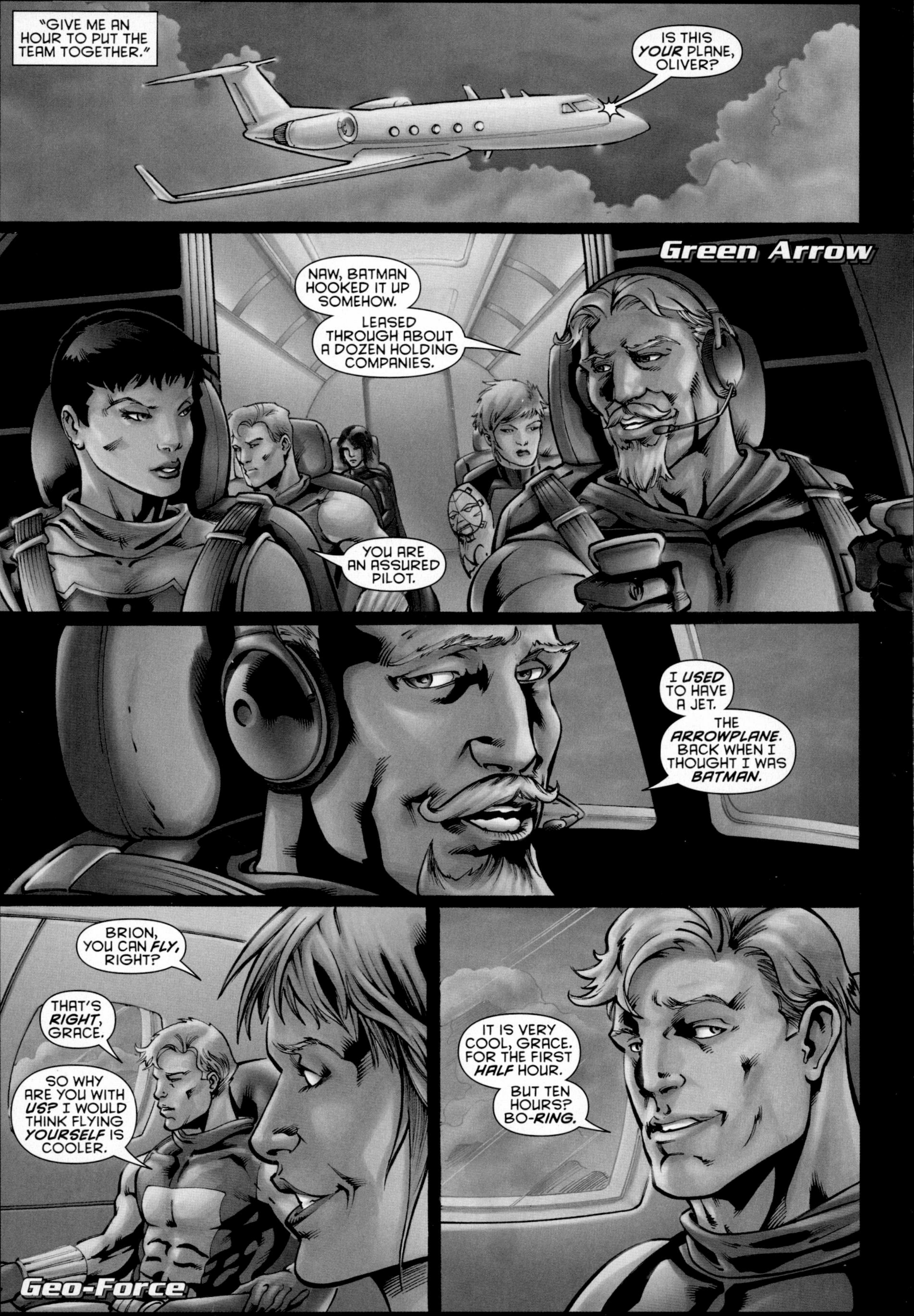
"GIVE ME AN HOUR TO PUT THE TEAM TOGETHER."
IS THIS YOUR PLANE, OLIVER?
Green Arrow
NAW, BATMAN HOOKED IT UP SOMEHOW.
LEASED THROUGH ABOUT A DOZEN HOLDING COMPANIES.
YOU ARE AN ASSURED PILOT.
I USED TO HAVE A JET.
THE ARROWPLANE. BACK WHEN I THOUGHT I WAS BATMAN.
BRION, YOU CAN FLY, RIGHT?
THAT'S RIGHT, GRACE.
SO WHY ARE YOU WITH US? I WOULD THINK FLYING YOURSELF IS COOLER.
IT IS VERY COOL, GRACE. FOR THE FIRST HALF HOUR.
BUT TEN HOURS? BO-RING.
Geo-Force

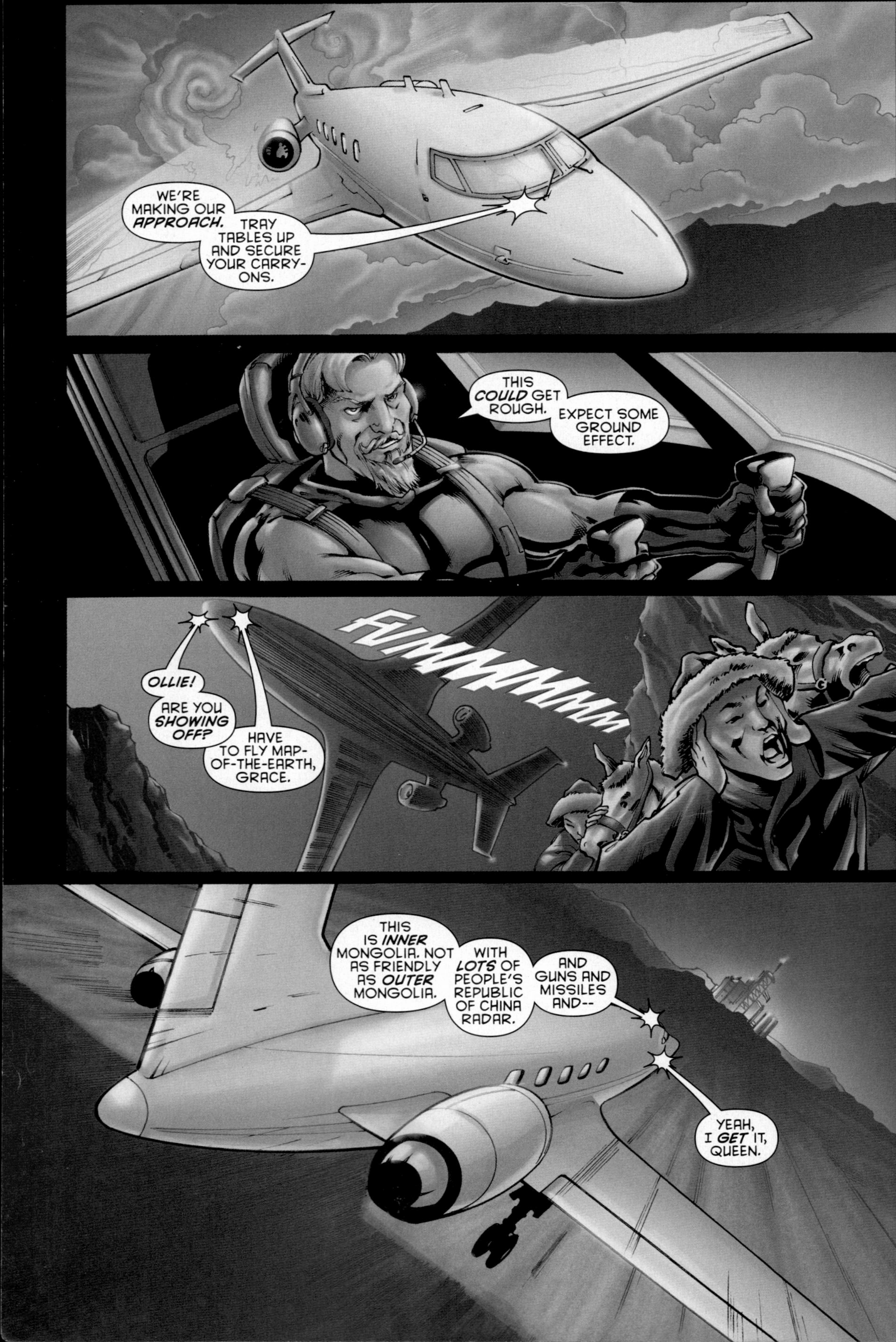
WE'RE MAKING OUR APPROACH.
TRAY TABLES UP AND SECURE YOUR CARRY-ONS.
THIS COULD GET ROUGH.
EXPECT SOME GROUND EFFECT.
FWMMMMMM
OLLIE!
ARE YOU SHOWING OFF?
HAVE TO FLY MAP-OF-THE-EARTH, GRACE.
THIS IS INNER MONGOLIA. NOT AS FRIENDLY AS OUTER MONGOLIA.
WITH LOTS OF PEOPLE'S REPUBLIC OF CHINA RADAR.
AND GUNS AND MISSILES AND--
YEAH, I GET IT, QUEEN.

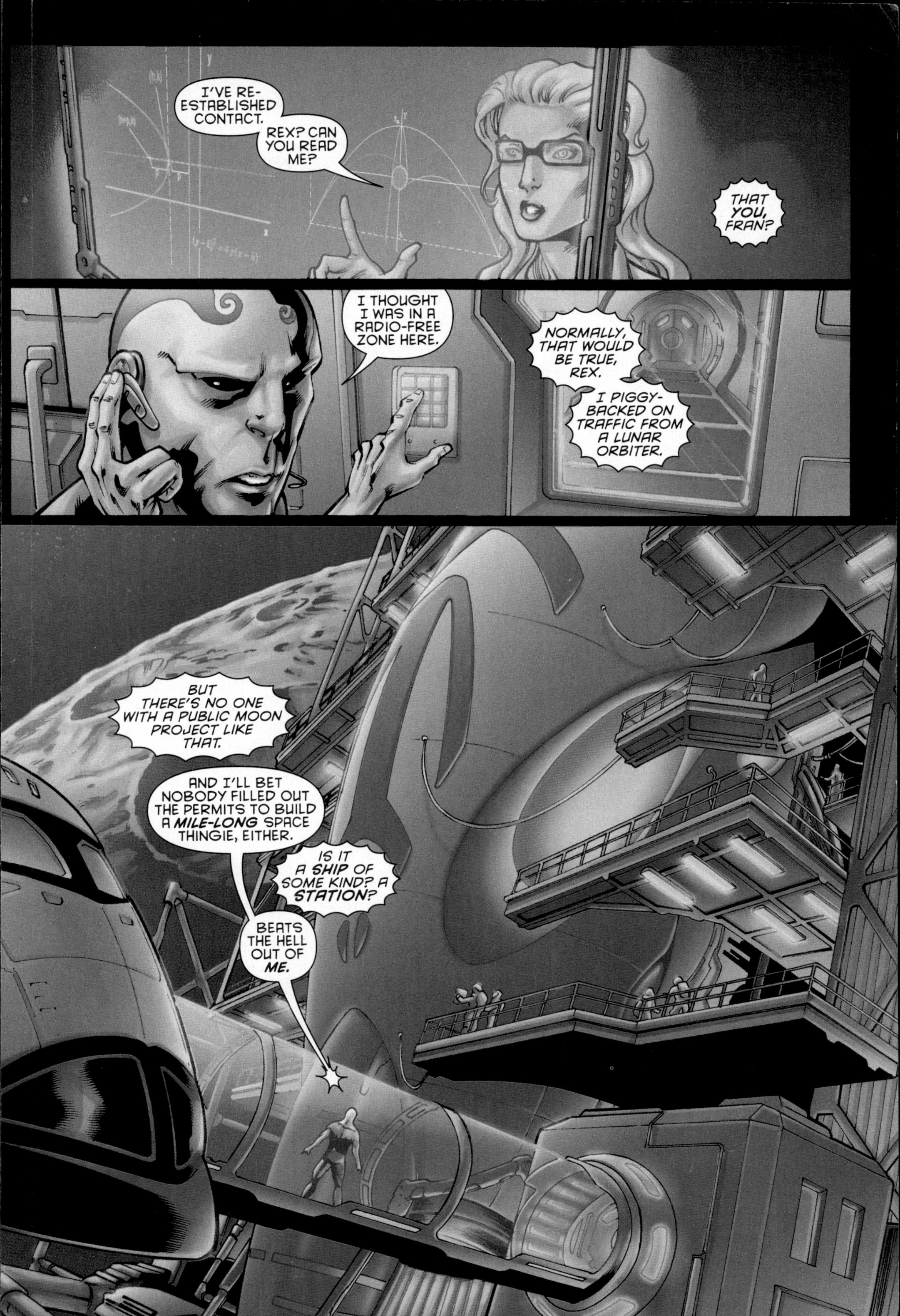
I'VE RE-ESTABLISHED CONTACT.
REX? CAN YOU READ ME?
THAT YOU, FRAN?
I THOUGHT I WAS IN A RADIO-FREE ZONE HERE.
NORMALLY, THAT WOULD BE TRUE, REX.
I PIGGY-BACKED ON TRAFFIC FROM A LUNAR ORBITER.
BUT THERE'S NO ONE WITH A PUBLIC MOON PROJECT LIKE THAT.
AND I'LL BET NOBODY FILLED OUT THE PERMITS TO BUILD A MILE-LONG SPACE THINGIE, EITHER.
IS IT A SHIP OF SOME KIND? A STATION?
BEATS THE HELL OUT OF ME.

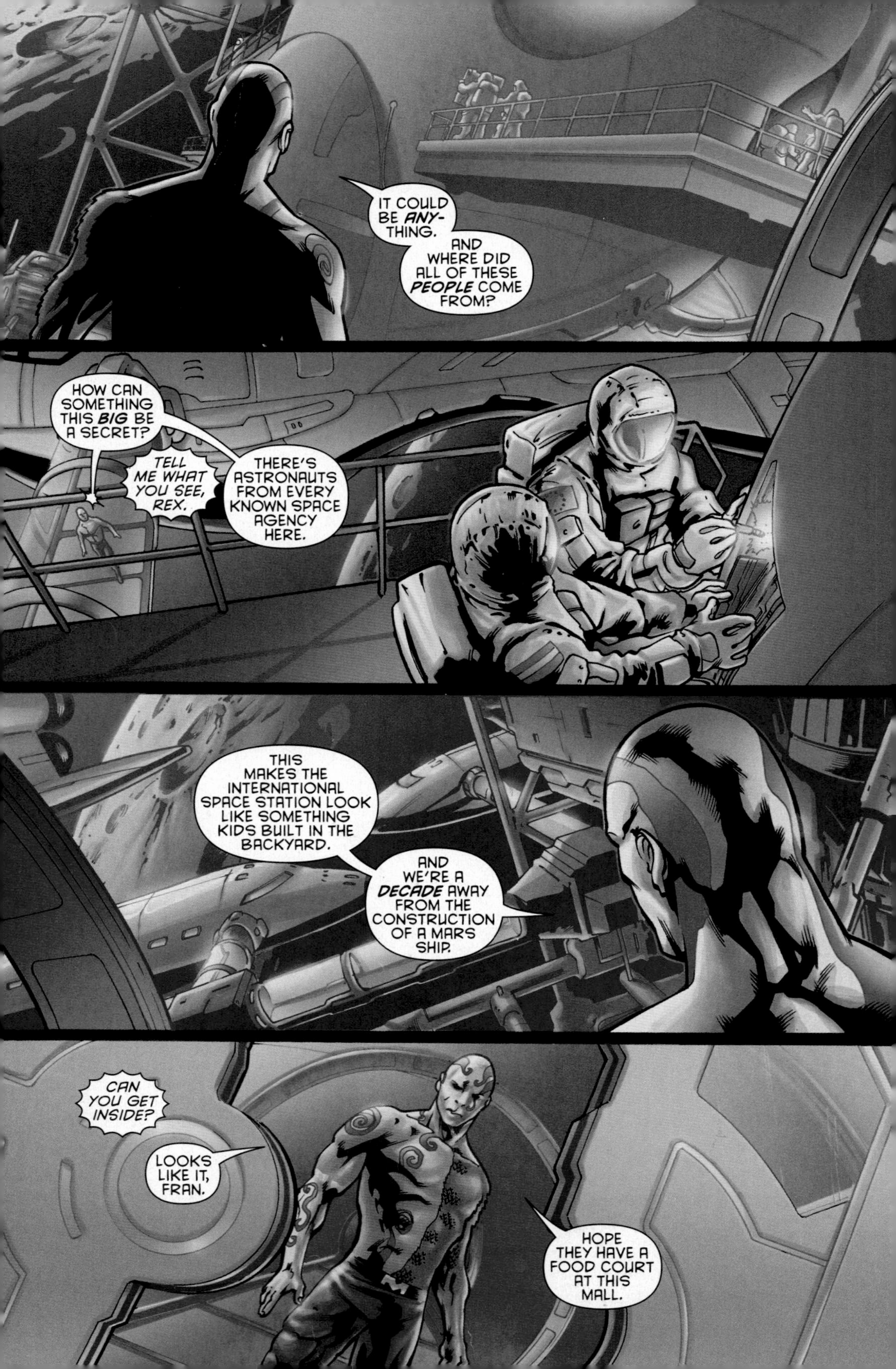
IT COULD BE ANY-THING.
AND WHERE DID ALL OF THESE PEOPLE COME FROM?
HOW CAN SOMETHING THIS BIG BE A SECRET?
TELL ME WHAT YOU SEE, REX.
THERE'S ASTRONAUTS FROM EVERY KNOWN SPACE AGENCY HERE.
THIS MAKES THE INTERNATIONAL SPACE STATION LOOK LIKE SOMETHING KIDS BUILT IN THE BACKYARD.
AND WE'RE A DECADE AWAY FROM THE CONSTRUCTION OF A MARS SHIP.
CAN YOU GET INSIDE?
LOOKS LIKE IT, FRAN.
HOPE THEY HAVE A FOOD COURT AT THIS MALL.

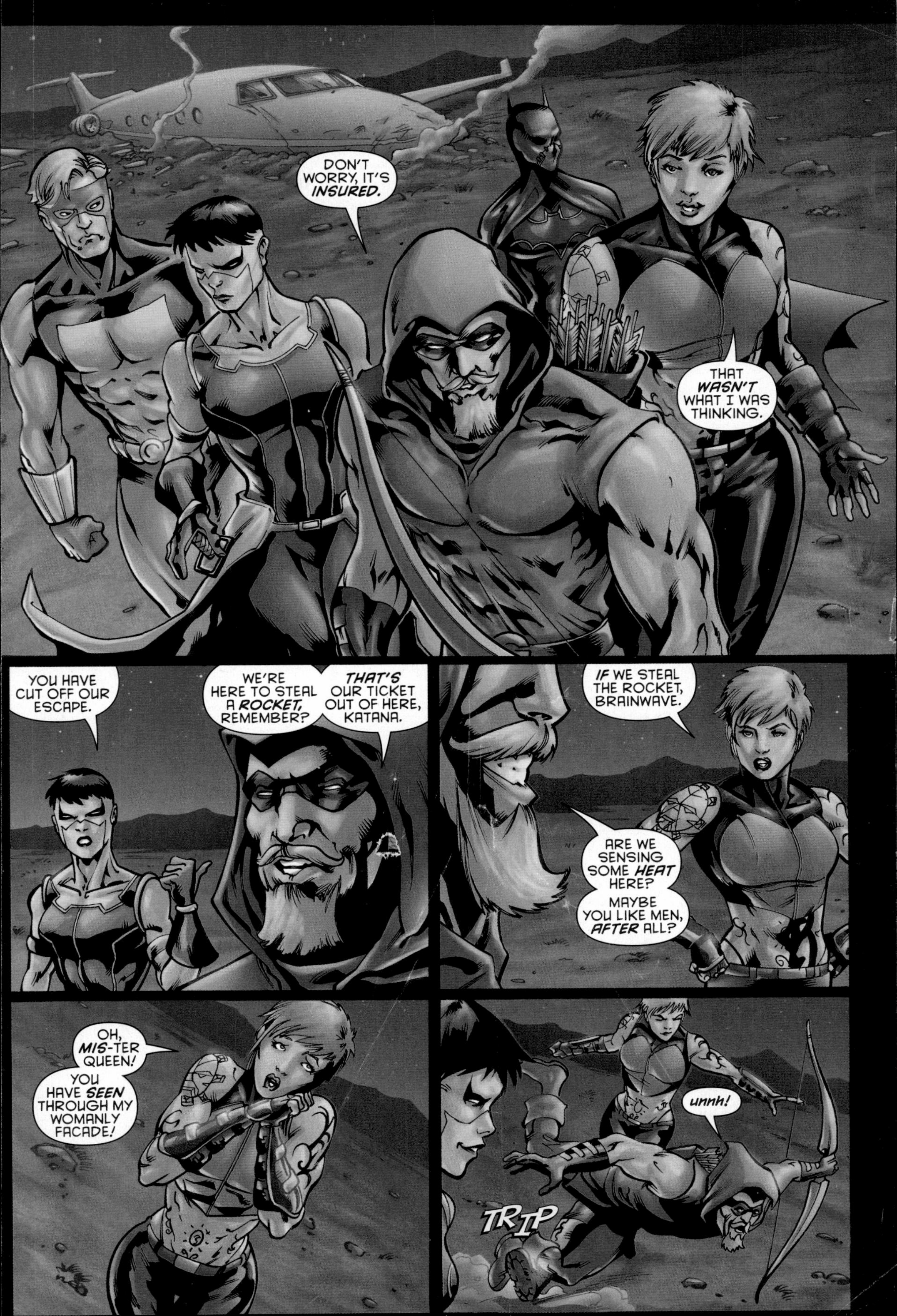
DON'T WORRY, IT'S INSURED.
THAT WASN'T WHAT I WAS THINKING.
YOU HAVE CUT OFF OUR ESCAPE.
WE'RE HERE TO STEAL A ROCKET, REMEMBER?
THAT'S OUR TICKET OUT OF HERE, KATANA.
IF WE STEAL THE ROCKET, BRAINWAVE.
ARE WE SENSING SOME HEAT HERE?
MAYBE YOU LIKE MEN, AFTER ALL?
OH, MIS-TER QUEEN!
YOU HAVE SEEN THROUGH MY WOMANLY FACADE!
unnh!
TRIP

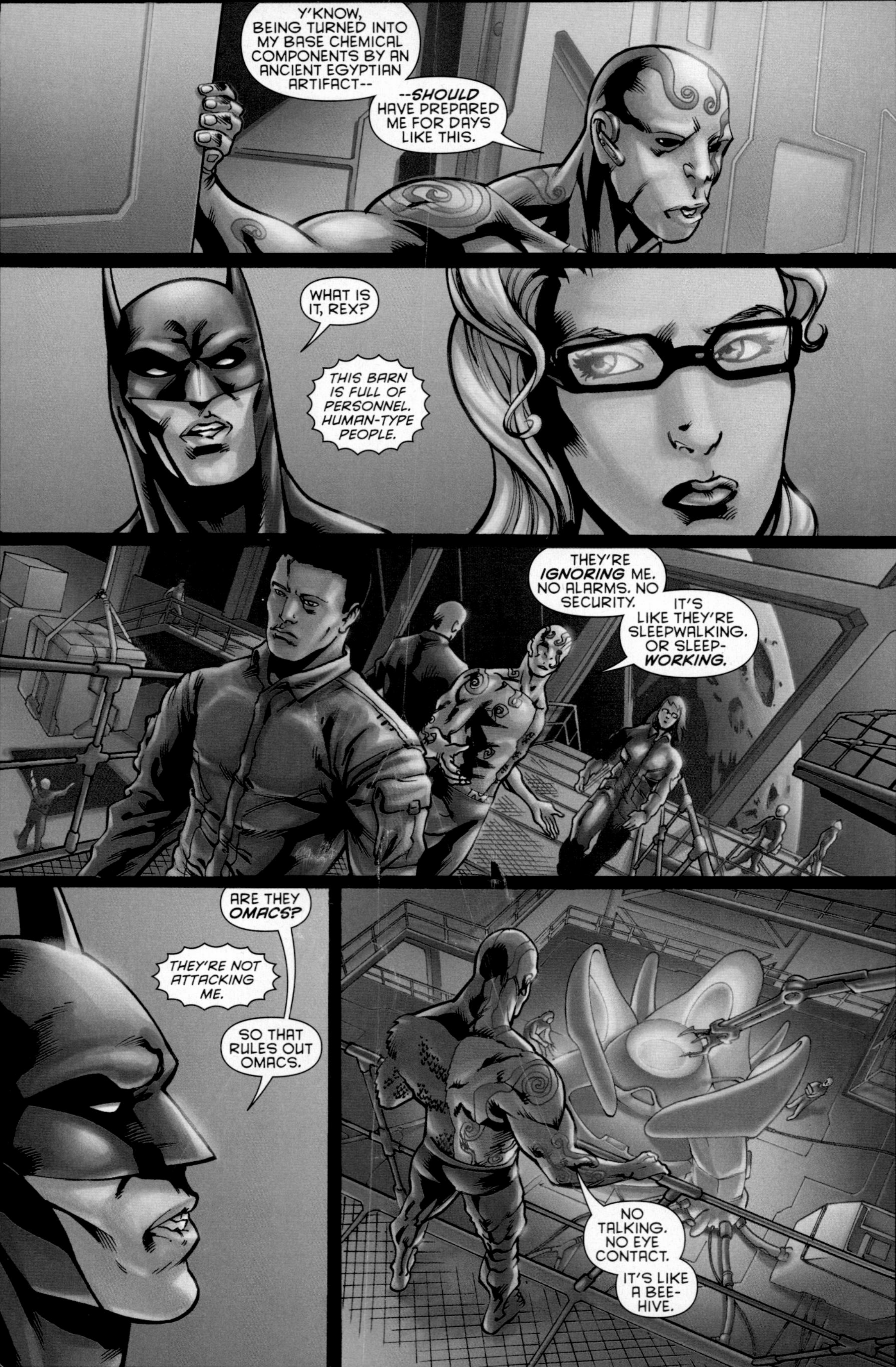
Y'KNOW, BEING TURNED INTO MY BASE CHEMICAL COMPONENTS BY AN ANCIENT EGYPTIAN ARTIFACT--
--SHOULD HAVE PREPARED ME FOR DAYS LIKE THIS.
WHAT IS IT, REX?
THIS BARN IS FULL OF PERSONNEL. HUMAN-TYPE PEOPLE.
THEY'RE IGNORING ME. NO ALARMS. NO SECURITY.
IT'S LIKE THEY'RE SLEEPWALKING. OR SLEEP-WORKING.
ARE THEY OMACS?
THEY'RE NOT ATTACKING ME.
SO THAT RULES OUT OMACS.
NO TALKING. NO EYE CONTACT.
IT'S LIKE A BEE-HIVE.

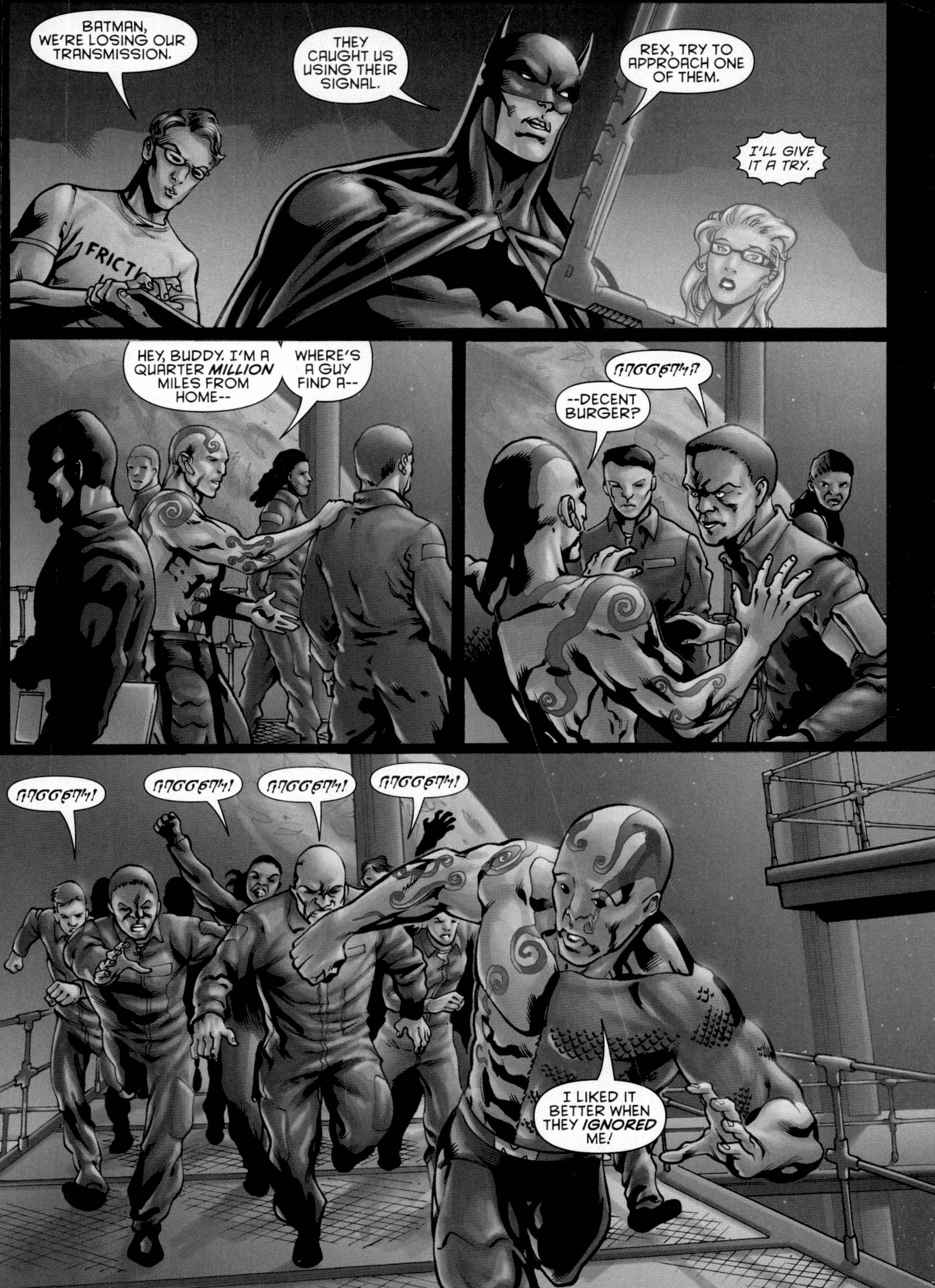
BATMAN, WE'RE LOSING OUR TRANSMISSION.
THEY CAUGHT US USING THEIR SIGNAL.
REX, TRY TO APPROACH ONE OF THEM.
I'LL GIVE IT A TRY.
HEY, BUDDY. I'M A QUARTER *MILLION* MILES FROM HOME--
WHERE'S A GUY FIND A--
--DECENT BURGER?
I LIKED IT BETTER WHEN THEY *IGNORED* ME!

"THINGS HAVE KIND OF GOTTEN MORE OUT OF CONTROL THAN USUAL."
IS ANYONE ELSE THINKING THE SAME THING?
WHAT ARE THE CHANCES OF FINDING ANOTHER SHUTTLE FUELED AND READY TO LAUNCH--
--INSIDE OF FORTY-EIGHT HOURS?
GOTTA ADMIT IT CROSSED MY MIND.
EVEN IF YOU BELIEVE IN CONSPIRACIES, LIKE I DO--THIS ONE'S HARD TO SWALLOW.
MAYBE JARDINE BOUGHT CARGO SPACE ON THIS RIDE, TOO?
WHICH MEANS BEIJING IS EITHER IN ON THIS OR BEING USED.
您在停止
ANYBODY SPEAK MANDARIN?
CANTONESE, MAYBE?

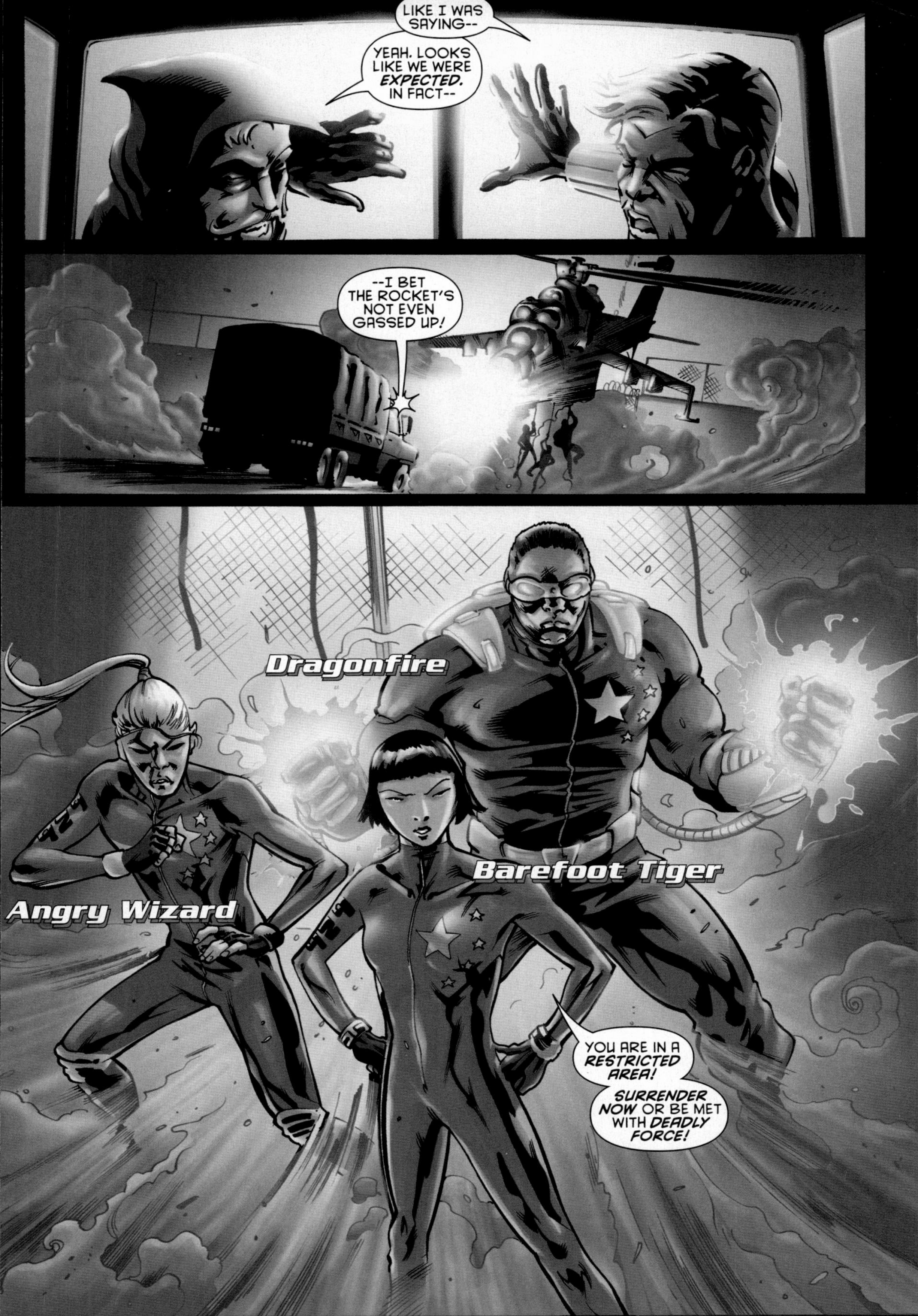

LIKE I WAS SAYING--
YEAH. LOOKS LIKE WE WERE *EXPECTED.* IN FACT--
--I BET THE ROCKET'S NOT EVEN GASSED UP!
Dragonfire
Barefoot Tiger
Angry Wizard
YOU ARE IN A *RESTRICTED AREA!*
*SURRENDER NOW* OR BE MET WITH *DEADLY FORCE!*

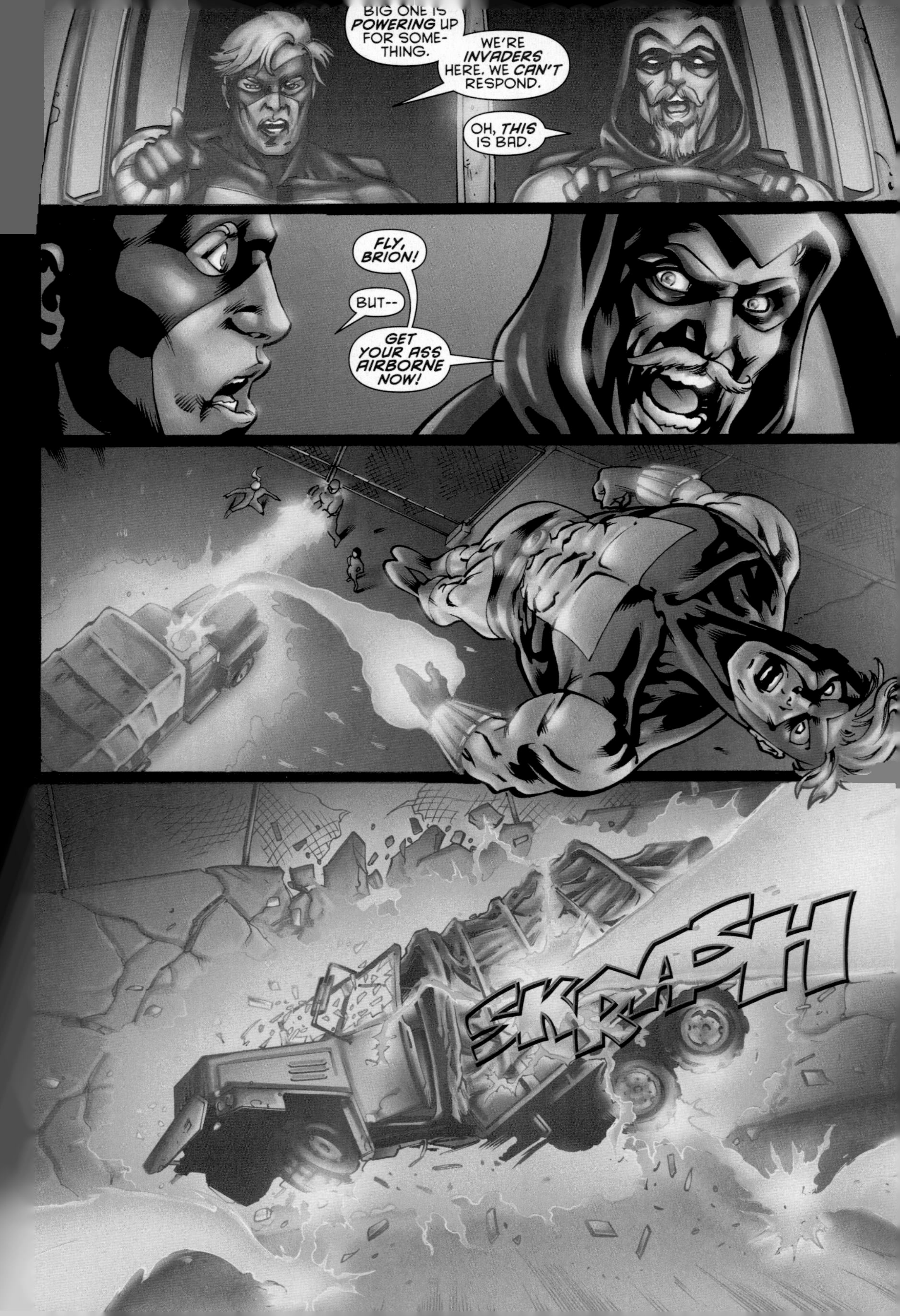
BIG ONE IS POWERING UP FOR SOME-THING.
WE'RE INVADERS HERE. WE CAN'T RESPOND.
OH, THIS IS BAD.
FLY, BRION!
BUT--
GET YOUR ASS AIRBORNE NOW!
SKRASH

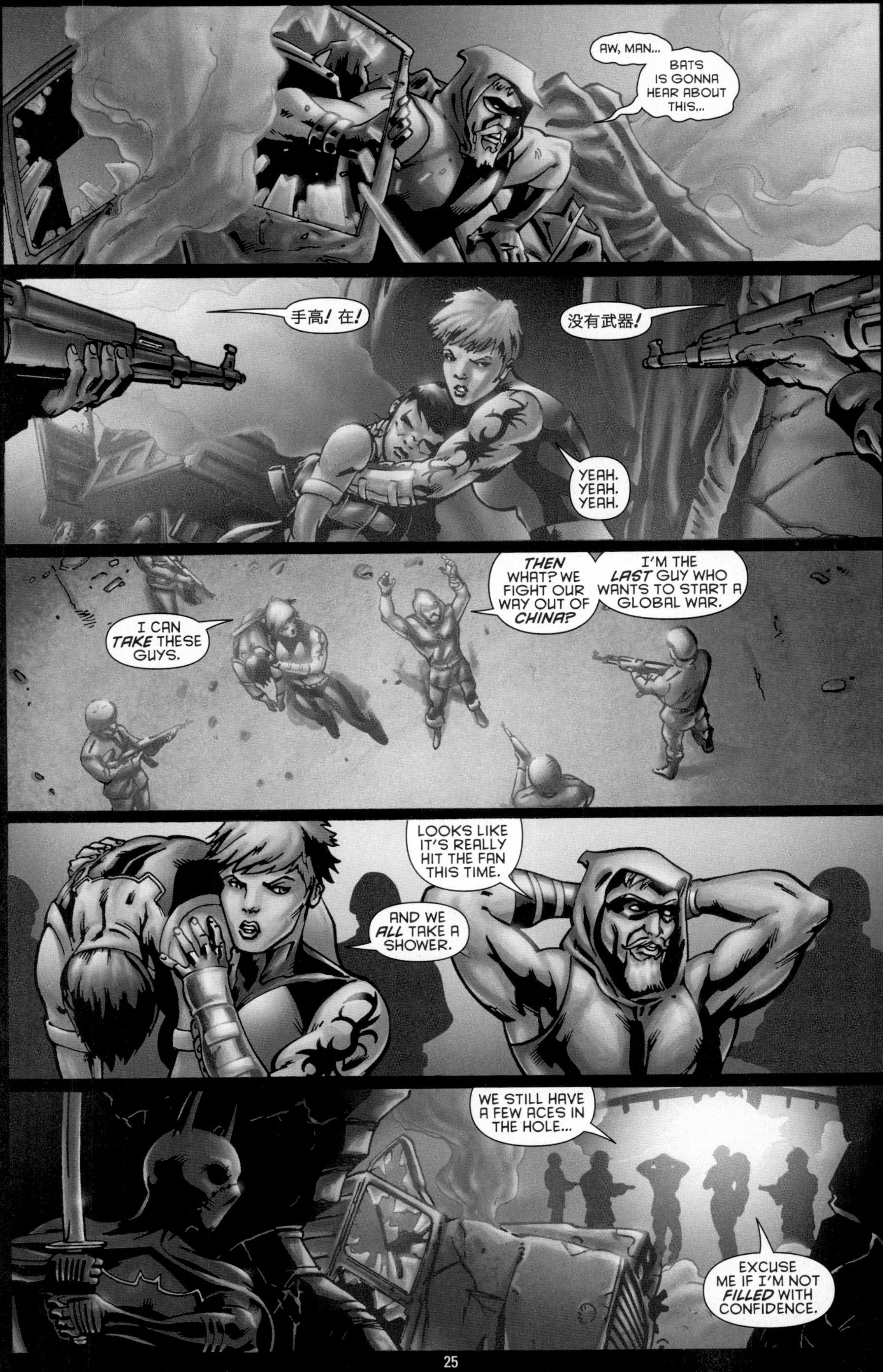
AW, MAN... BATS IS GONNA HEAR ABOUT THIS...
手高! 在!
没有武器!
YEAH. YEAH. YEAH.
I CAN TAKE THESE GUYS.
THEN WHAT? WE FIGHT OUR WAY OUT OF CHINA?
I'M THE LAST GUY WHO WANTS TO START A GLOBAL WAR.
LOOKS LIKE IT'S REALLY HIT THE FAN THIS TIME.
AND WE ALL TAKE A SHOWER.
WE STILL HAVE A FEW ACES IN THE HOLE...
EXCUSE ME IF I'M NOT FILLED WITH CONFIDENCE.

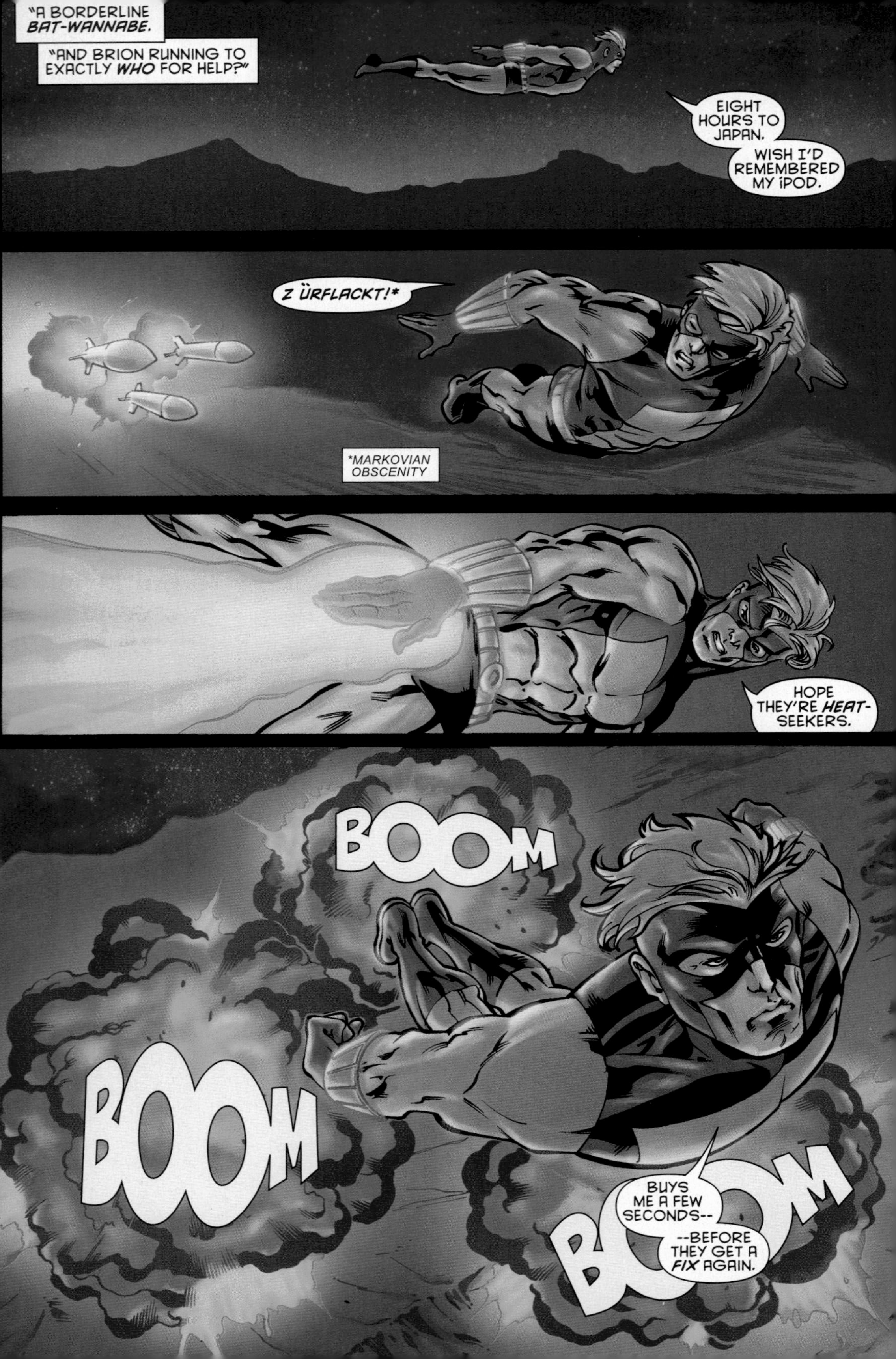
"A BORDERLINE *BAT-WANNABE*.
"AND BRION RUNNING TO EXACTLY *WHO* FOR HELP?"
EIGHT HOURS TO JAPAN.
WISH I'D REMEMBERED MY iPOD.
Z ÜRFLACKT!*
*MARKOVIAN OBSCENITY
HOPE THEY'RE *HEAT*-SEEKERS.
BOOM
BOOM
BOOM
BUYS ME A FEW SECONDS--
--BEFORE THEY GET A *FIX* AGAIN.

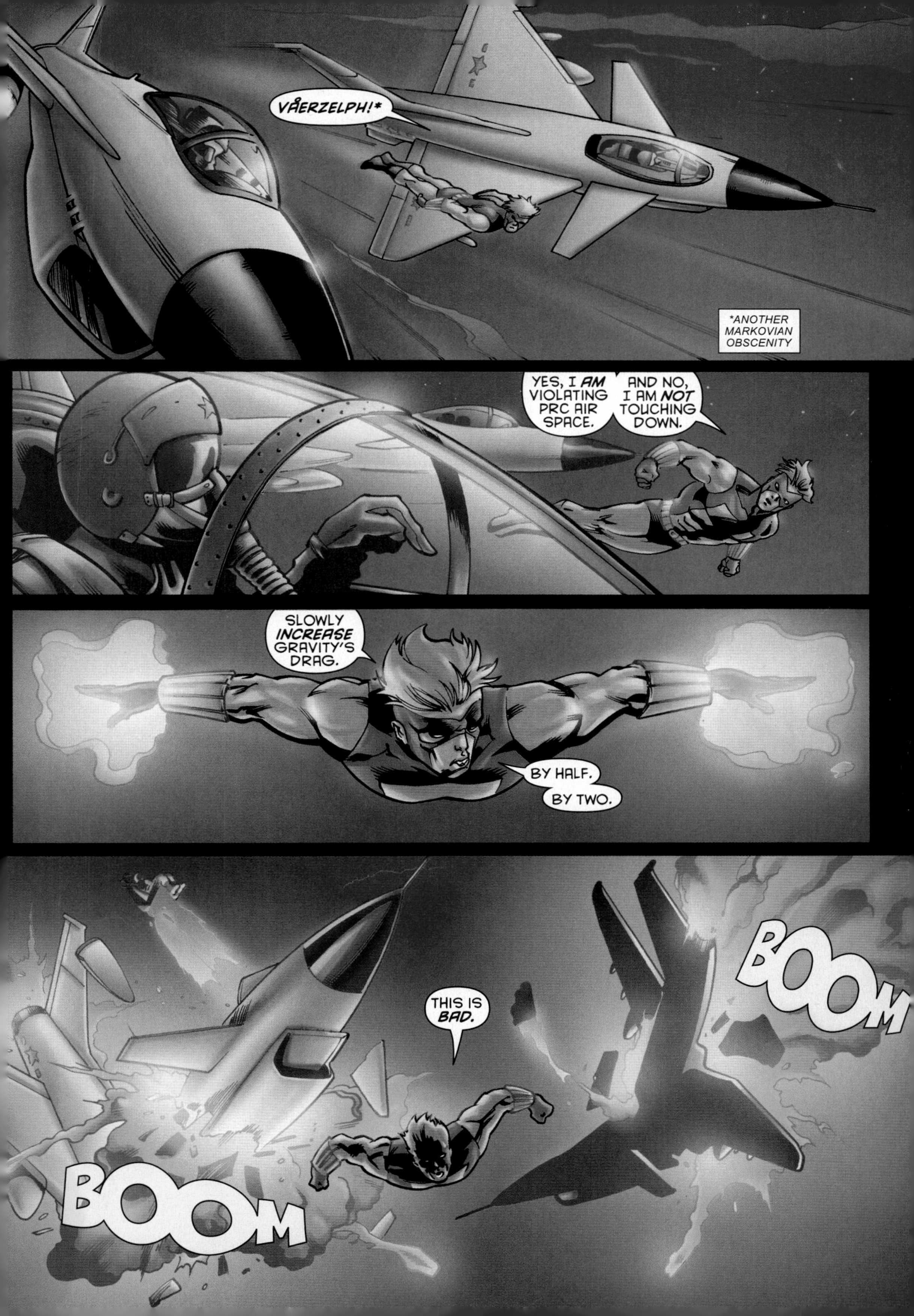

VÅERZELPH!*
*ANOTHER MARKOVIAN OBSCENITY
YES, I AM VIOLATING PRC AIR SPACE.
AND NO, I AM NOT TOUCHING DOWN.
SLOWLY INCREASE GRAVITY'S DRAG.
BY HALF.
BY TWO.
BOOM
THIS IS BAD.
BOOM

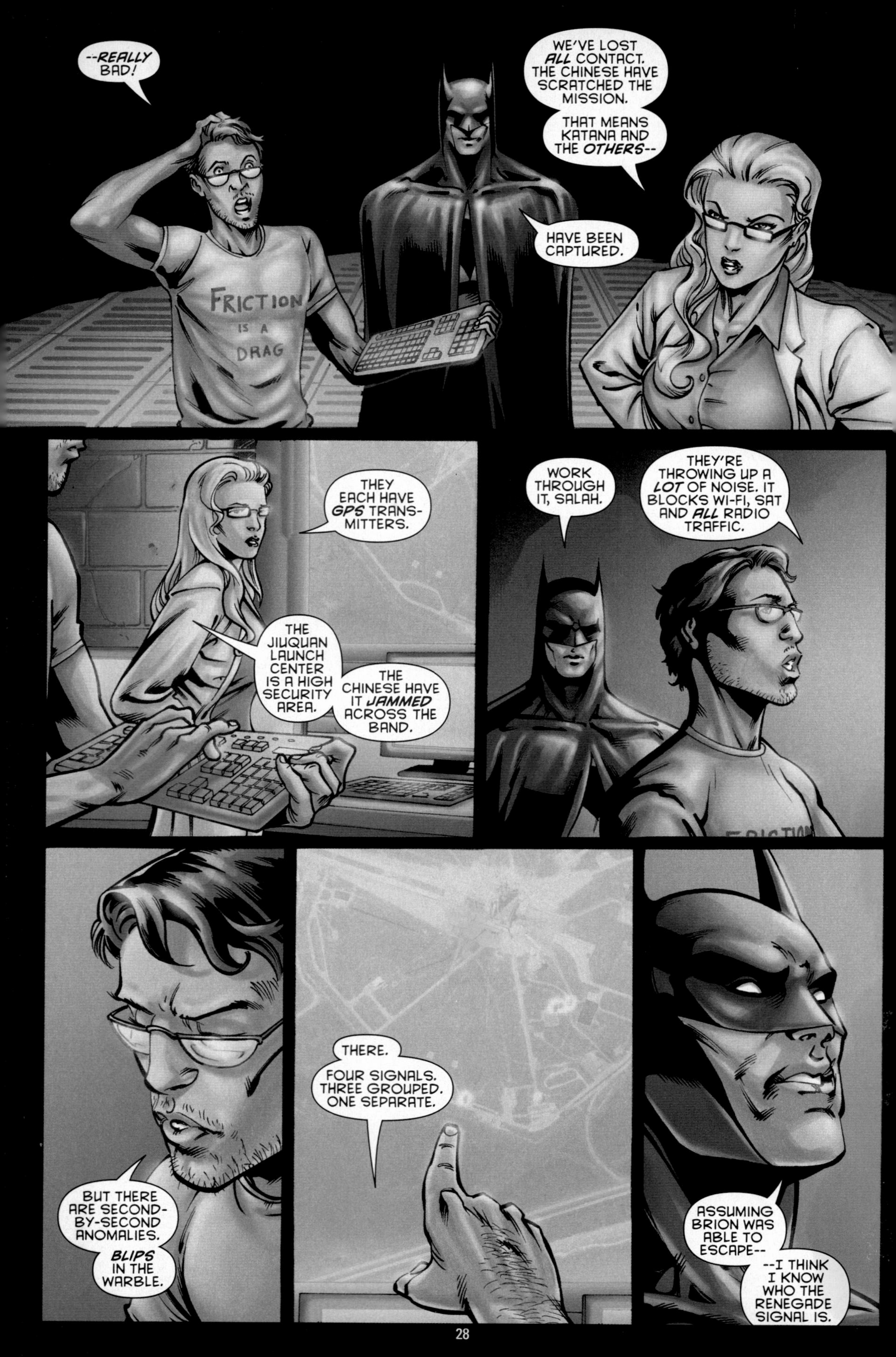
--REALLY BAD!
WE'VE LOST ALL CONTACT. THE CHINESE HAVE SCRATCHED THE MISSION.
THAT MEANS KATANA AND THE OTHERS--
HAVE BEEN CAPTURED.
FRICTION IS A DRAG
THEY EACH HAVE GPS TRANSMITTERS.
THE JIUQUAN LAUNCH CENTER IS A HIGH SECURITY AREA.
THE CHINESE HAVE IT JAMMED ACROSS THE BAND.
WORK THROUGH IT, SALAH.
THEY'RE THROWING UP A LOT OF NOISE. IT BLOCKS WI-FI, SAT AND ALL RADIO TRAFFIC.
BUT THERE ARE SECOND-BY-SECOND ANOMALIES.
BLIPS IN THE WARBLE.
THERE.
FOUR SIGNALS. THREE GROUPED. ONE SEPARATE.
ASSUMING BRION WAS ABLE TO ESCAPE--
--I THINK I KNOW WHO THE RENEGADE SIGNAL IS.

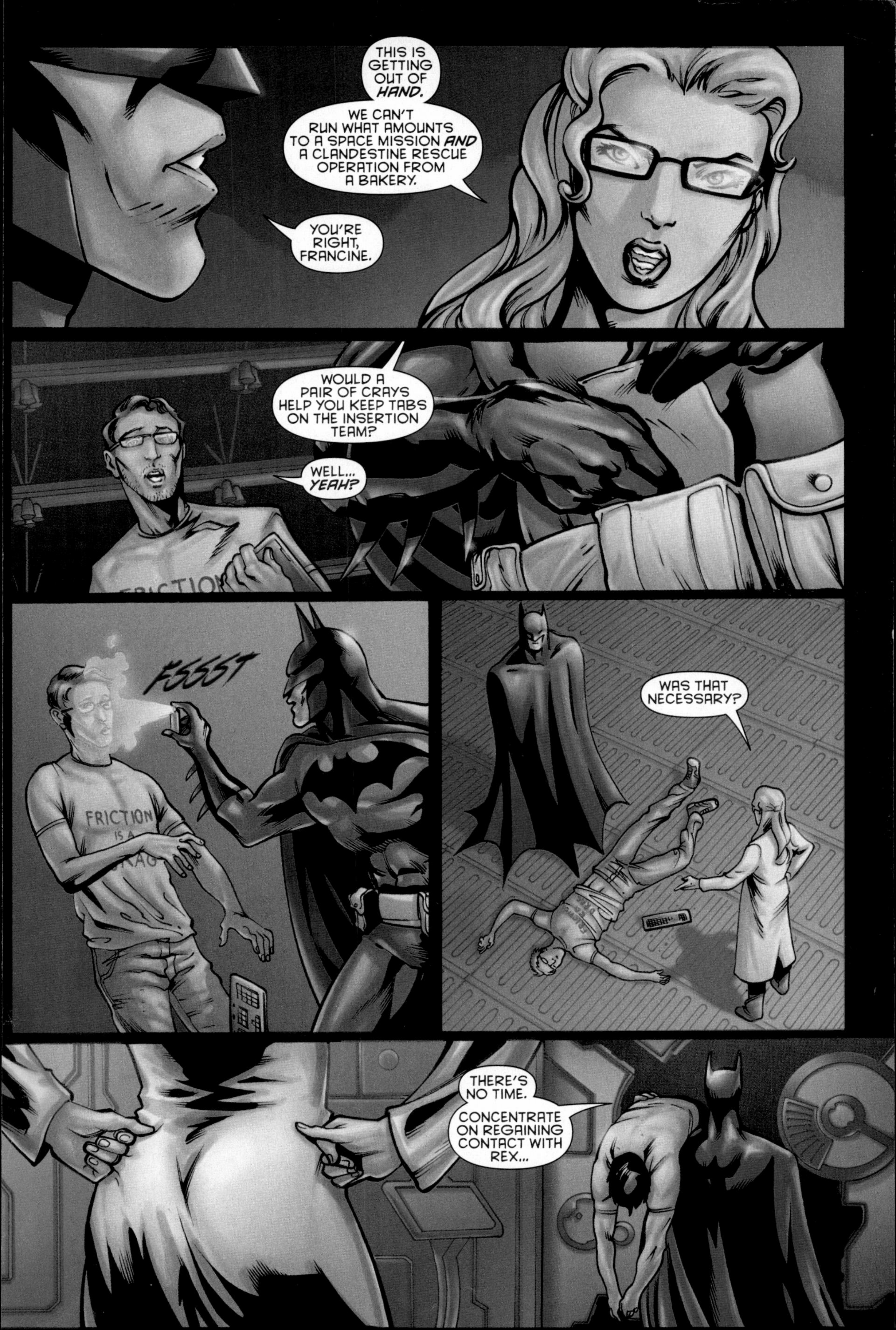
THIS IS GETTING OUT OF *HAND.*
WE CAN'T RUN WHAT AMOUNTS TO A SPACE MISSION *AND* A CLANDESTINE RESCUE OPERATION FROM A BAKERY.
YOU'RE RIGHT, FRANCINE.
WOULD A PAIR OF CRAYS HELP YOU KEEP TABS ON THE INSERTION TEAM?
WELL... *YEAH?*
FSSST
FRICTION IS A
WAS THAT NECESSARY?
THERE'S NO TIME.
CONCENTRATE ON REGAINING CONTACT WITH REX...

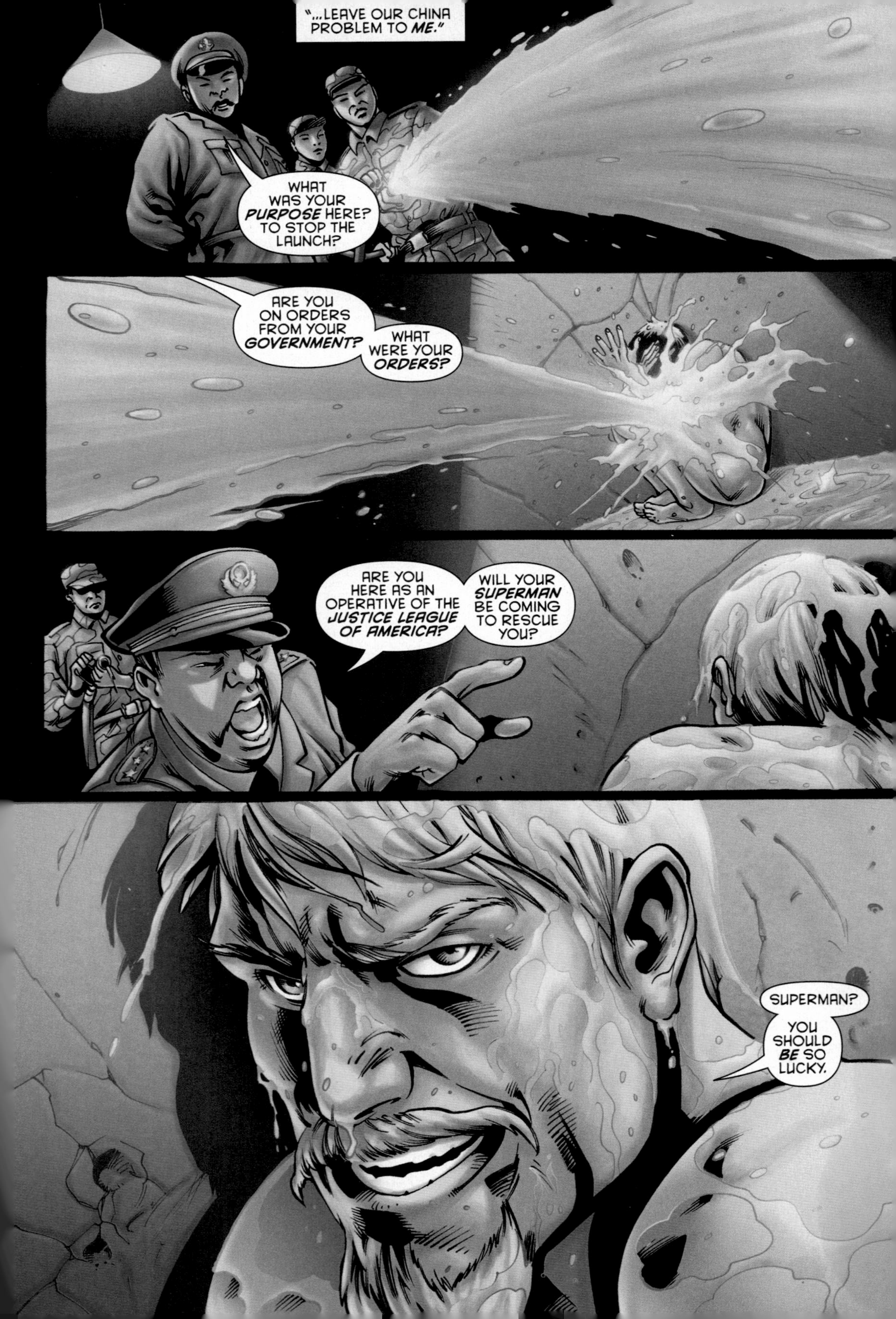
"...LEAVE OUR CHINA PROBLEM TO *ME.*"
WHAT WAS YOUR *PURPOSE* HERE? TO STOP THE LAUNCH?
ARE YOU ON ORDERS FROM YOUR *GOVERNMENT?*
WHAT WERE YOUR *ORDERS?*
ARE YOU HERE AS AN OPERATIVE OF THE *JUSTICE LEAGUE OF AMERICA?*
WILL YOUR *SUPERMAN* BE COMING TO RESCUE YOU?
SUPERMAN?
YOU SHOULD *BE* SO LUCKY.

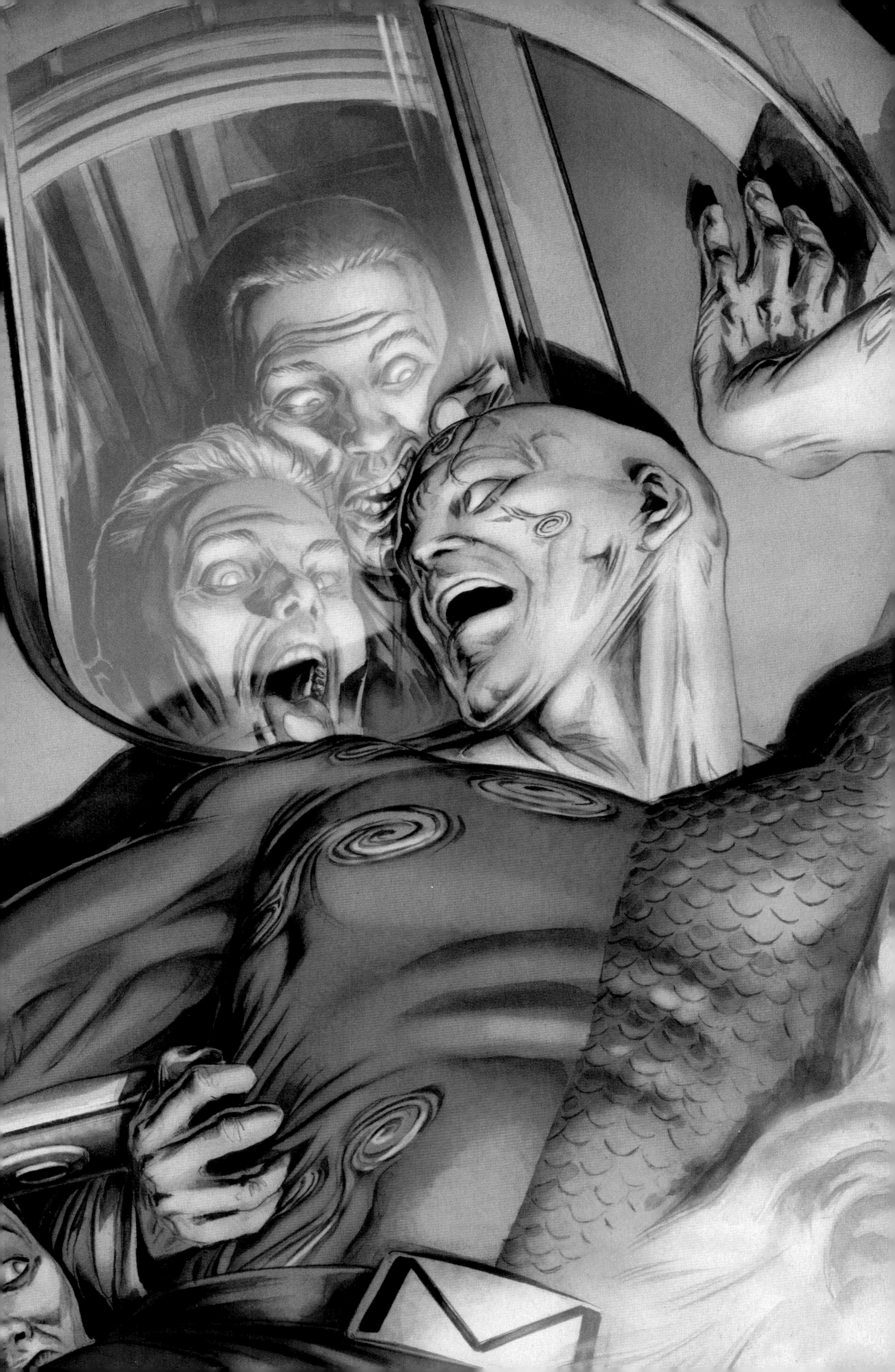

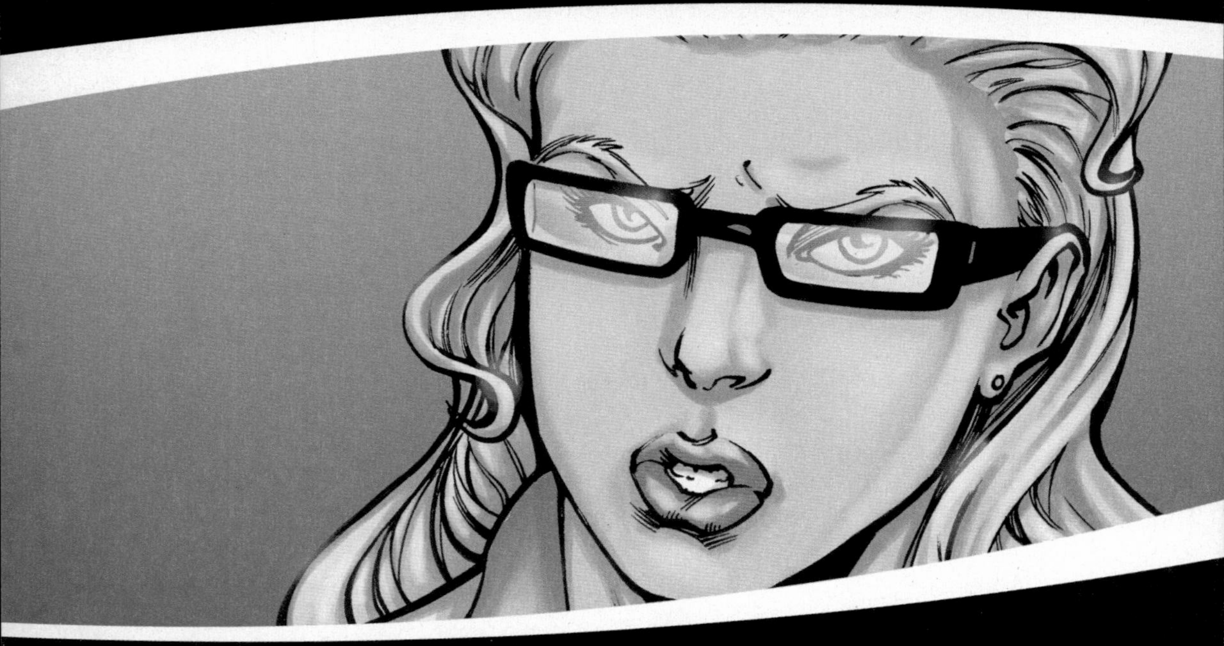

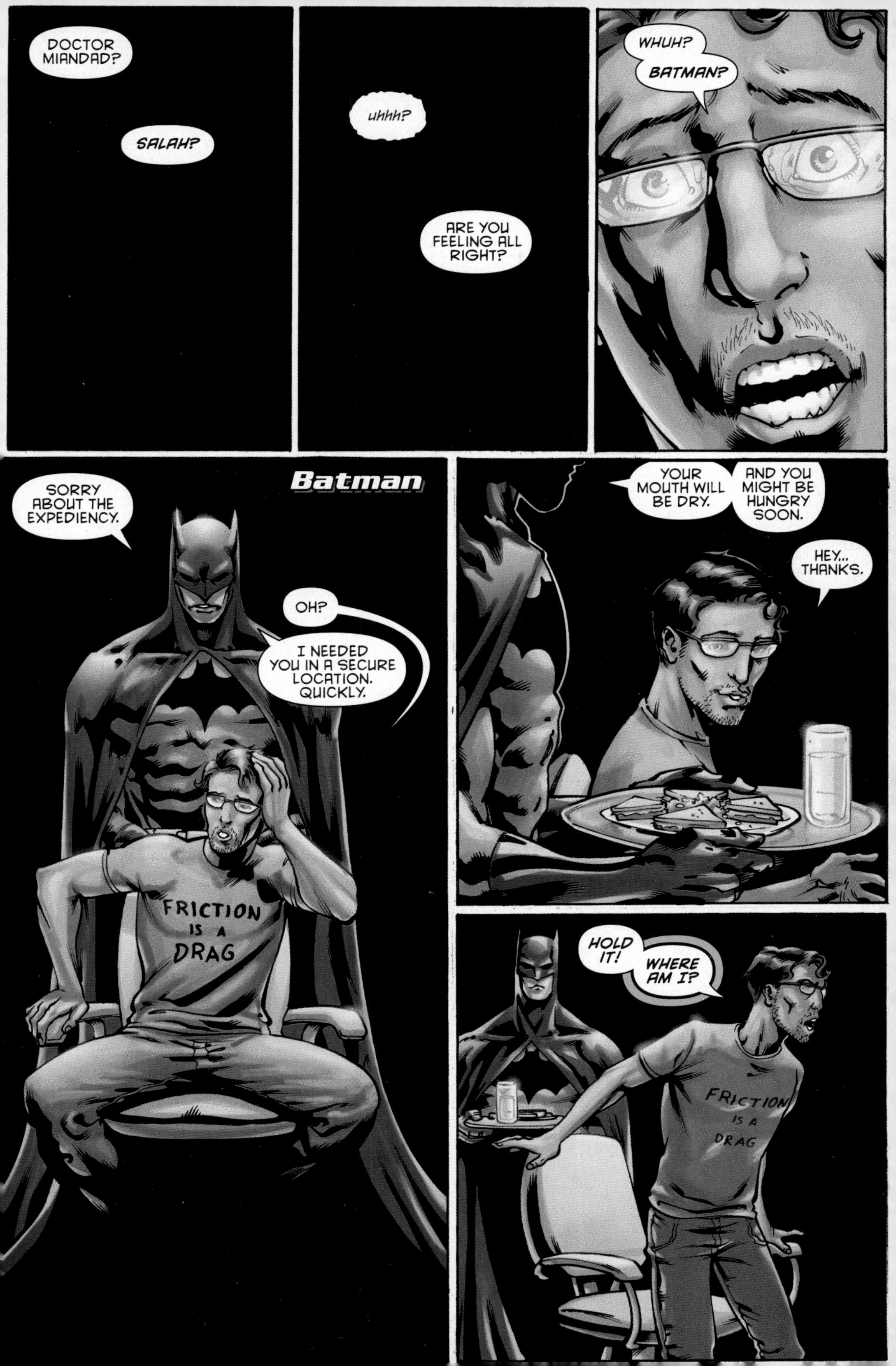
DOCTOR MIANDAD?
SALAH?
uhhh?
ARE YOU FEELING ALL RIGHT?
WHUH?
BATMAN?
Batman
SORRY ABOUT THE EXPEDIENCY.
OH?
I NEEDED YOU IN A SECURE LOCATION. QUICKLY.
FRICTION IS A DRAG
YOUR MOUTH WILL BE DRY.
AND YOU MIGHT BE HUNGRY SOON.
HEY... THANKS.
HOLD IT!
WHERE AM I?
FRICTION IS A DRAG

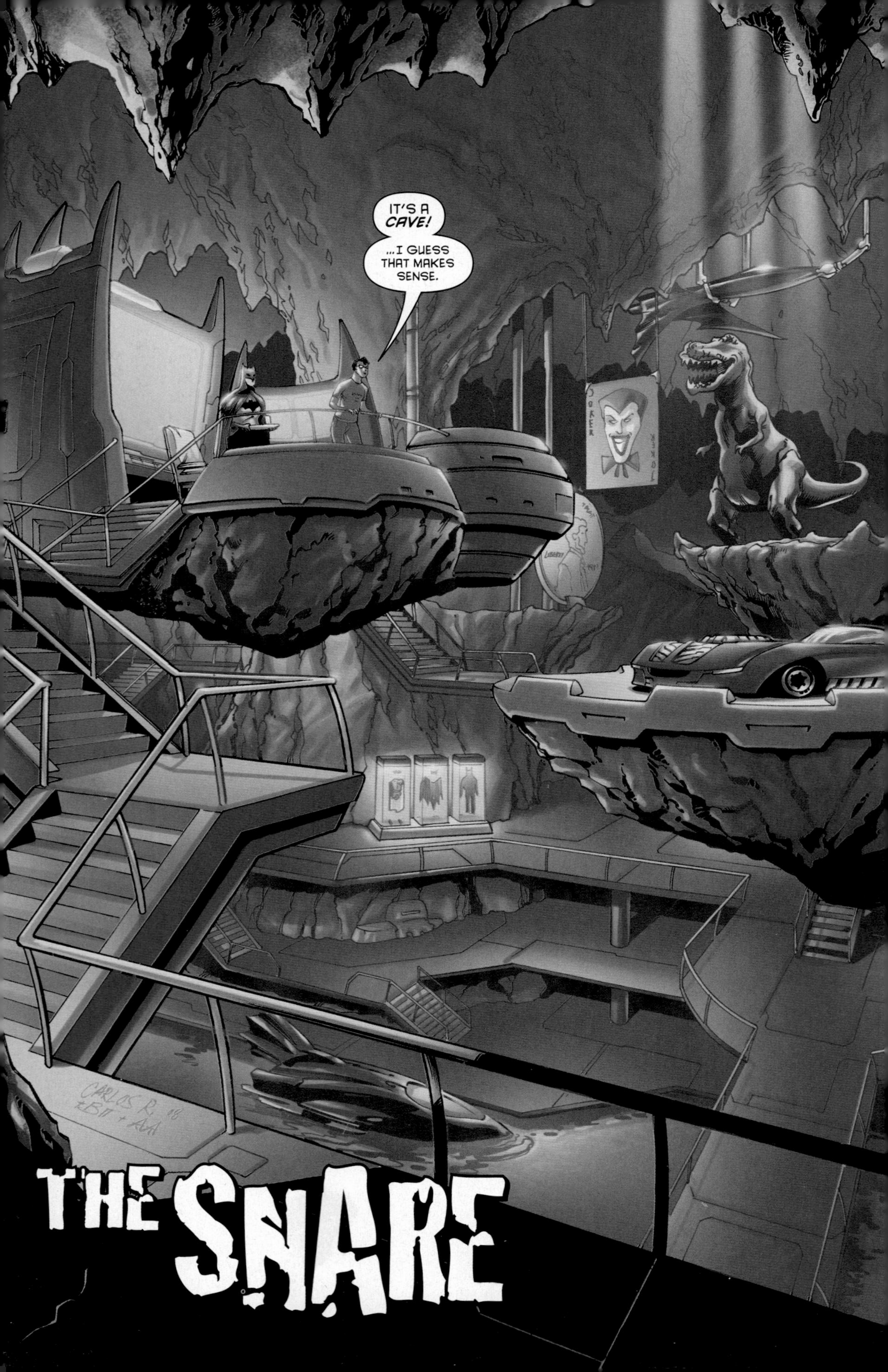
IT'S A CAVE!
...I GUESS THAT MAKES SENSE.
THE SNARE

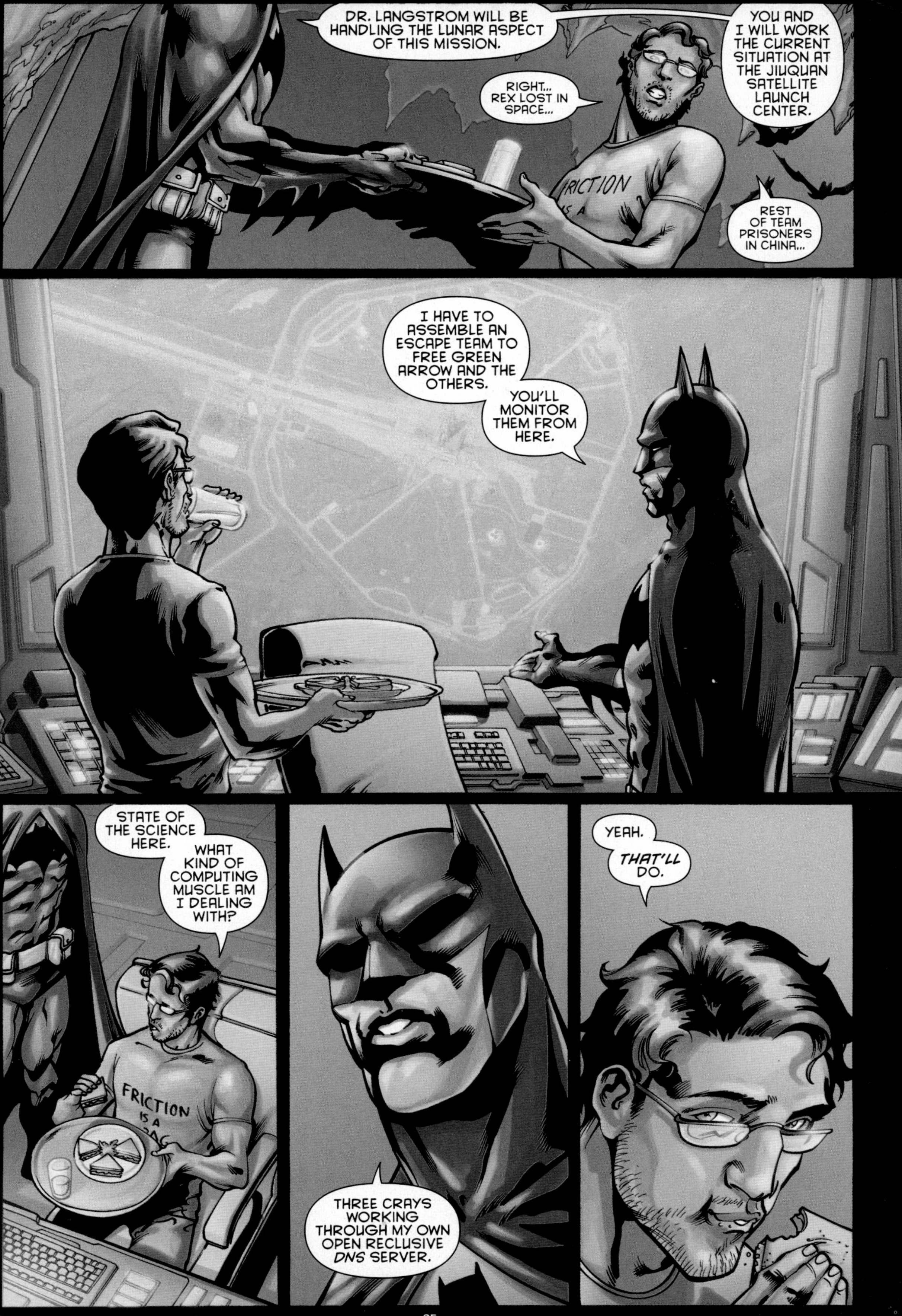
DR. LANGSTROM WILL BE HANDLING THE LUNAR ASPECT OF THIS MISSION.
RIGHT... REX LOST IN SPACE...
YOU AND I WILL WORK THE CURRENT SITUATION AT THE JIUQUAN SATELLITE LAUNCH CENTER.
REST OF TEAM PRISONERS IN CHINA...
I HAVE TO ASSEMBLE AN ESCAPE TEAM TO FREE GREEN ARROW AND THE OTHERS.
YOU'LL MONITOR THEM FROM HERE.
STATE OF THE SCIENCE HERE.
WHAT KIND OF COMPUTING MUSCLE AM I DEALING WITH?
FRICTION IS A
THREE CRAYS WORKING THROUGH MY OWN OPEN RECLUSIVE *DNS* SERVER.
YEAH.
*THAT'LL* DO.

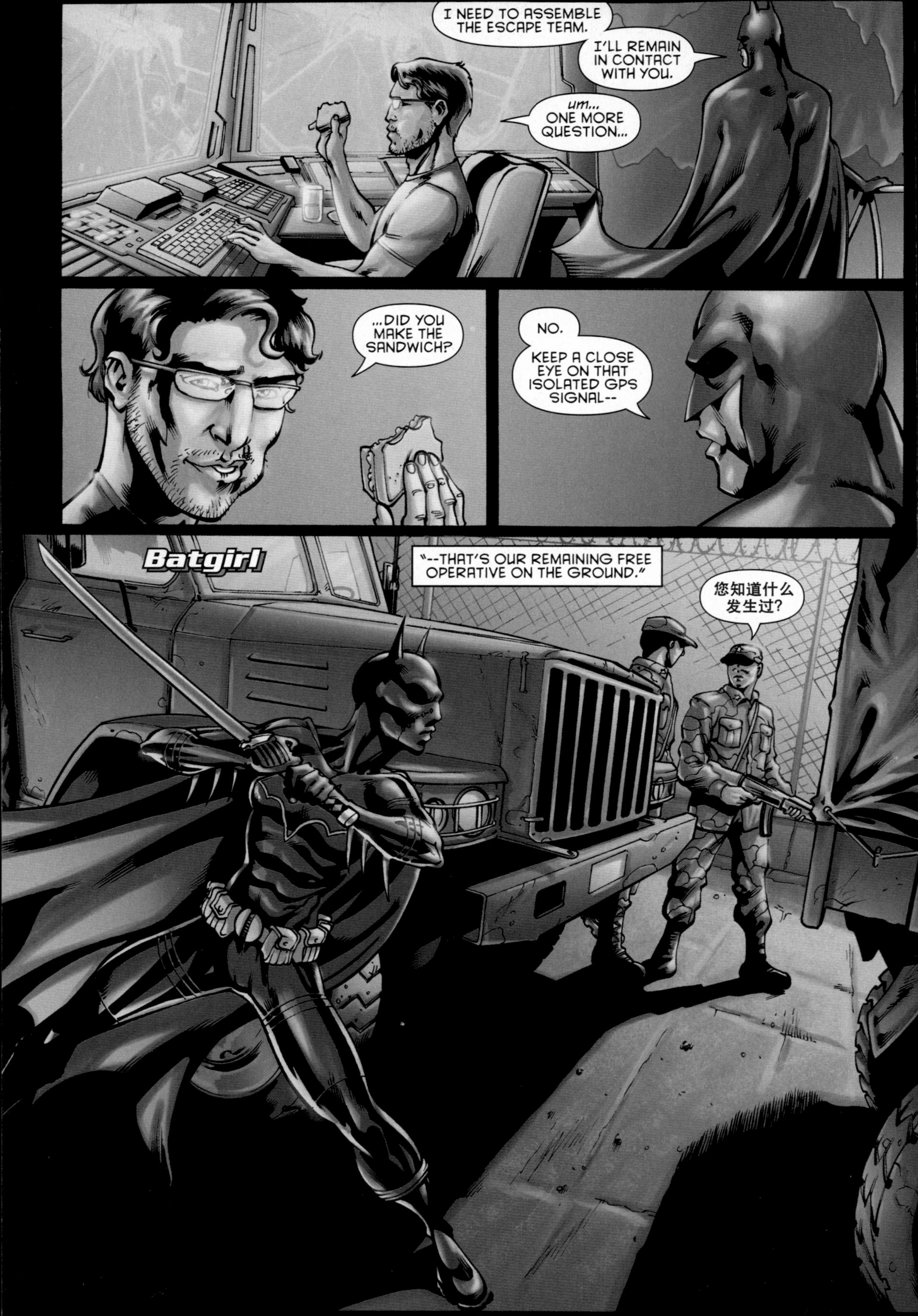
I NEED TO ASSEMBLE THE ESCAPE TEAM.
I'LL REMAIN IN CONTACT WITH YOU.
um... ONE MORE QUESTION...
...DID YOU MAKE THE SANDWICH?
NO.
KEEP A CLOSE EYE ON THAT ISOLATED GPS SIGNAL--
Batgirl
"--THAT'S OUR REMAINING FREE OPERATIVE ON THE GROUND."
您知道什么发生过?

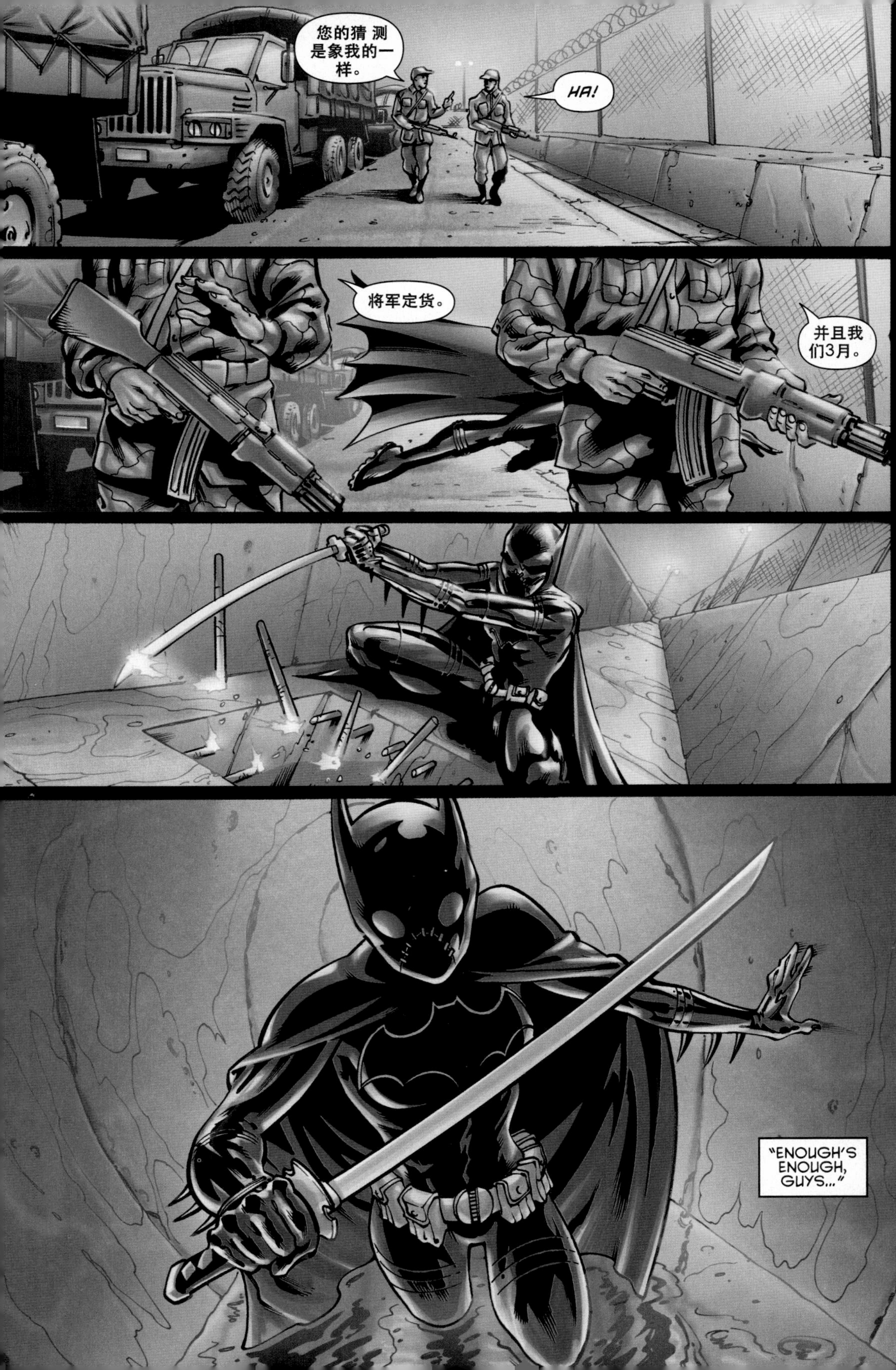
您的猜 测
是象我的一
样。
HA!
将军定货。
并且我
们3月。
"ENOUGH'S ENOUGH, GUYS..."

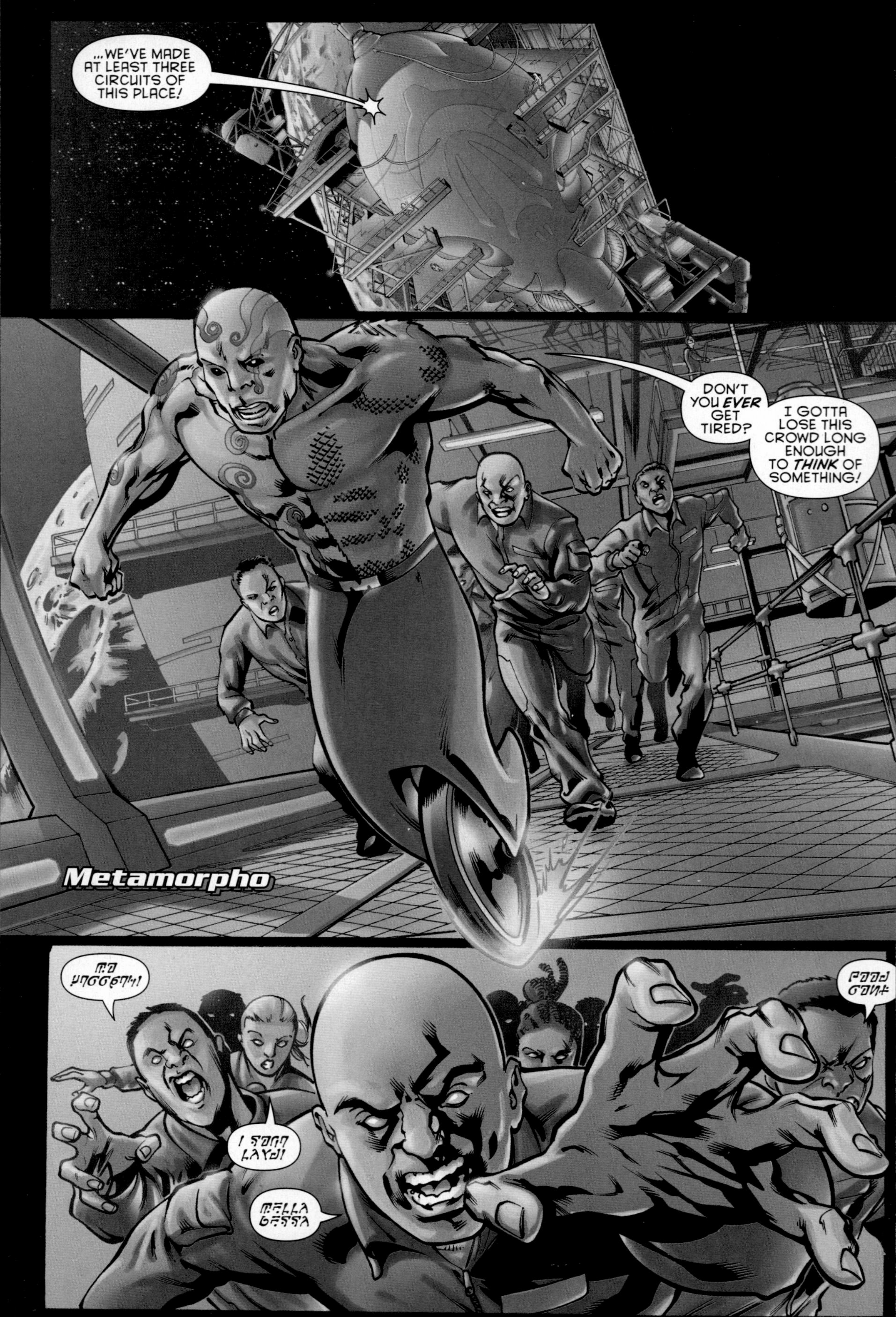
...WE'VE MADE AT LEAST THREE CIRCUITS OF THIS PLACE!
DON'T YOU EVER GET TIRED?
I GOTTA LOSE THIS CROWD LONG ENOUGH TO THINK OF SOMETHING!
Metamorpho

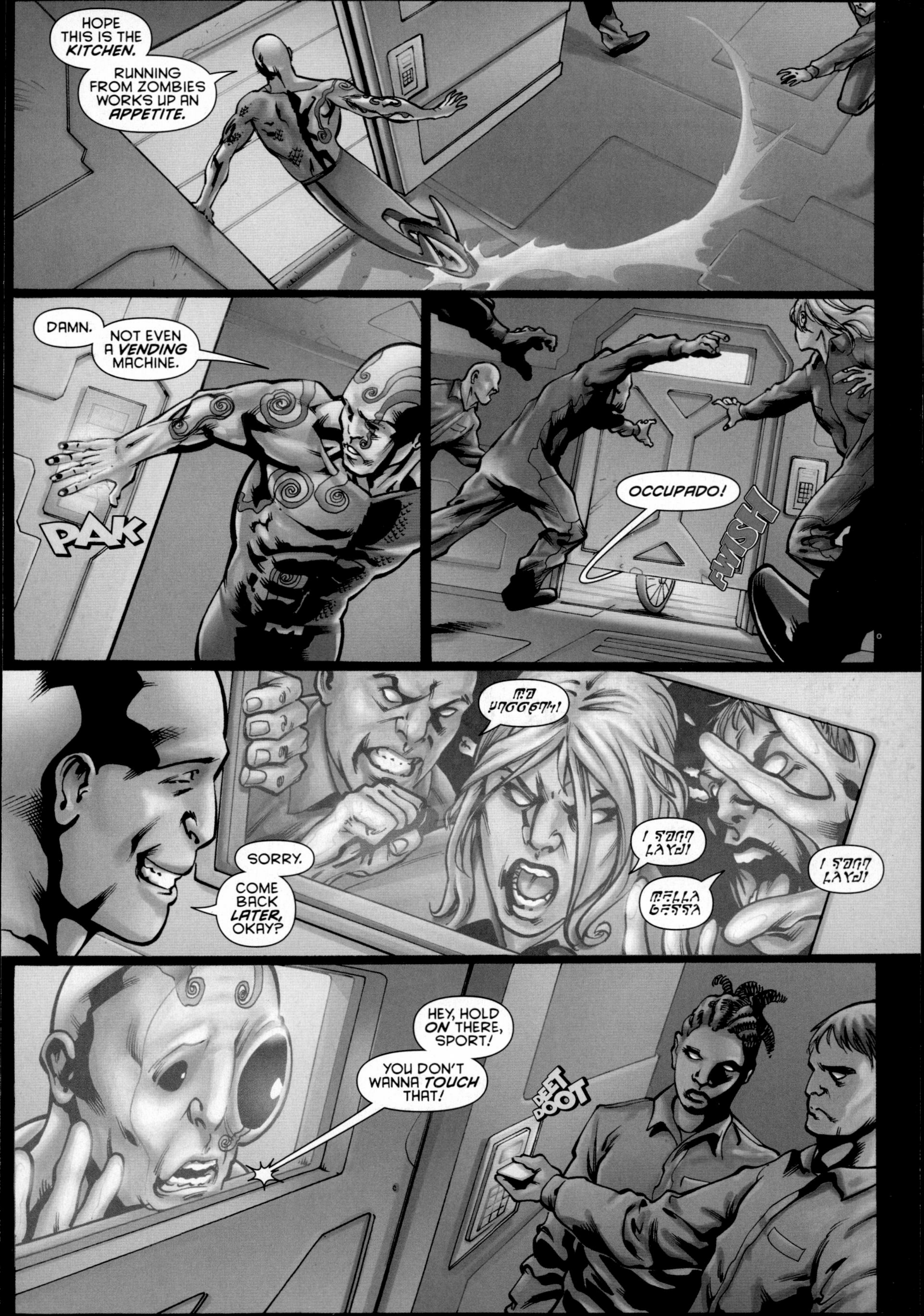
HOPE THIS IS THE *KITCHEN.*
RUNNING FROM ZOMBIES WORKS UP AN *APPETITE.*
DAMN.
NOT EVEN A *VENDING* MACHINE.
PAK
OCCUPADO!
FWISH
SORRY.
COME BACK *LATER,* OKAY?
HEY, HOLD *ON* THERE, SPORT!
YOU DON'T WANNA *TOUCH* THAT!
DEET DOOT

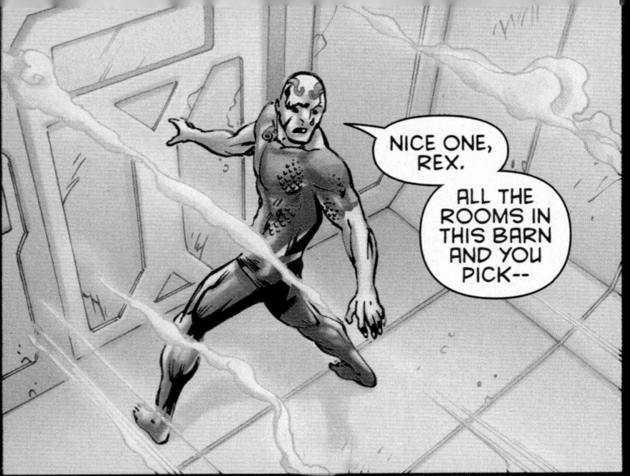
NICE ONE, REX.
ALL THE ROOMS IN THIS BARN AND YOU PICK--
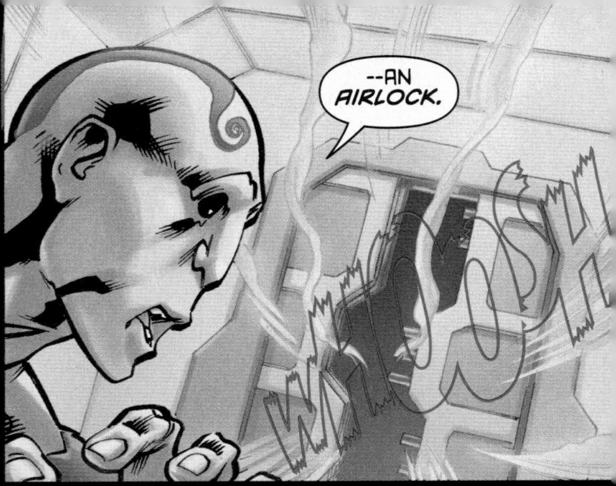
--AN *AIRLOCK.*
WHOOSH
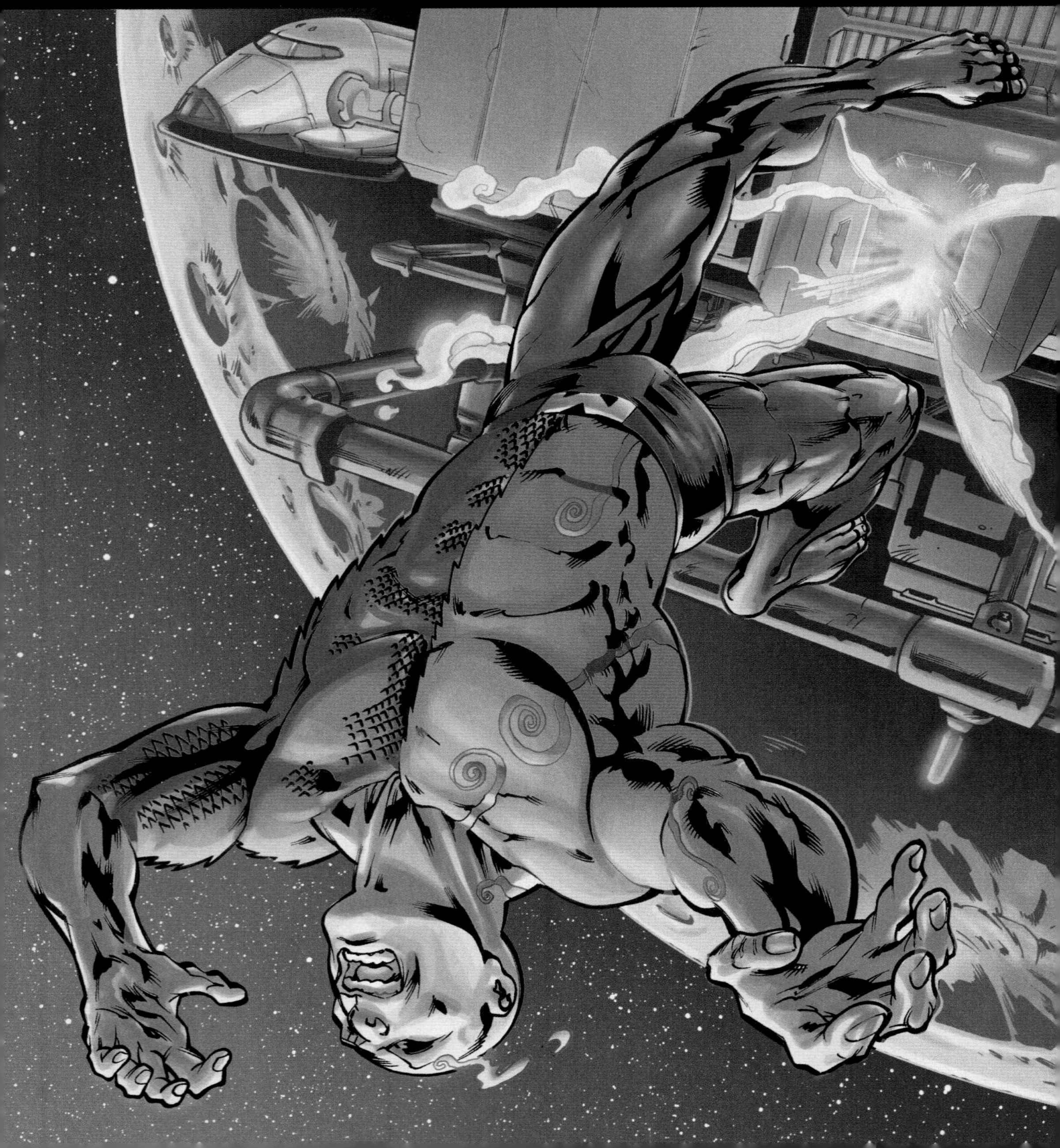

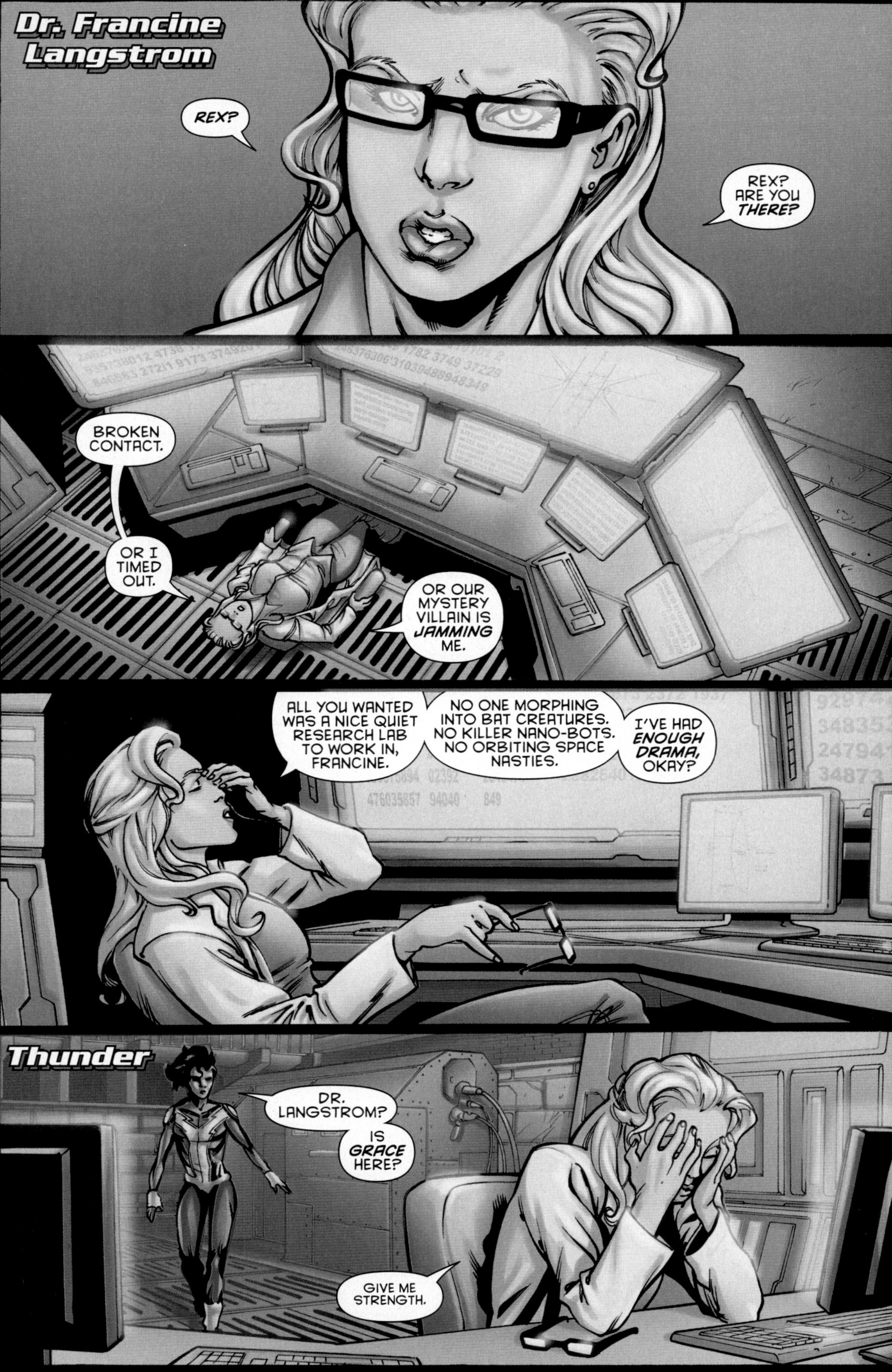

Dr. Francine Langstrom
REX?
REX? ARE YOU THERE?
BROKEN CONTACT.
OR I TIMED OUT.
OR OUR MYSTERY VILLAIN IS JAMMING ME.
ALL YOU WANTED WAS A NICE QUIET RESEARCH LAB TO WORK IN, FRANCINE.
NO ONE MORPHING INTO BAT CREATURES. NO KILLER NANO-BOTS. NO ORBITING SPACE NASTIES.
I'VE HAD ENOUGH DRAMA, OKAY?
Thunder
DR. LANGSTROM?
IS GRACE HERE?
GIVE ME STRENGTH.

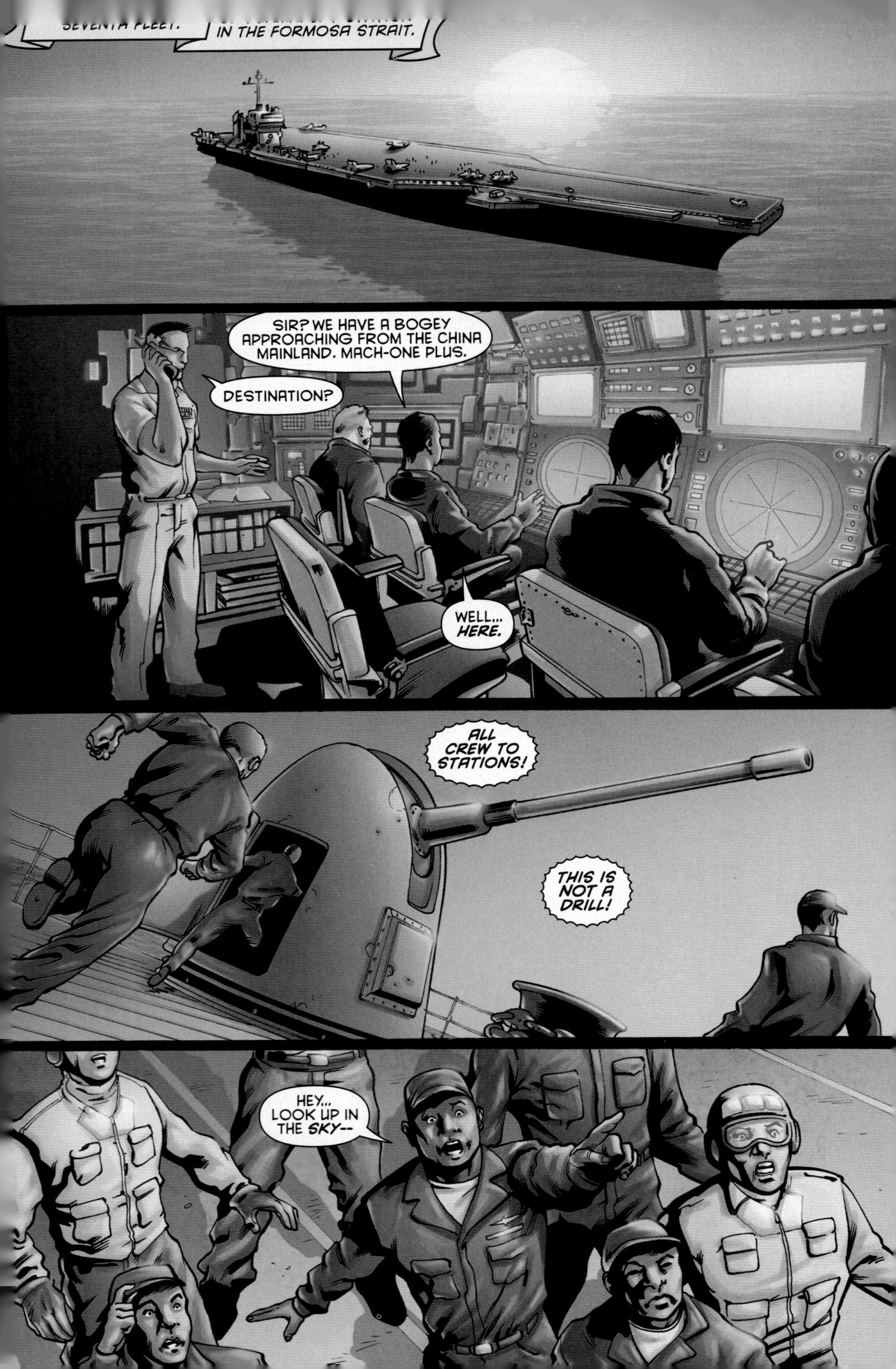

IN THE FORMOSA STRAIT.
SIR? WE HAVE A BOGEY APPROACHING FROM THE CHINA MAINLAND. MACH-ONE PLUS.
DESTINATION?
WELL... HERE.
ALL CREW TO STATIONS!
THIS IS NOT A DRILL!
HEY... LOOK UP IN THE SKY--

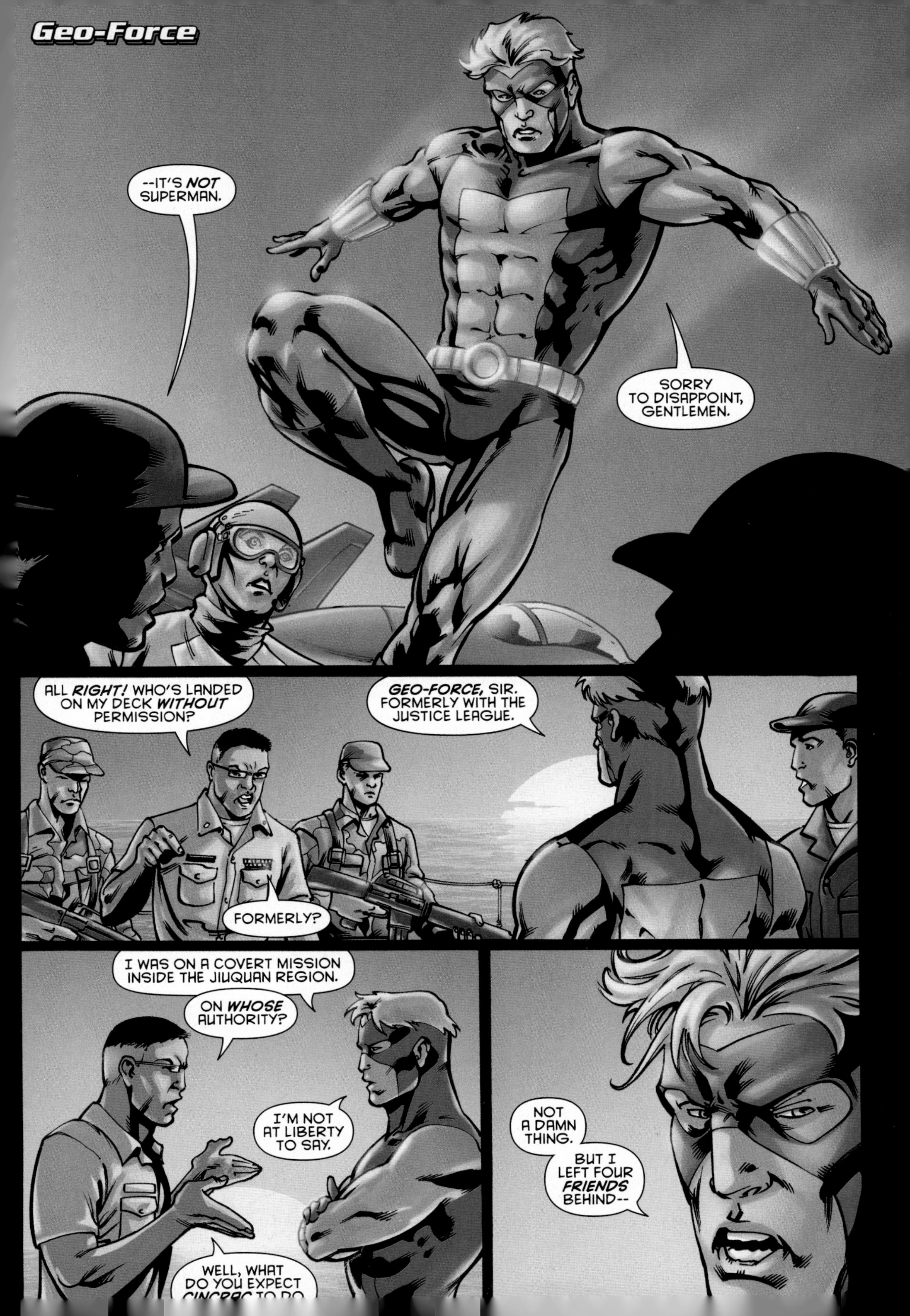
--IT'S NOT SUPERMAN.
SORRY TO DISAPPOINT, GENTLEMEN.
ALL RIGHT! WHO'S LANDED ON MY DECK WITHOUT PERMISSION?
GEO-FORCE, SIR. FORMERLY WITH THE JUSTICE LEAGUE.
FORMERLY?
I WAS ON A COVERT MISSION INSIDE THE JIUQUAN REGION.
ON WHOSE AUTHORITY?
I'M NOT AT LIBERTY TO SAY.
WELL, WHAT DO YOU EXPECT
NOT A DAMN THING.
BUT I LEFT FOUR FRIENDS BEHIND--

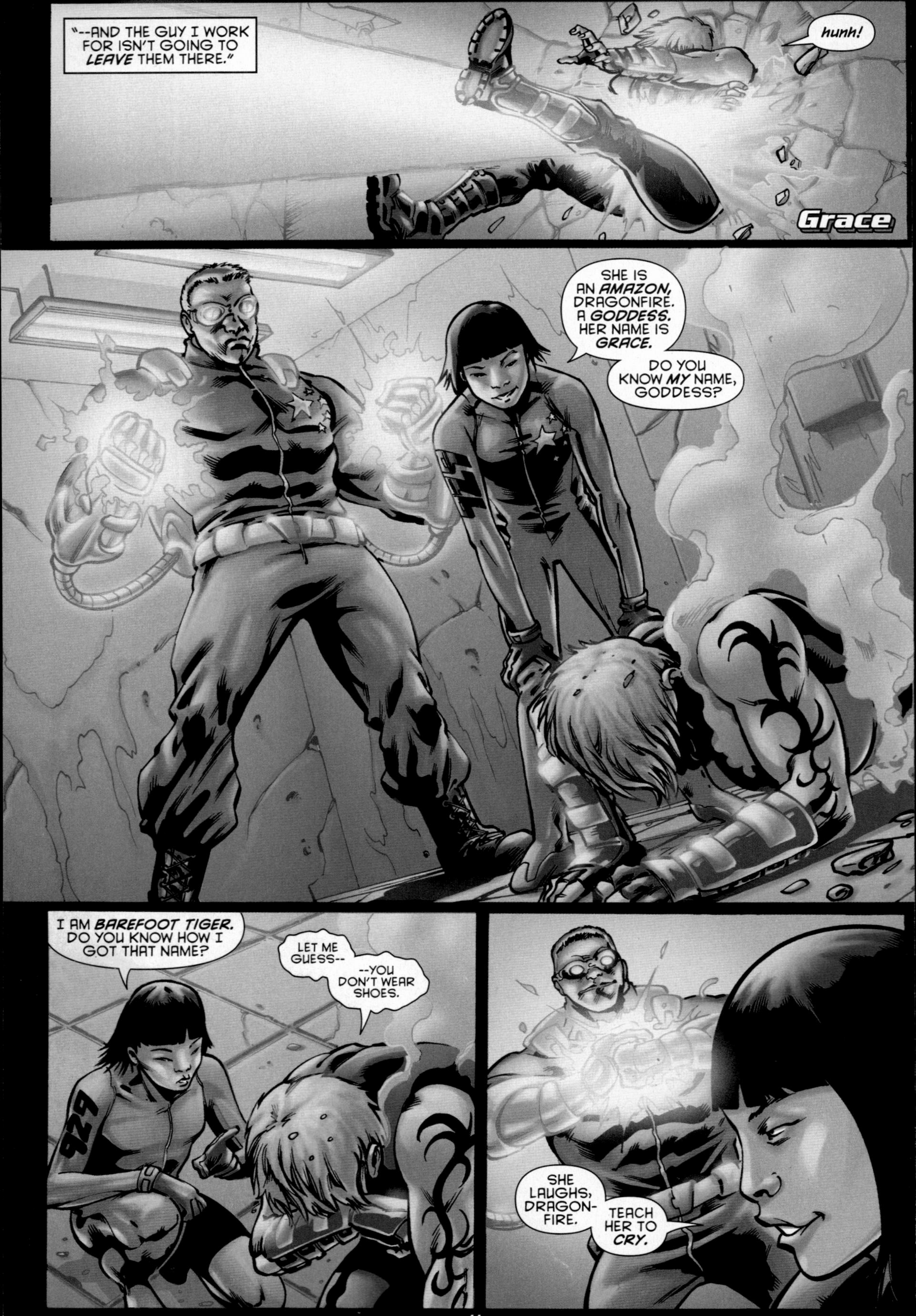
"--AND THE GUY I WORK FOR ISN'T GOING TO LEAVE THEM THERE."
hunh!
Grace
SHE IS AN AMAZON, DRAGONFIRE. A GODDESS. HER NAME IS GRACE.
DO YOU KNOW MY NAME, GODDESS?
I AM BAREFOOT TIGER. DO YOU KNOW HOW I GOT THAT NAME?
LET ME GUESS--
--YOU DON'T WEAR SHOES.
929
SHE LAUGHS, DRAGON-FIRE.
TEACH HER TO CRY.

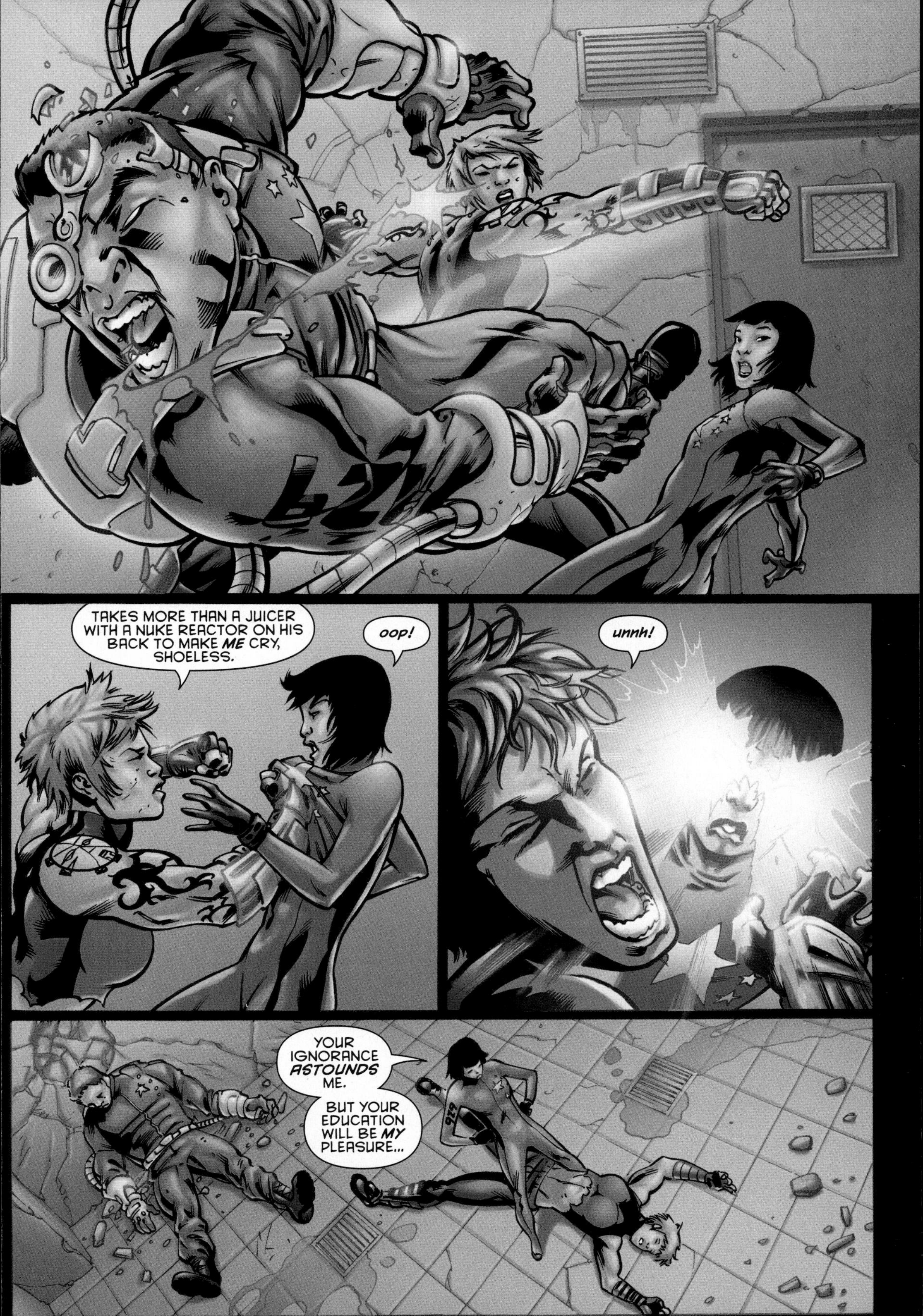
TAKES MORE THAN A JUICER WITH A NUKE REACTOR ON HIS BACK TO MAKE *ME* CRY, SHOELESS.
*oop!*
*unnh!*
YOUR IGNORANCE ***ASTOUNDS*** ME.
BUT YOUR EDUCATION WILL BE ***MY*** PLEASURE...

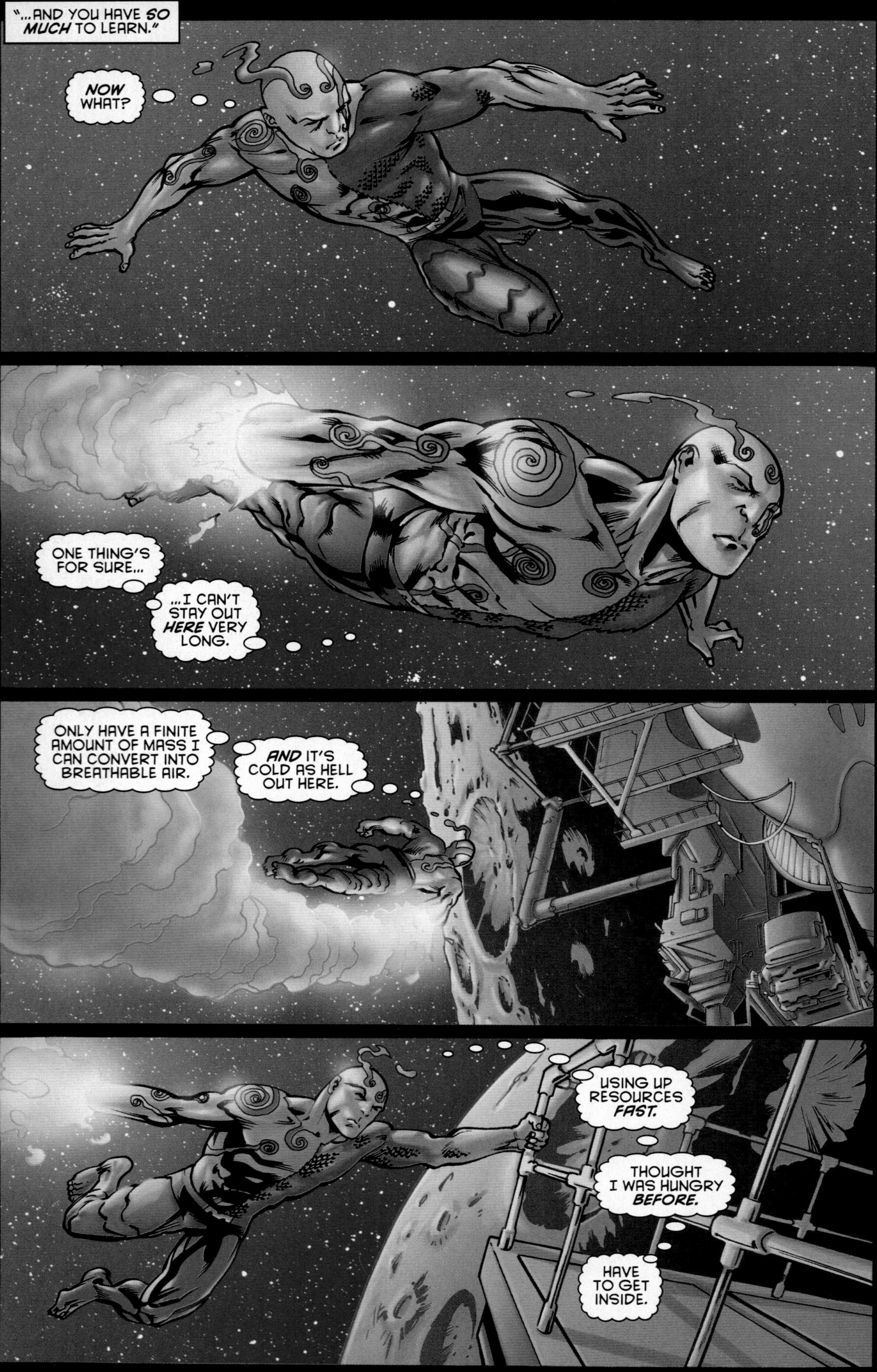
"...AND YOU HAVE SO MUCH TO LEARN."
NOW WHAT?
ONE THING'S FOR SURE...
...I CAN'T STAY OUT HERE VERY LONG.
ONLY HAVE A FINITE AMOUNT OF MASS I CAN CONVERT INTO BREATHABLE AIR.
AND IT'S COLD AS HELL OUT HERE.
USING UP RESOURCES FAST.
THOUGHT I WAS HUNGRY BEFORE.
HAVE TO GET INSIDE.

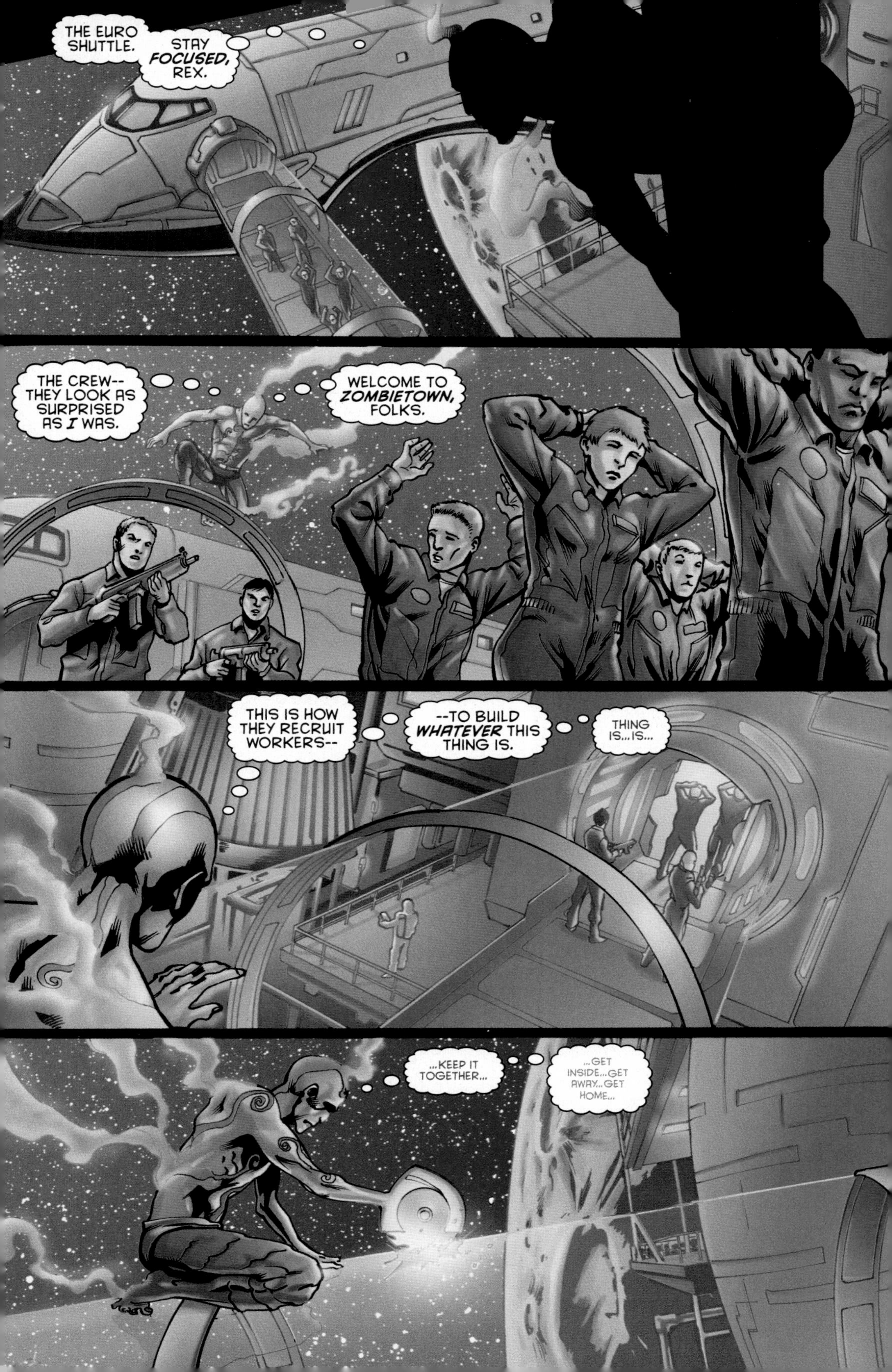
THE EURO SHUTTLE.
STAY *FOCUSED*, REX.
THE CREW-- THEY LOOK AS SURPRISED AS *I* WAS.
WELCOME TO *ZOMBIETOWN*, FOLKS.
THIS IS HOW THEY RECRUIT WORKERS--
--TO BUILD *WHATEVER* THIS THING IS.
THING IS...IS...
...KEEP IT TOGETHER...
...GET INSIDE...GET AWAY...GET HOME...

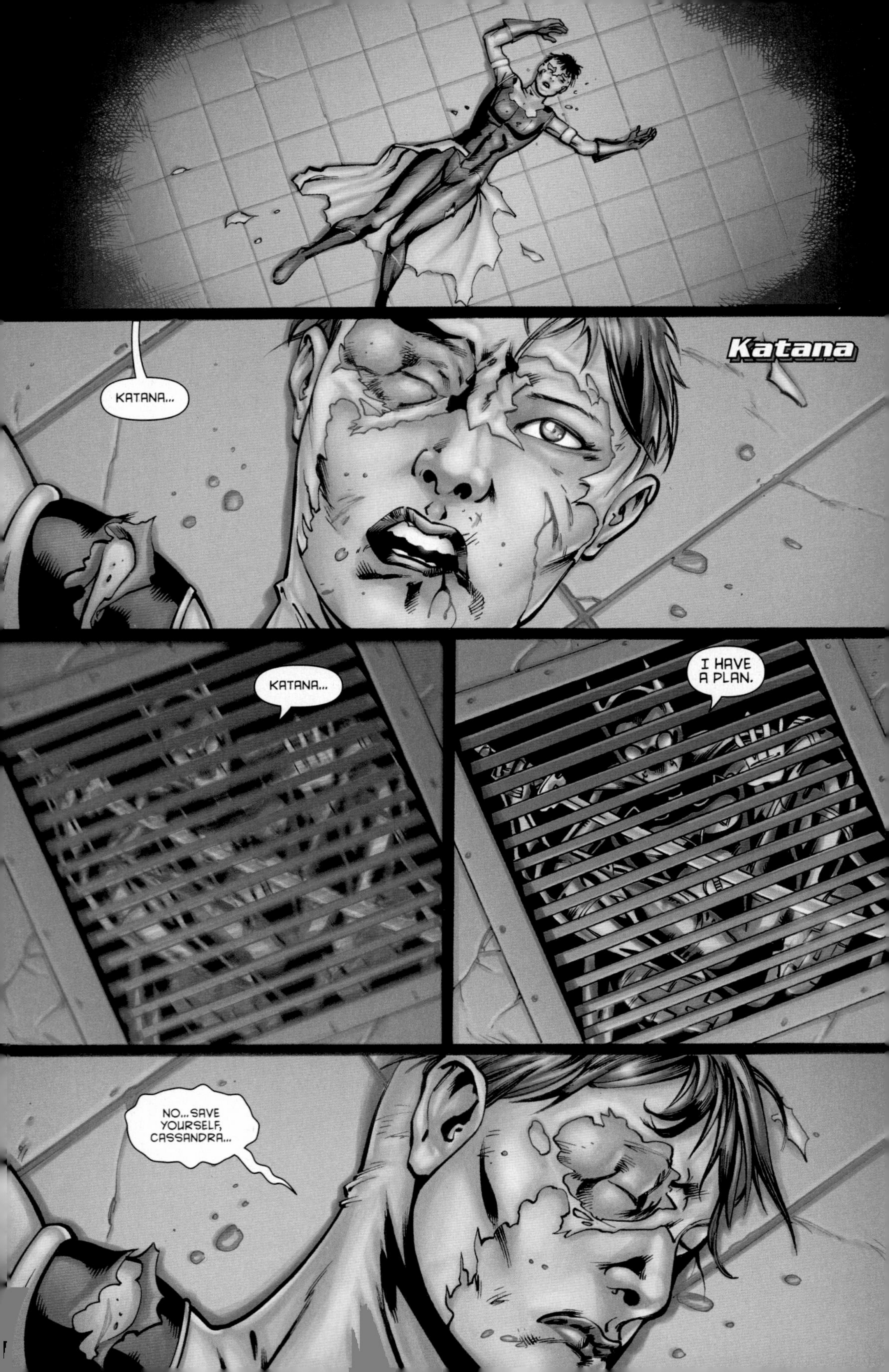
Katana
KATANA...
KATANA...
I HAVE A PLAN.
NO...SAVE YOURSELF, CASSANDRA...

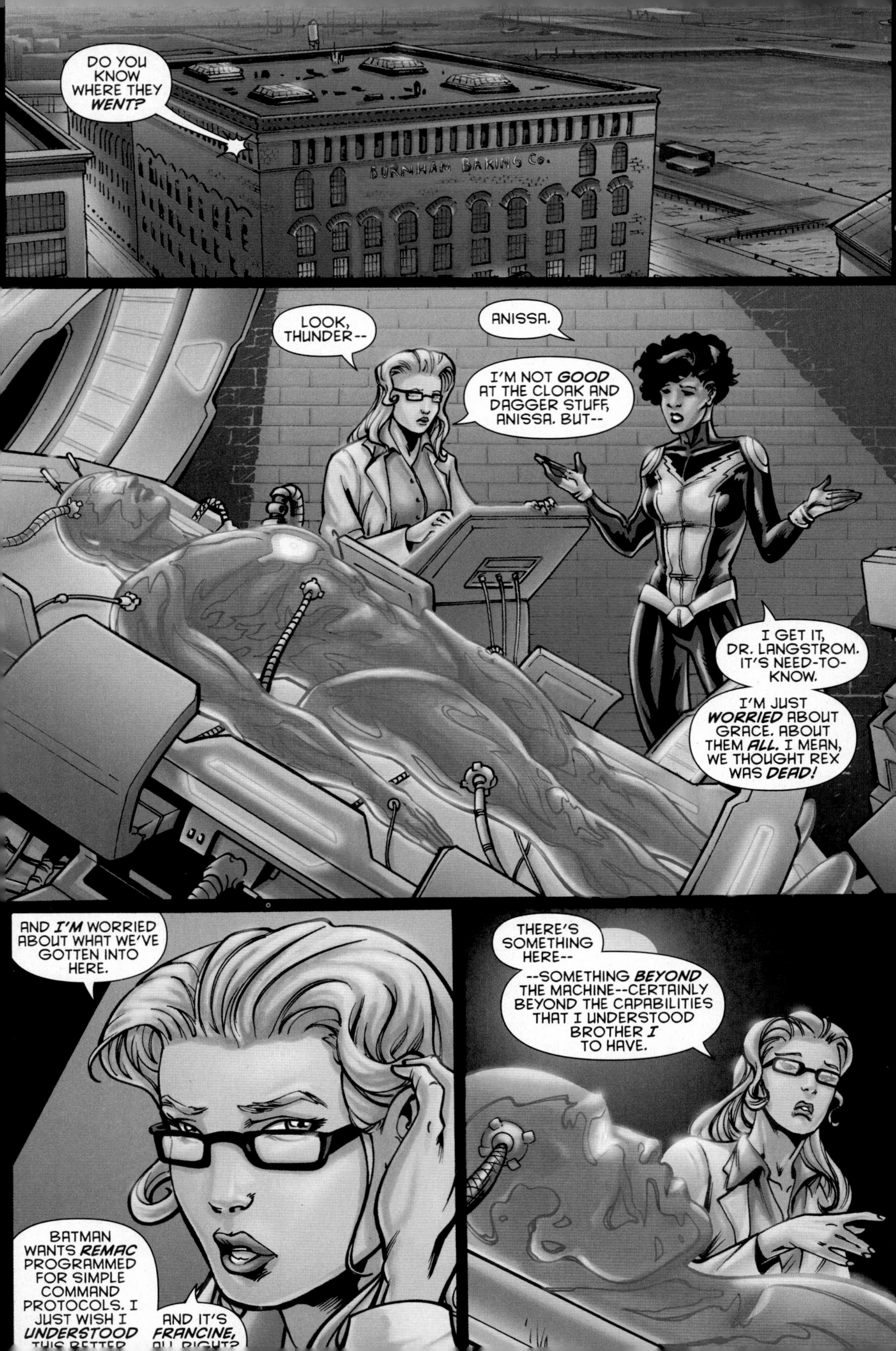
DO YOU KNOW WHERE THEY *WENT?*
BURNHAM BAKING Co.
LOOK, THUNDER--
ANISSA.
I'M NOT *GOOD* AT THE CLOAK AND DAGGER STUFF, ANISSA. BUT--
I GET IT, DR. LANGSTROM. IT'S NEED-TO-KNOW.
I'M JUST *WORRIED* ABOUT GRACE. ABOUT THEM *ALL.* I MEAN, WE THOUGHT REX WAS *DEAD!*
AND *I'M* WORRIED ABOUT WHAT WE'VE GOTTEN INTO HERE.
BATMAN WANTS *REMAC* PROGRAMMED FOR SIMPLE COMMAND PROTOCOLS. I JUST WISH I *UNDERSTOOD*
AND IT'S *FRANCINE,*
THERE'S SOMETHING HERE--
--SOMETHING *BEYOND* THE MACHINE--CERTAINLY BEYOND THE CAPABILITIES THAT I UNDERSTOOD BROTHER *I* TO HAVE.

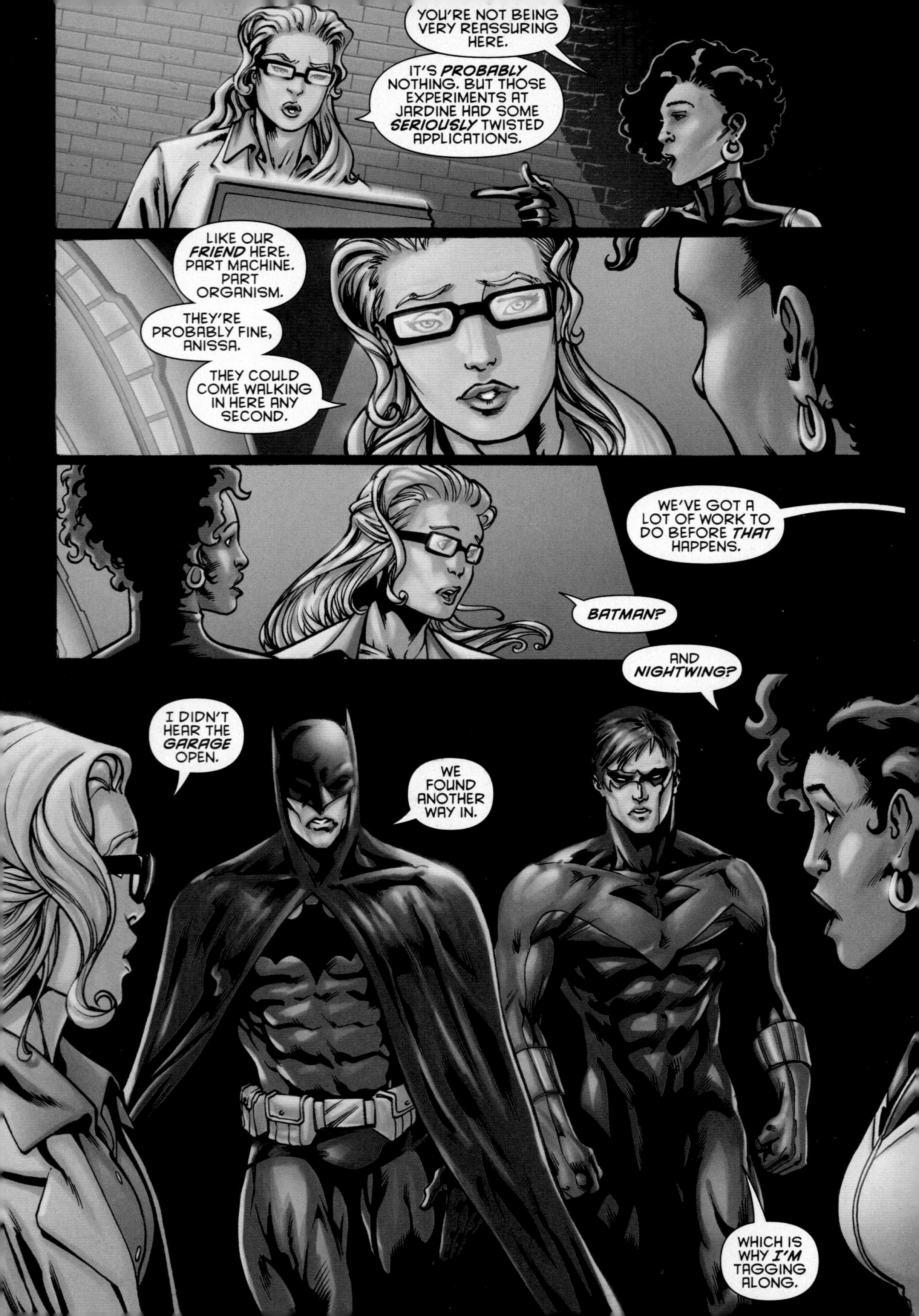

YOU'RE NOT BEING VERY REASSURING HERE.
IT'S PROBABLY NOTHING. BUT THOSE EXPERIMENTS AT JARDINE HAD SOME SERIOUSLY TWISTED APPLICATIONS.
LIKE OUR FRIEND HERE. PART MACHINE. PART ORGANISM.
THEY'RE PROBABLY FINE, ANISSA.
THEY COULD COME WALKING IN HERE ANY SECOND.
WE'VE GOT A LOT OF WORK TO DO BEFORE THAT HAPPENS.
BATMAN?
AND NIGHTWING?
I DIDN'T HEAR THE GARAGE OPEN.
WE FOUND ANOTHER WAY IN.
WHICH IS WHY I'M TAGGING ALONG.

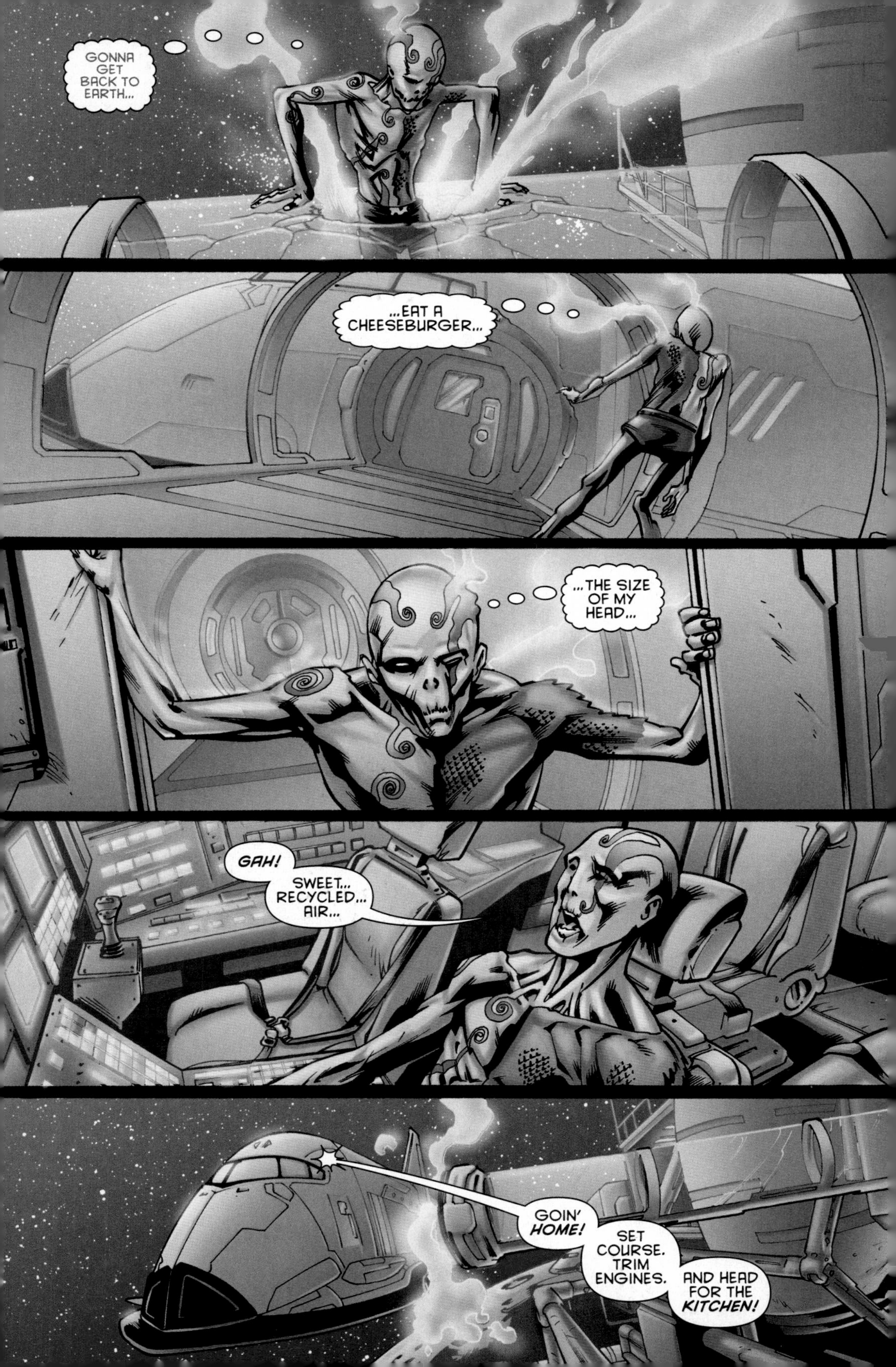
GONNA GET BACK TO EARTH...
...EAT A CHEESEBURGER...
...THE SIZE OF MY HEAD...
GAH!
SWEET... RECYCLED... AIR...
GOIN' *HOME!*
SET COURSE. TRIM ENGINES.
AND HEAD FOR THE *KITCHEN!*

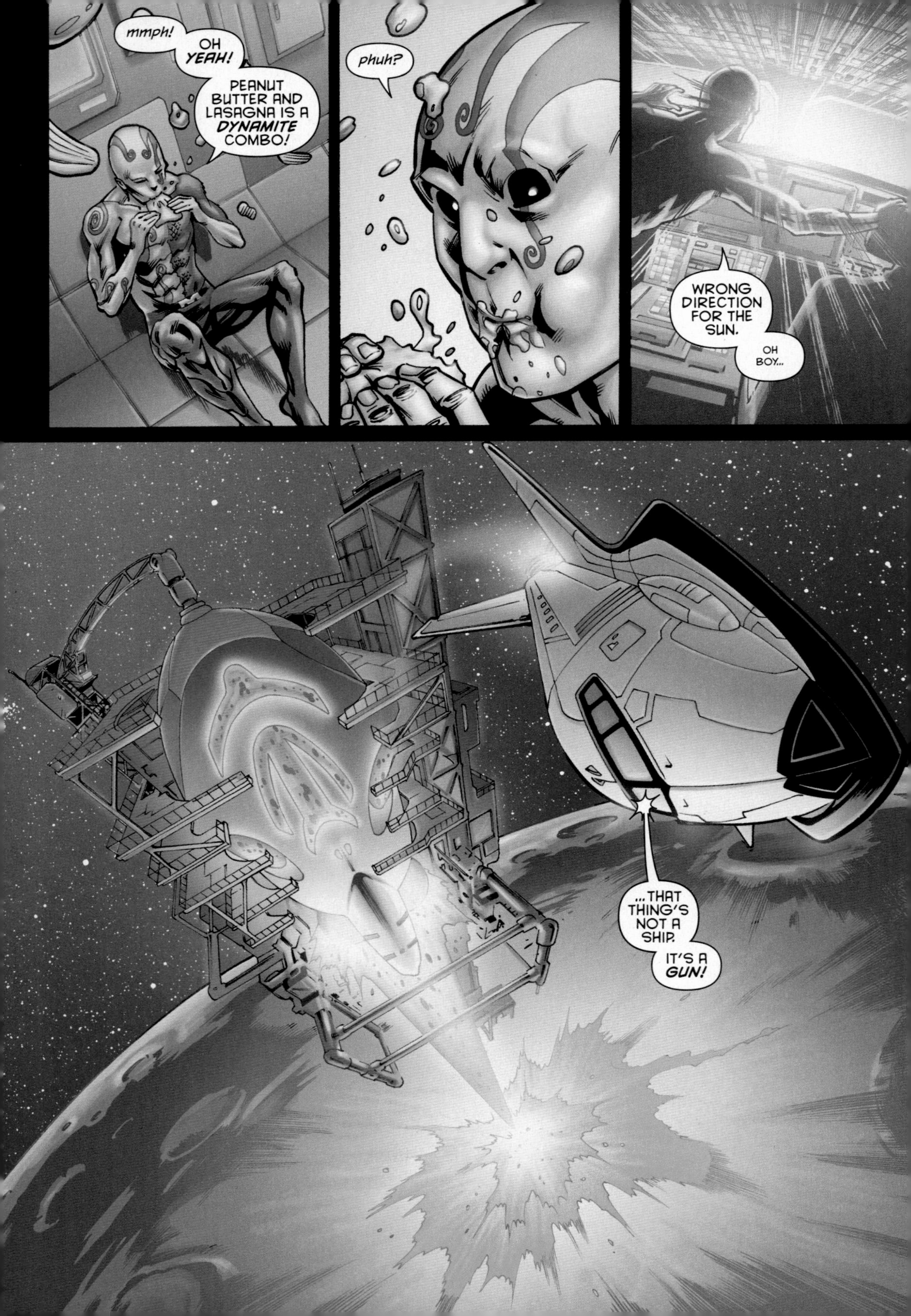
mmph!
OH YEAH!
PEANUT BUTTER AND LASAGNA IS A DYNAMITE COMBO!
phuh?
WRONG DIRECTION FOR THE SUN.
OH BOY...
...THAT THING'S NOT A SHIP.
IT'S A GUN!

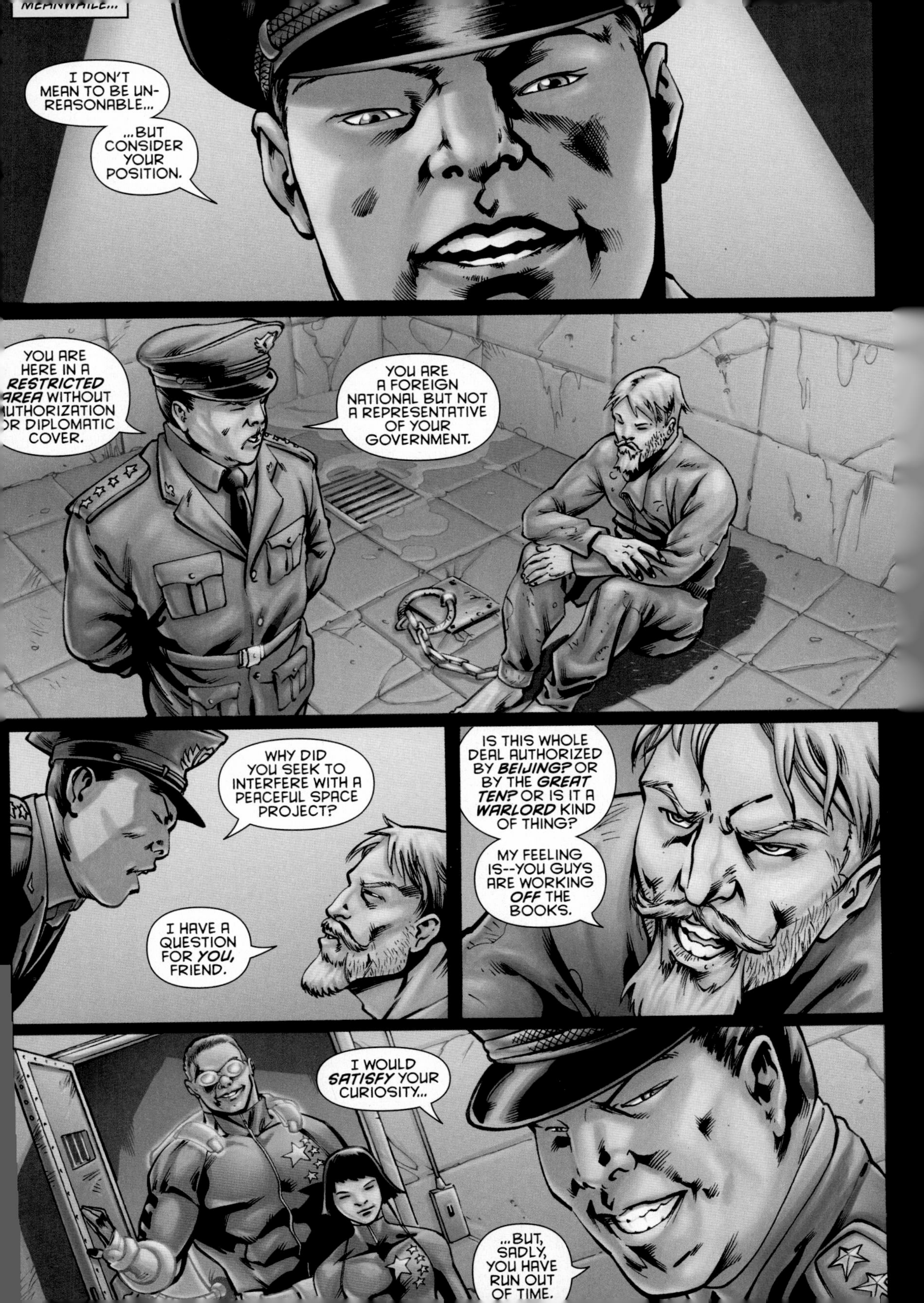
MEANWHILE...
I DON'T MEAN TO BE UN-REASONABLE...
...BUT CONSIDER YOUR POSITION.
YOU ARE HERE IN A RESTRICTED AREA WITHOUT AUTHORIZATION OR DIPLOMATIC COVER.
YOU ARE A FOREIGN NATIONAL BUT NOT A REPRESENTATIVE OF YOUR GOVERNMENT.
WHY DID YOU SEEK TO INTERFERE WITH A PEACEFUL SPACE PROJECT?
I HAVE A QUESTION FOR YOU, FRIEND.
IS THIS WHOLE DEAL AUTHORIZED BY BEIJING? OR BY THE GREAT TEN? OR IS IT A WARLORD KIND OF THING?
MY FEELING IS--YOU GUYS ARE WORKING OFF THE BOOKS.
I WOULD SATISFY YOUR CURIOSITY...
...BUT, SADLY, YOU HAVE RUN OUT OF TIME.

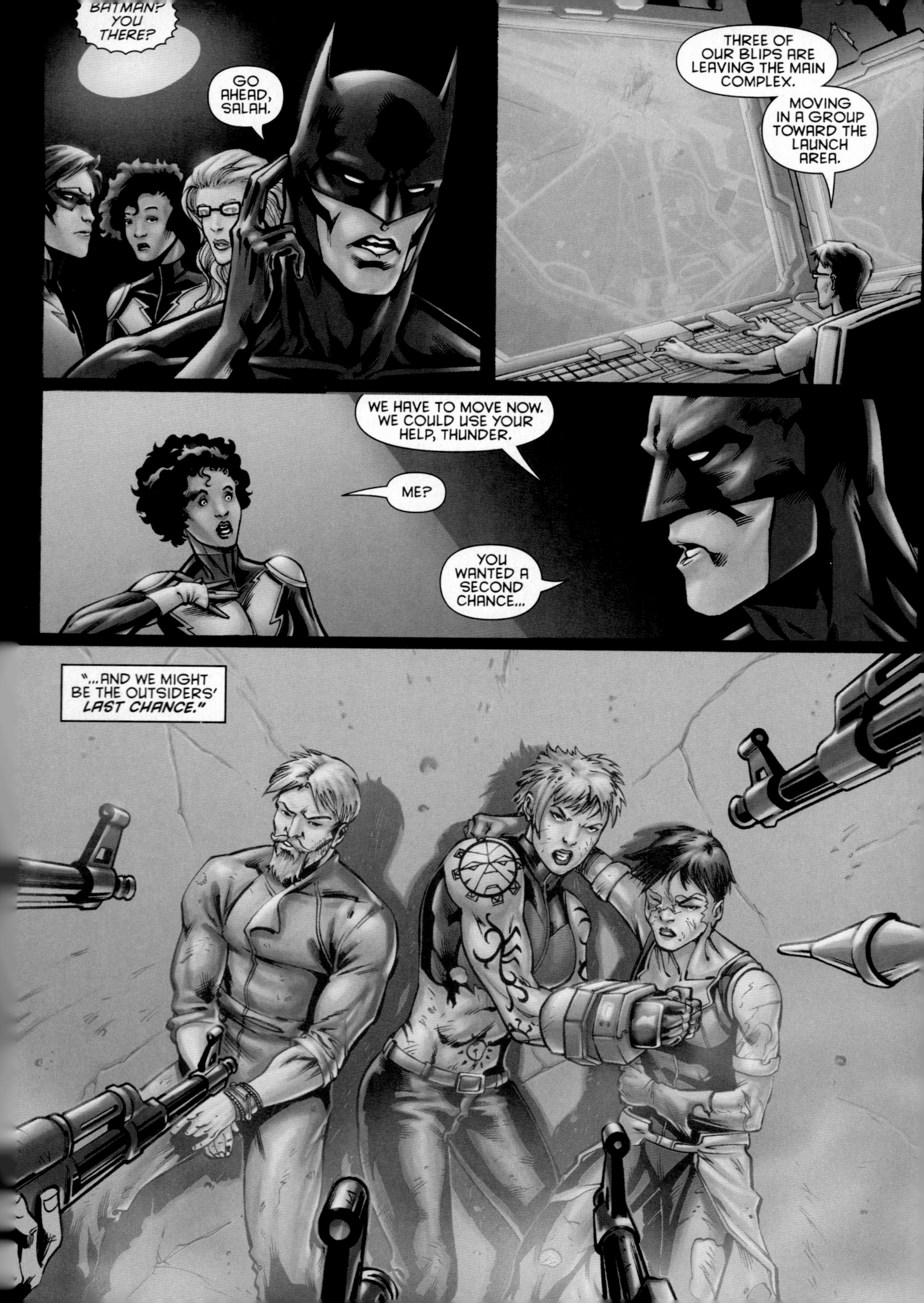
BATMAN? YOU THERE?
GO AHEAD, SALAH.
THREE OF OUR BLIPS ARE LEAVING THE MAIN COMPLEX.
MOVING IN A GROUP TOWARD THE LAUNCH AREA.
WE HAVE TO MOVE NOW. WE COULD USE YOUR HELP, THUNDER.
ME?
YOU WANTED A SECOND CHANCE...
"...AND WE MIGHT BE THE OUTSIDERS' LAST CHANCE."

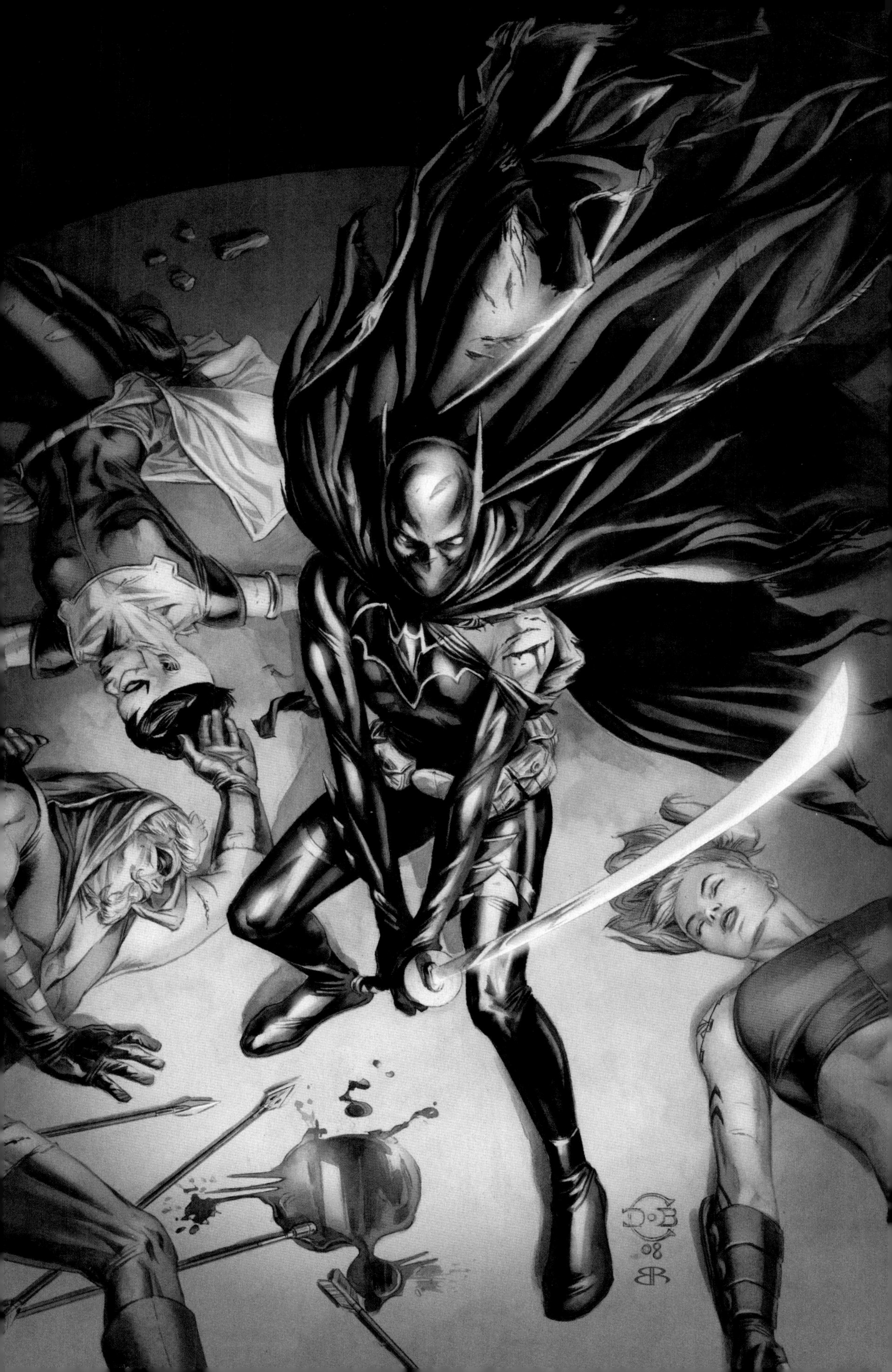

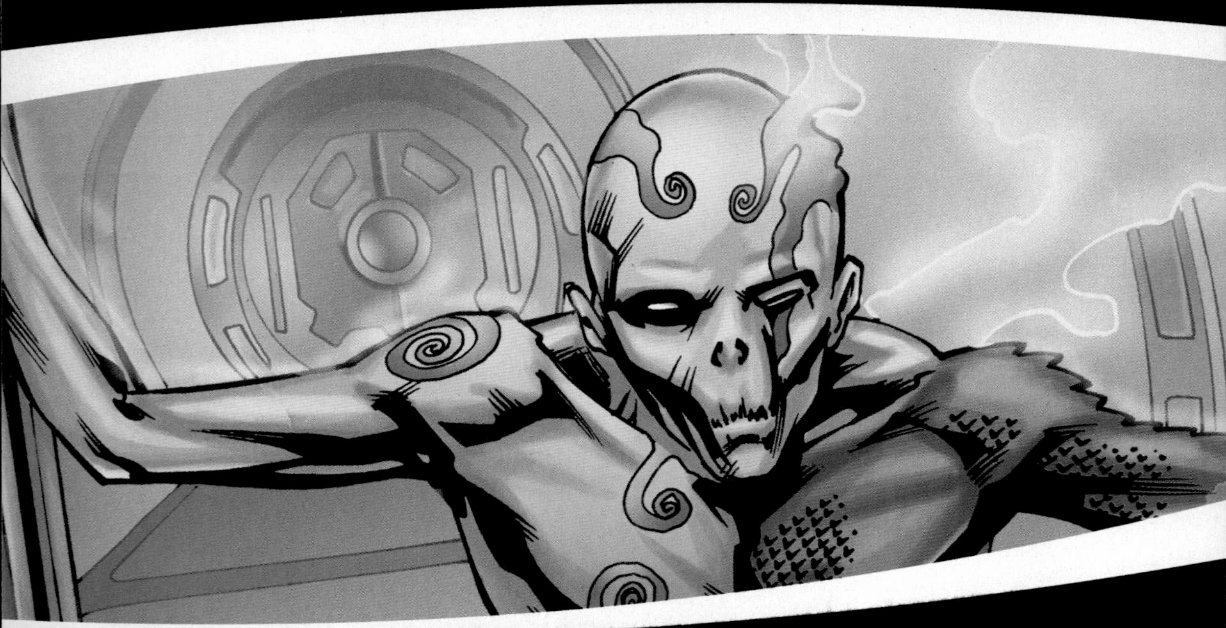

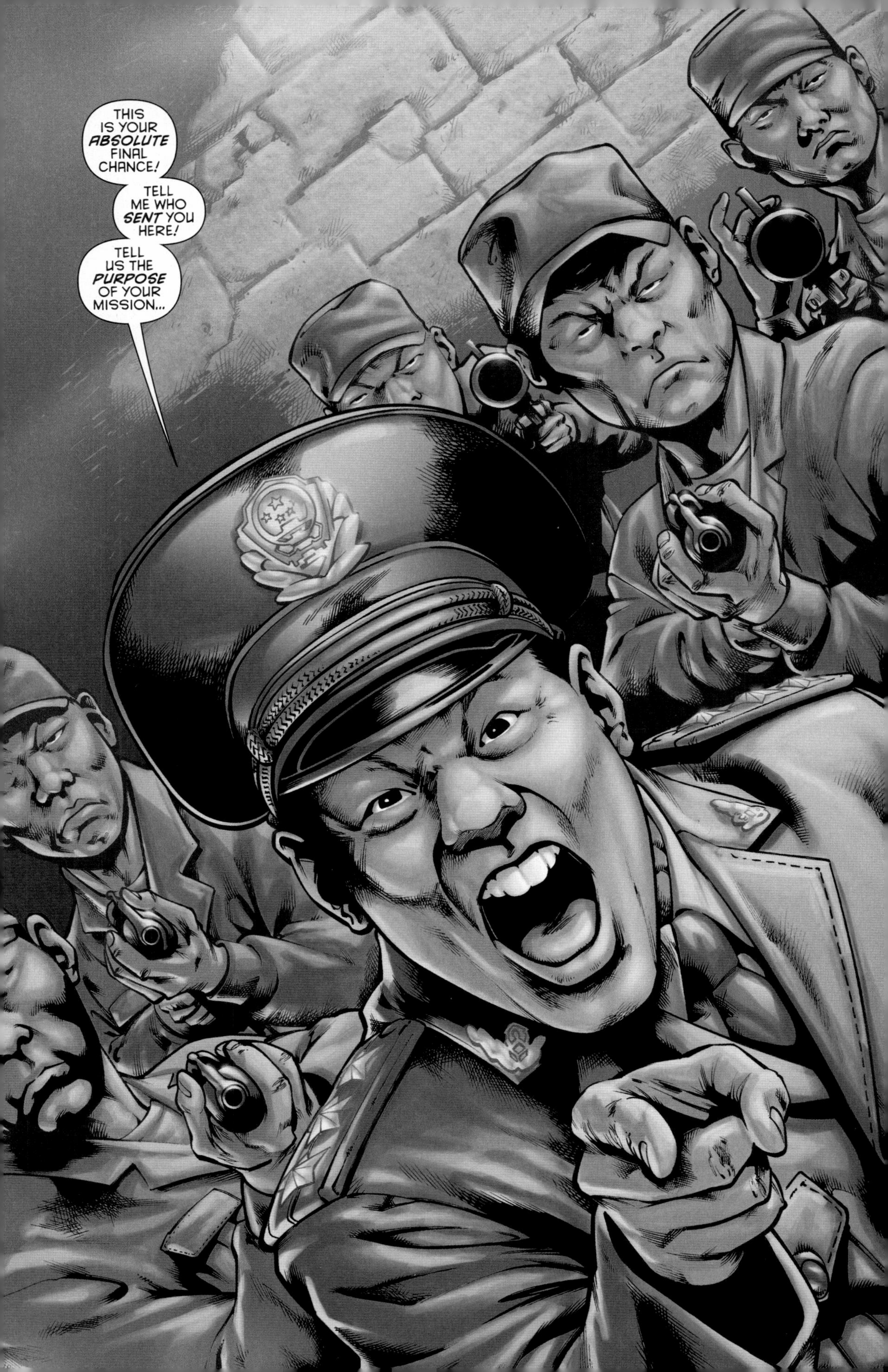
THIS IS YOUR ABSOLUTE FINAL CHANCE!
TELL ME WHO SENT YOU HERE!
TELL US THE PURPOSE OF YOUR MISSION...

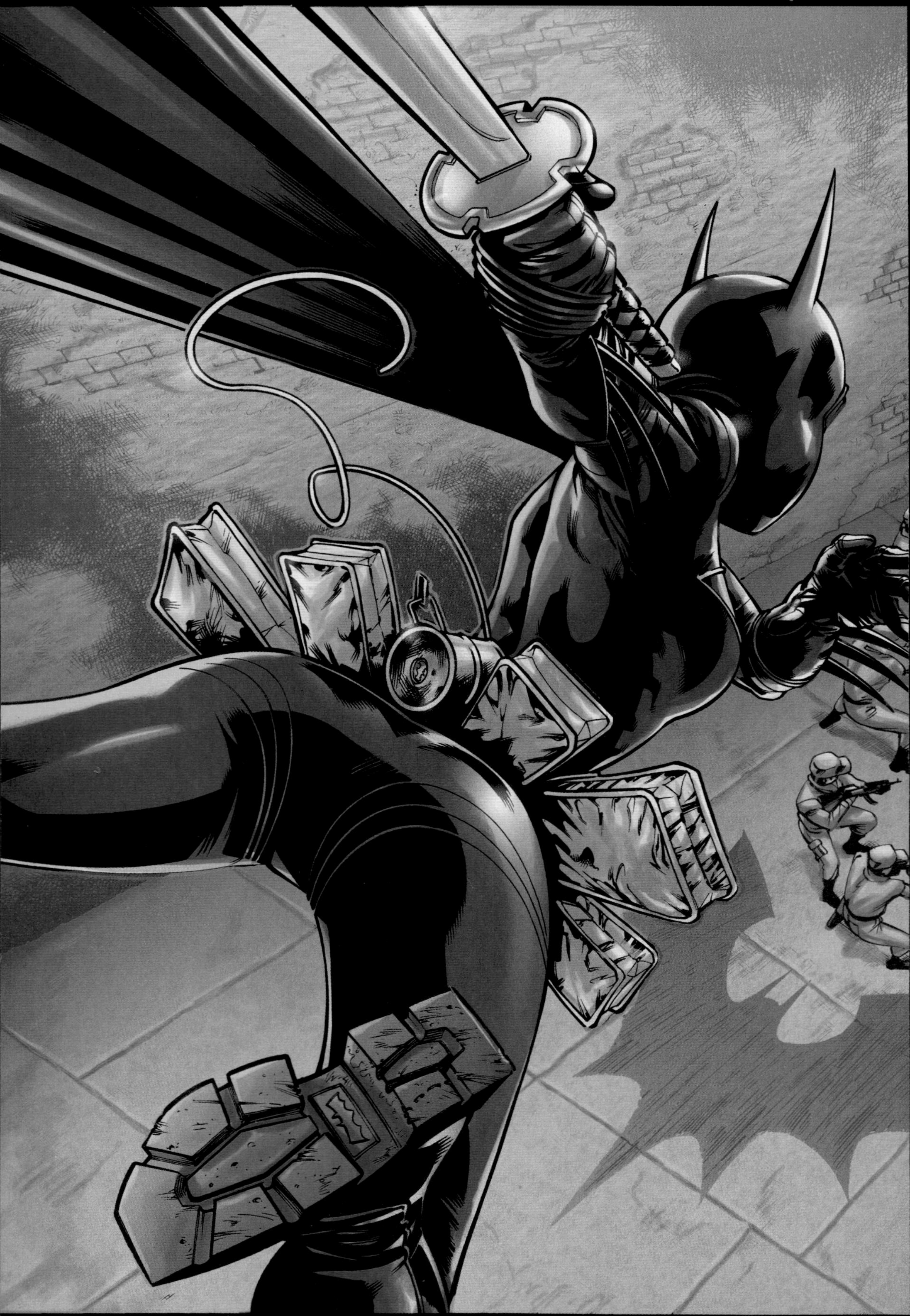

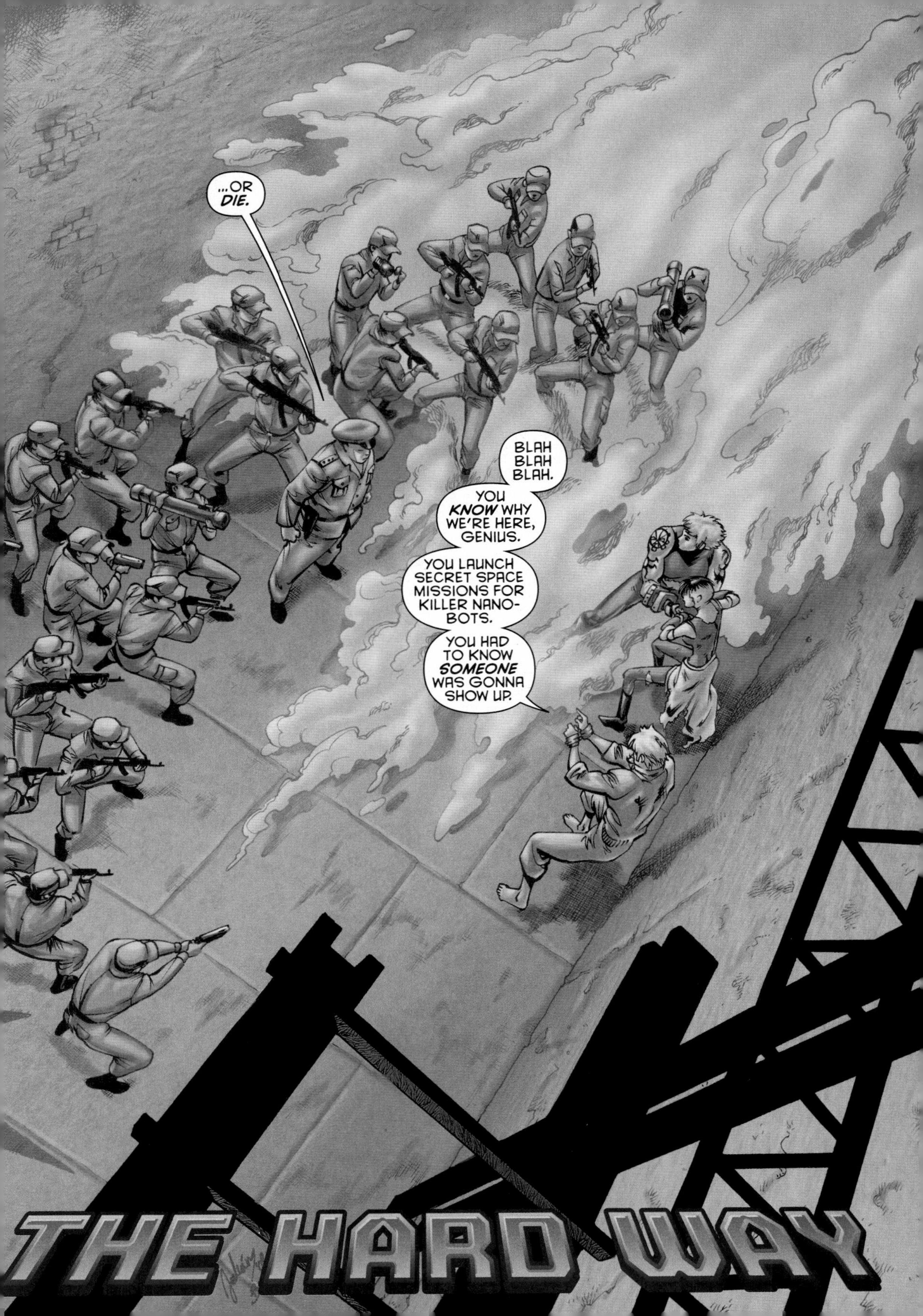
...OR DIE.
BLAH BLAH BLAH.
YOU KNOW WHY WE'RE HERE, GENIUS.
YOU LAUNCH SECRET SPACE MISSIONS FOR KILLER NANO-BOTS.
YOU HAD TO KNOW SOMEONE WAS GONNA SHOW UP.
THE HARD WAY

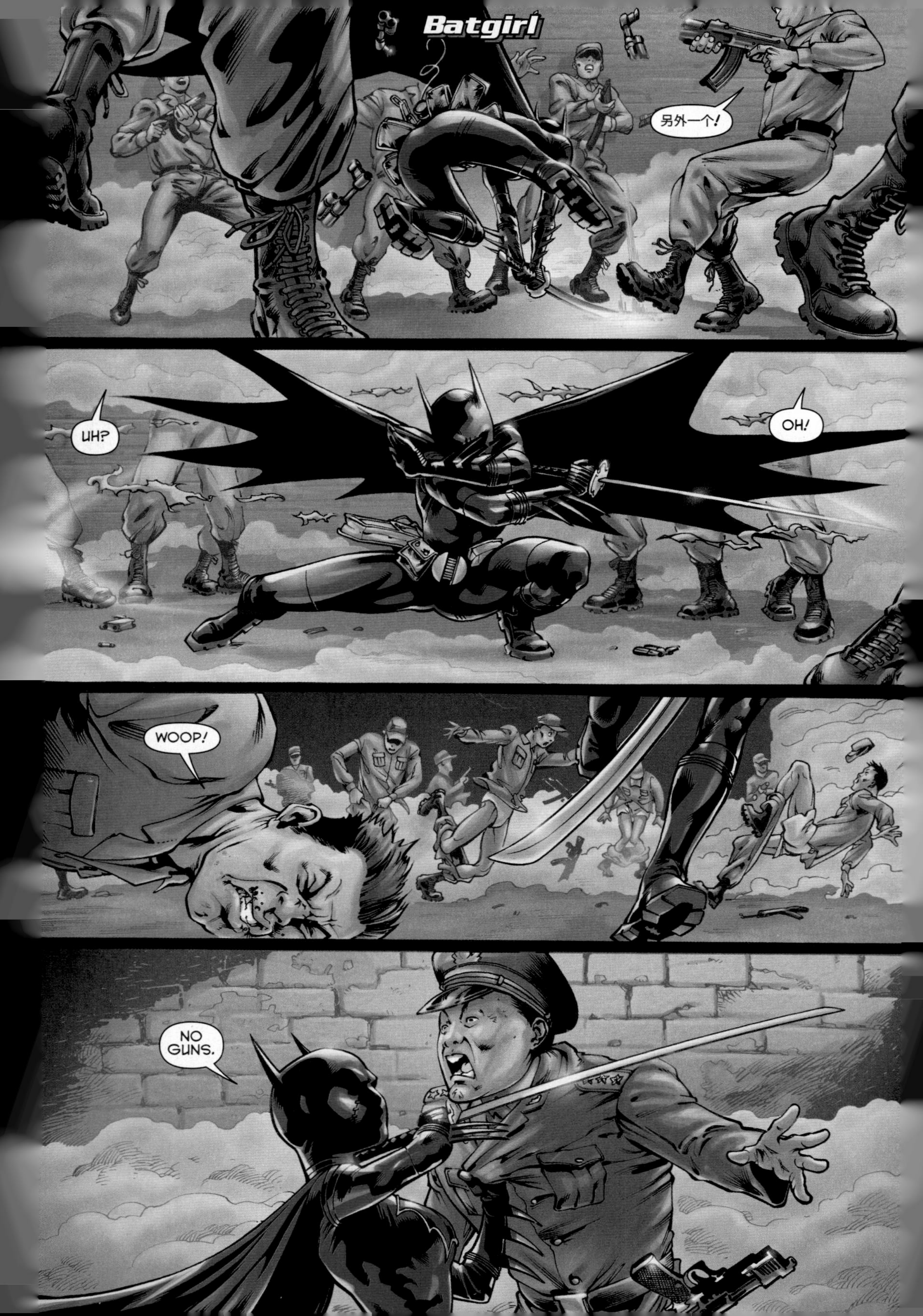

Batgirl
另外一个!
UH?
OH!
WOOP!
NO GUNS.

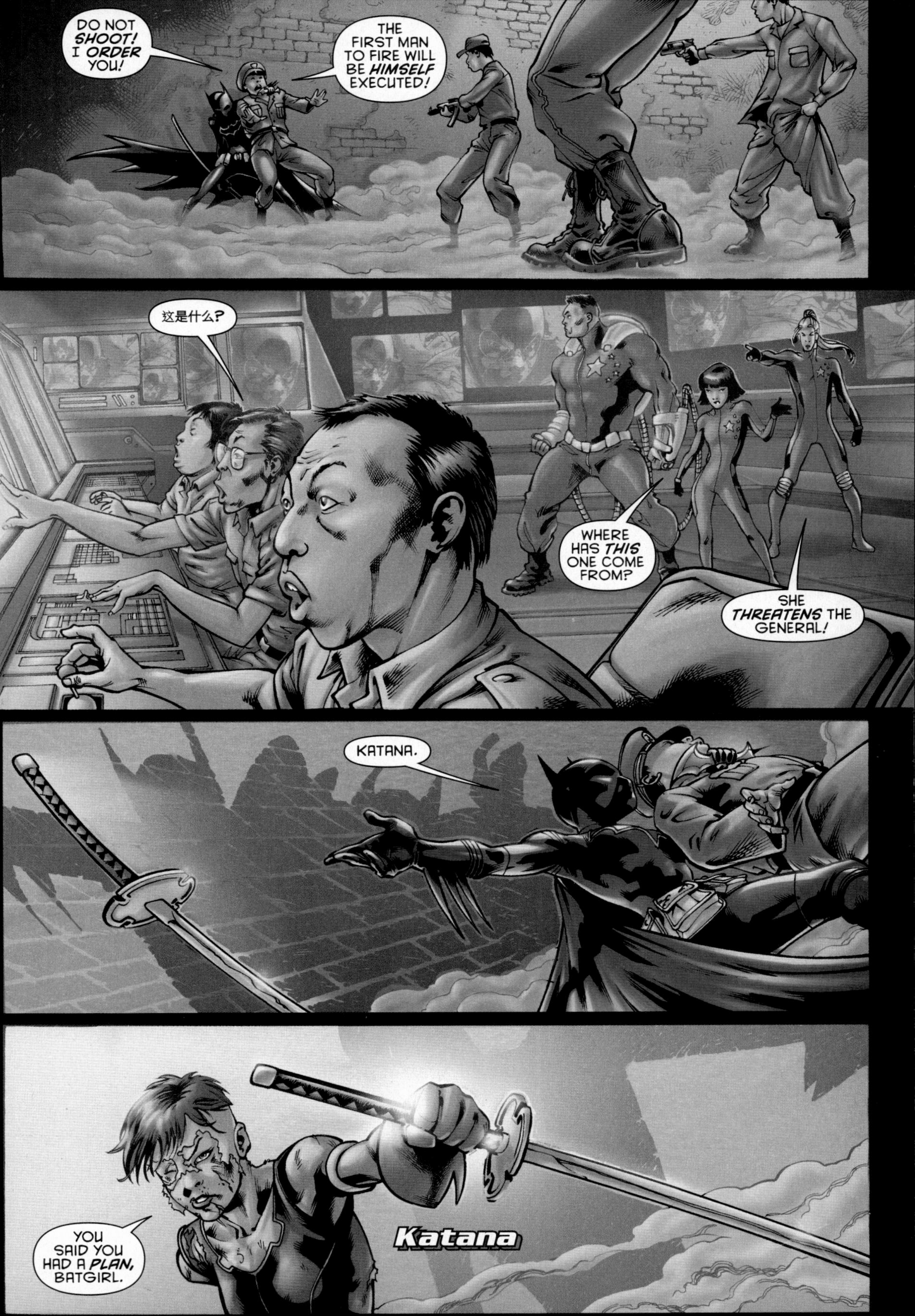
DO NOT SHOOT! I ORDER YOU!
THE FIRST MAN TO FIRE WILL BE HIMSELF EXECUTED!
这是什么?
WHERE HAS THIS ONE COME FROM?
SHE THREATENS THE GENERAL!
KATANA.
YOU SAID YOU HAD A PLAN, BATGIRL.
Katana

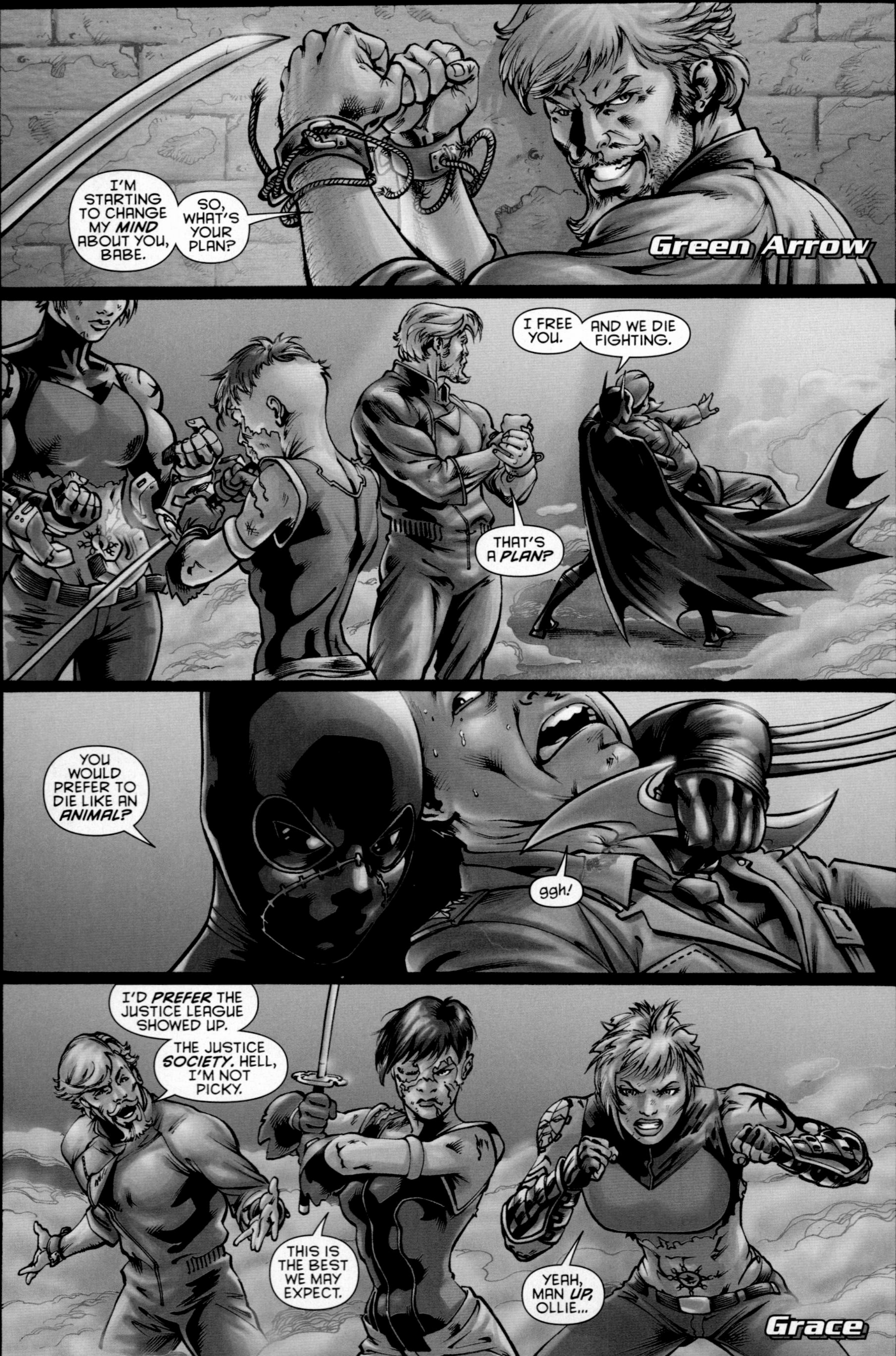
I'M STARTING TO CHANGE MY MIND ABOUT YOU, BABE.
SO, WHAT'S YOUR PLAN?
Green Arrow
I FREE YOU.
AND WE DIE FIGHTING.
THAT'S A PLAN?
YOU WOULD PREFER TO DIE LIKE AN ANIMAL?
ggh!
I'D PREFER THE JUSTICE LEAGUE SHOWED UP.
THE JUSTICE SOCIETY. HELL, I'M NOT PICKY.
THIS IS THE BEST WE MAY EXPECT.
YEAH, MAN UP, OLLIE...
Grace

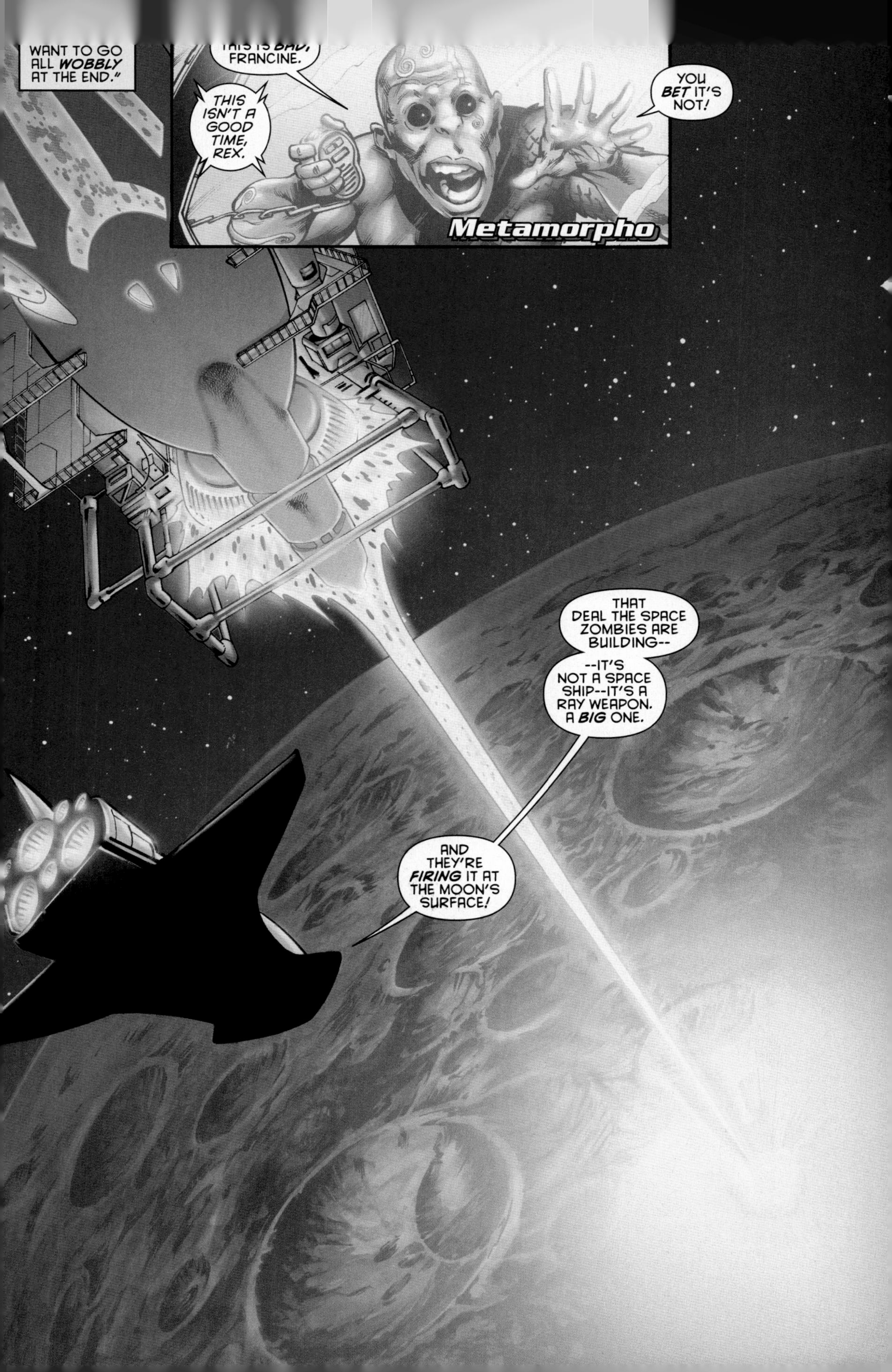
WANT TO GO ALL WOBBLY AT THE END."
FRANCINE.
THIS ISN'T A GOOD TIME, REX.
YOU BET IT'S NOT!
Metamorpho
THAT DEAL THE SPACE ZOMBIES ARE BUILDING--
--IT'S NOT A SPACE SHIP--IT'S A RAY WEAPON. A BIG ONE.
AND THEY'RE FIRING IT AT THE MOON'S SURFACE!

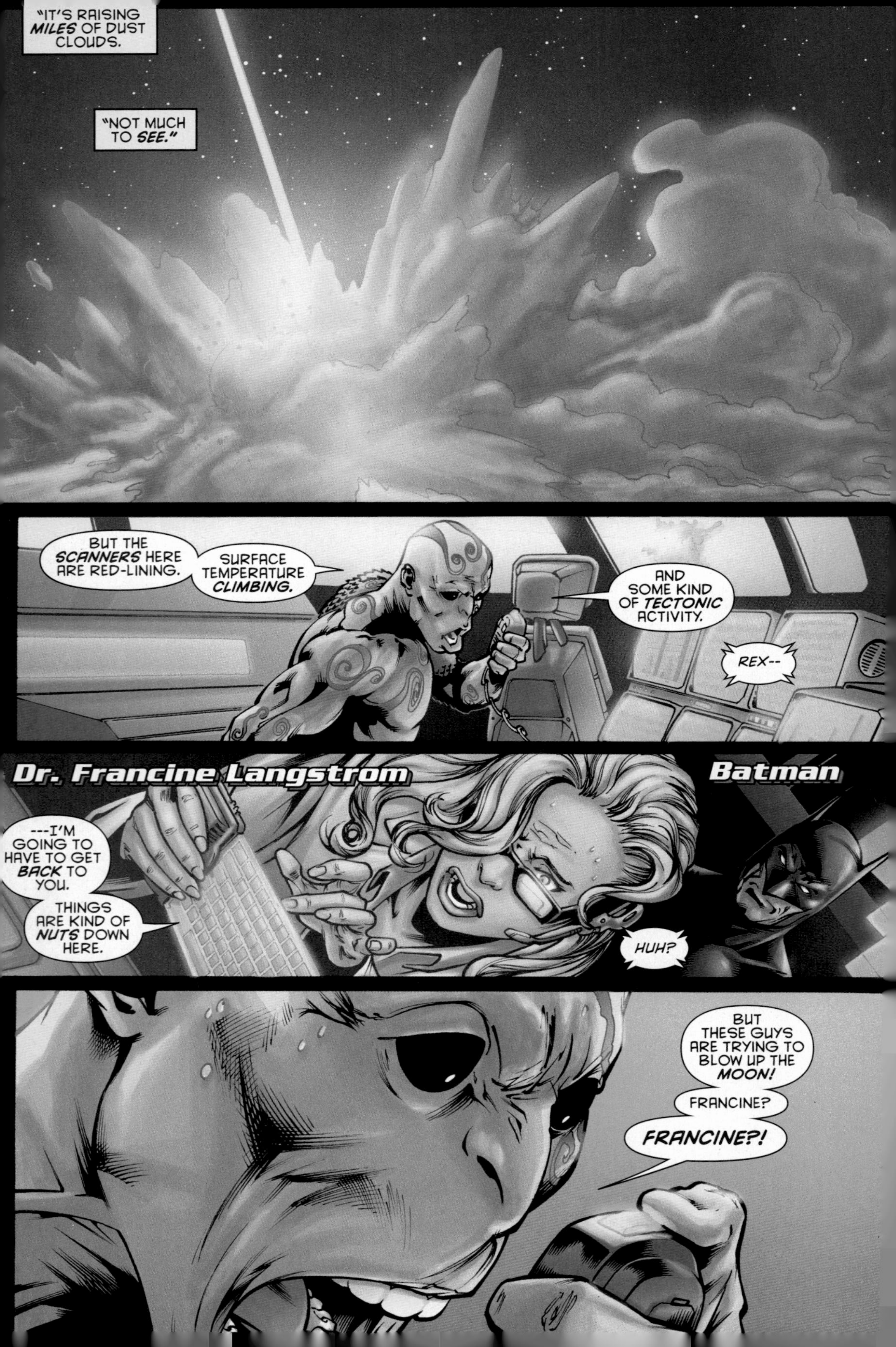
"IT'S RAISING MILES OF DUST CLOUDS.
"NOT MUCH TO SEE."
BUT THE SCANNERS HERE ARE RED-LINING.
SURFACE TEMPERATURE CLIMBING.
AND SOME KIND OF TECTONIC ACTIVITY.
REX--
Dr. Francine Langstrom
Batman
---I'M GOING TO HAVE TO GET BACK TO YOU.
THINGS ARE KIND OF NUTS DOWN HERE.
HUH?
BUT THESE GUYS ARE TRYING TO BLOW UP THE MOON!
FRANCINE?
FRANCINE?!

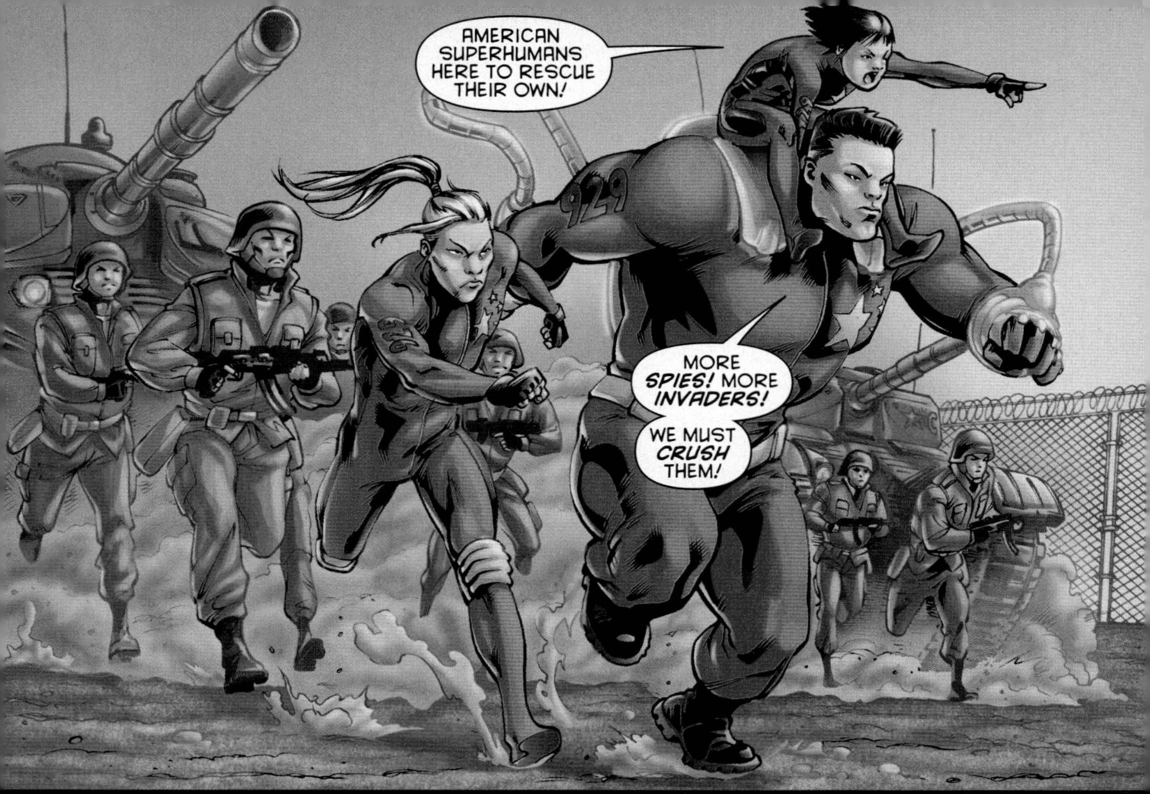
AMERICAN SUPERHUMANS HERE TO RESCUE THEIR OWN!
MORE SPIES! MORE INVADERS!
WE MUST CRUSH THEM!

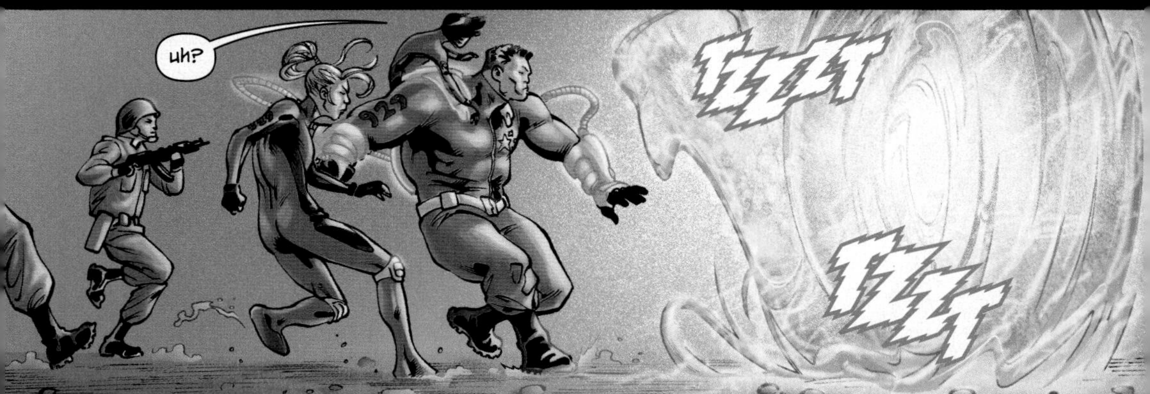
uh?
TZZZT
TZZZT

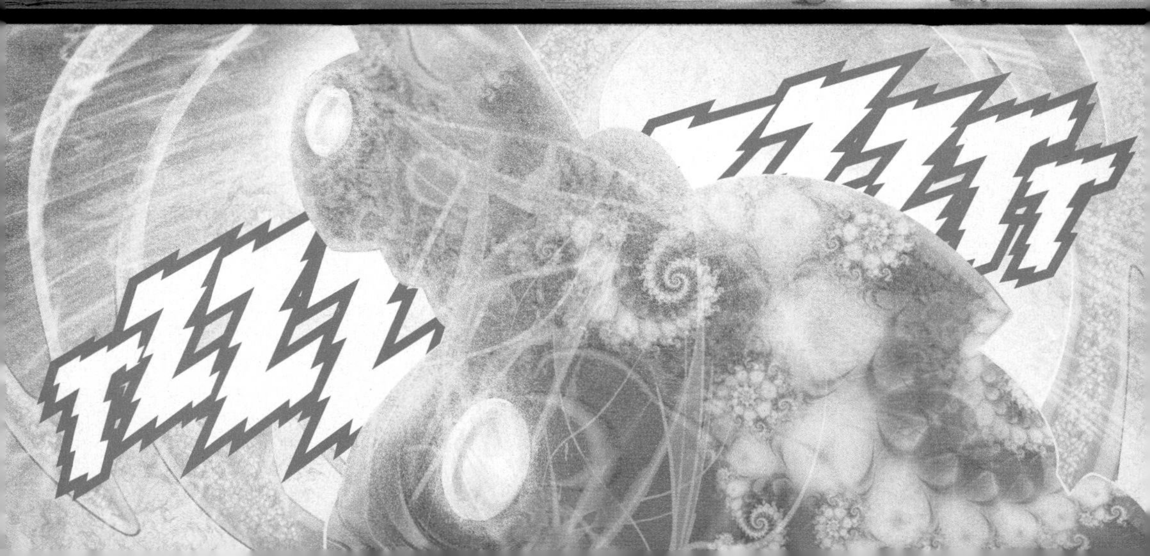
TZZZZZZZZT

Remac
ARE WE *HERE,* NIGHTWING?
WE'RE *SOME*WHERE, THUNDER.
I'M NOT *THAT* EXPERIENCED WITH THIS THING. ESPECIALLY OVER LONG DISTANCES.
I ONLY HACKED THE *JLA* TELEPORT CODES RECENTLY.
AND ASIA *IS* A BIG PLACE.
Thunder
Nightwing

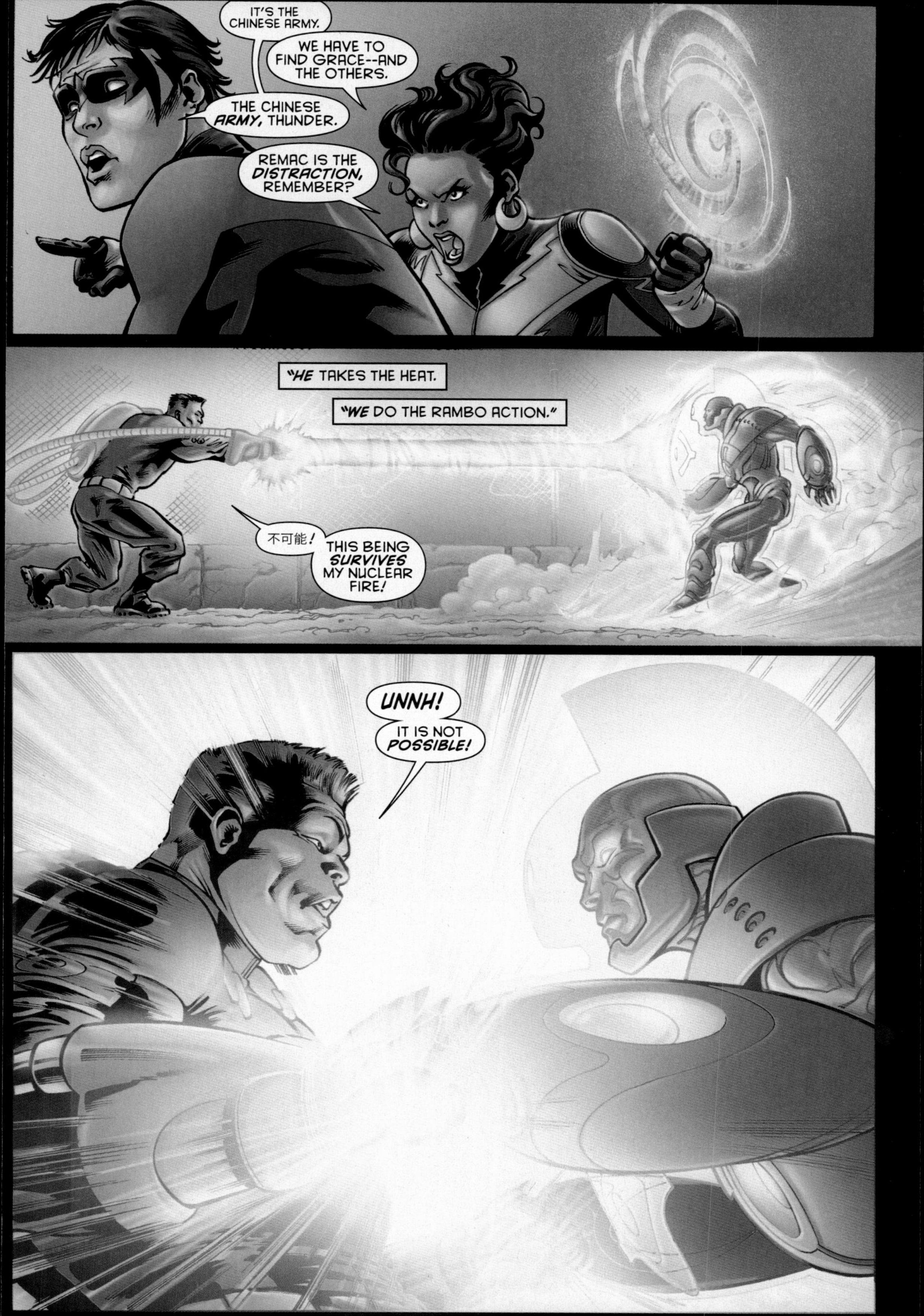

IT'S THE CHINESE ARMY.
WE HAVE TO FIND GRACE--AND THE OTHERS.
THE CHINESE ARMY, THUNDER.
REMAC IS THE DISTRACTION, REMEMBER?
"HE TAKES THE HEAT.
"WE DO THE RAMBO ACTION."
不可能! THIS BEING SURVIVES MY NUCLEAR FIRE!
UNNH! IT IS NOT POSSIBLE!

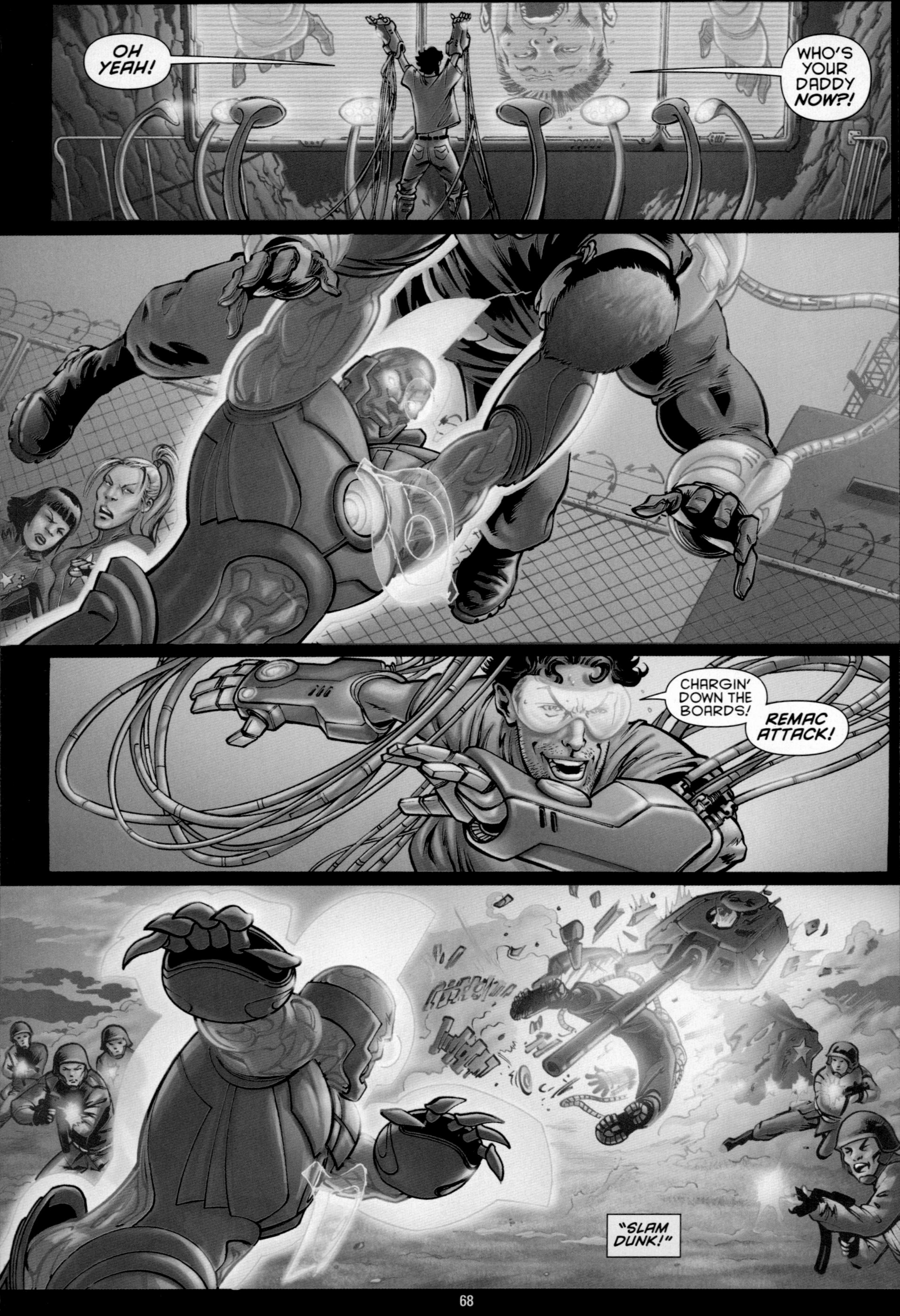
OH YEAH!
WHO'S YOUR DADDY NOW?!
CHARGIN' DOWN THE BOARDS!
REMAC ATTACK!
"SLAM DUNK!"

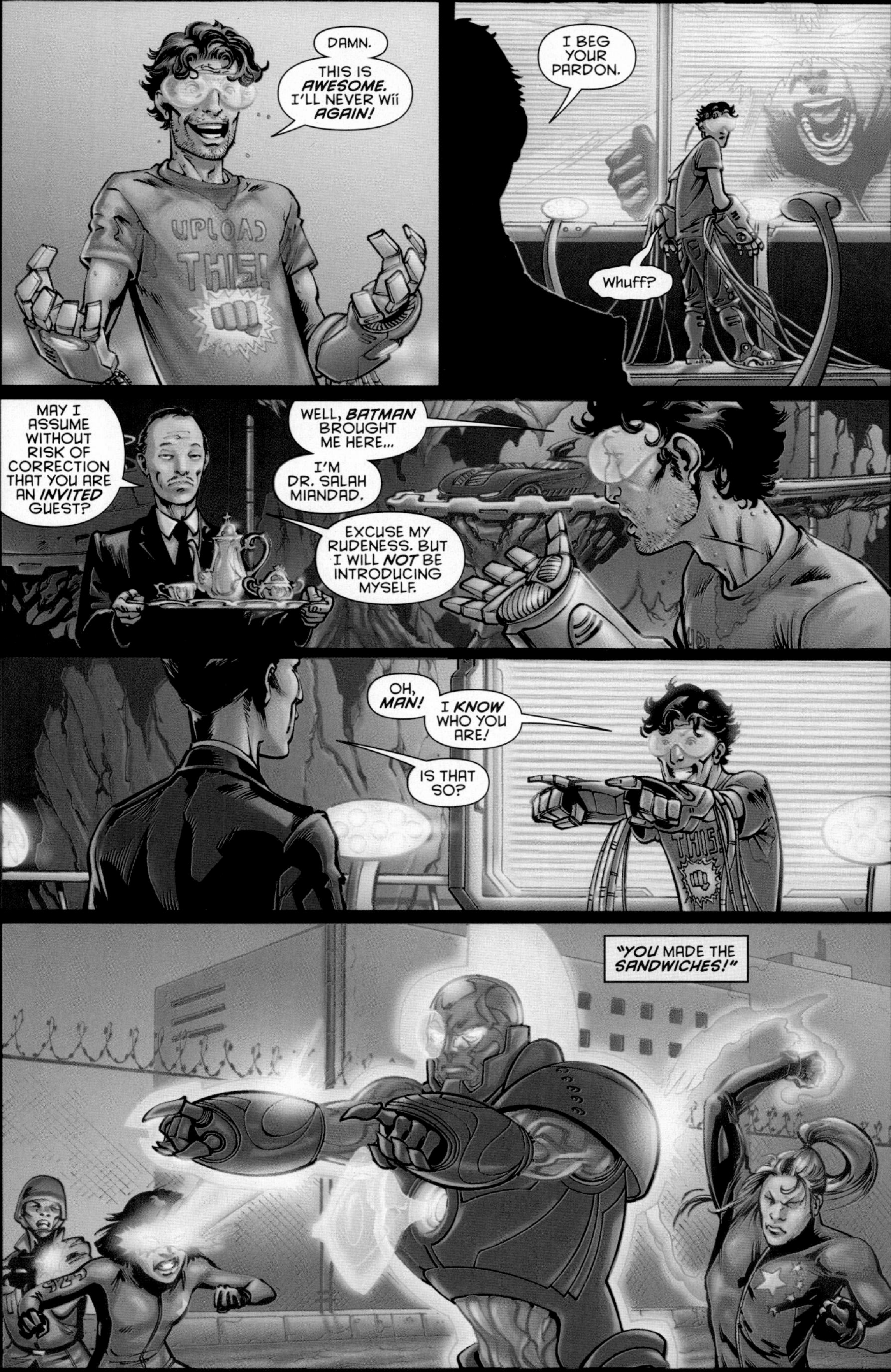
DAMN.
THIS IS AWESOME. I'LL NEVER Wii AGAIN!
I BEG YOUR PARDON.
Whuff?
MAY I ASSUME WITHOUT RISK OF CORRECTION THAT YOU ARE AN INVITED GUEST?
WELL, BATMAN BROUGHT ME HERE...
I'M DR. SALAH MIANDAD.
EXCUSE MY RUDENESS. BUT I WILL NOT BE INTRODUCING MYSELF.
OH, MAN!
I KNOW WHO YOU ARE!
IS THAT SO?
"YOU MADE THE SANDWICHES!"

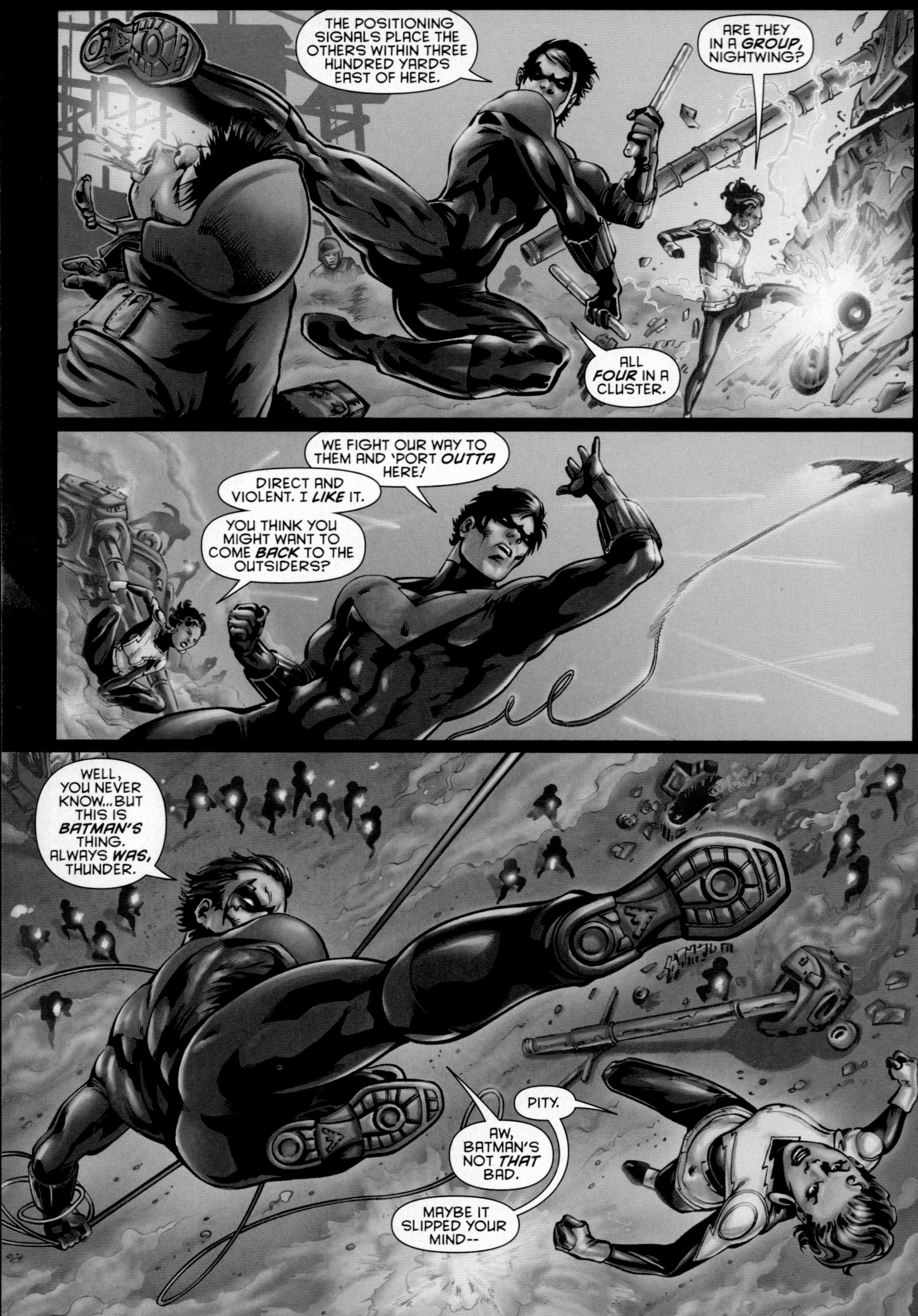
THE POSITIONING SIGNALS PLACE THE OTHERS WITHIN THREE HUNDRED YARDS EAST OF HERE.
ARE THEY IN A GROUP, NIGHTWING?
ALL FOUR IN A CLUSTER.
WE FIGHT OUR WAY TO THEM AND 'PORT OUTTA HERE!
DIRECT AND VIOLENT. I LIKE IT.
YOU THINK YOU MIGHT WANT TO COME BACK TO THE OUTSIDERS?
WELL, YOU NEVER KNOW...BUT THIS IS BATMAN'S THING. ALWAYS WAS, THUNDER.
PITY.
AW, BATMAN'S NOT THAT BAD.
MAYBE IT SLIPPED YOUR MIND--

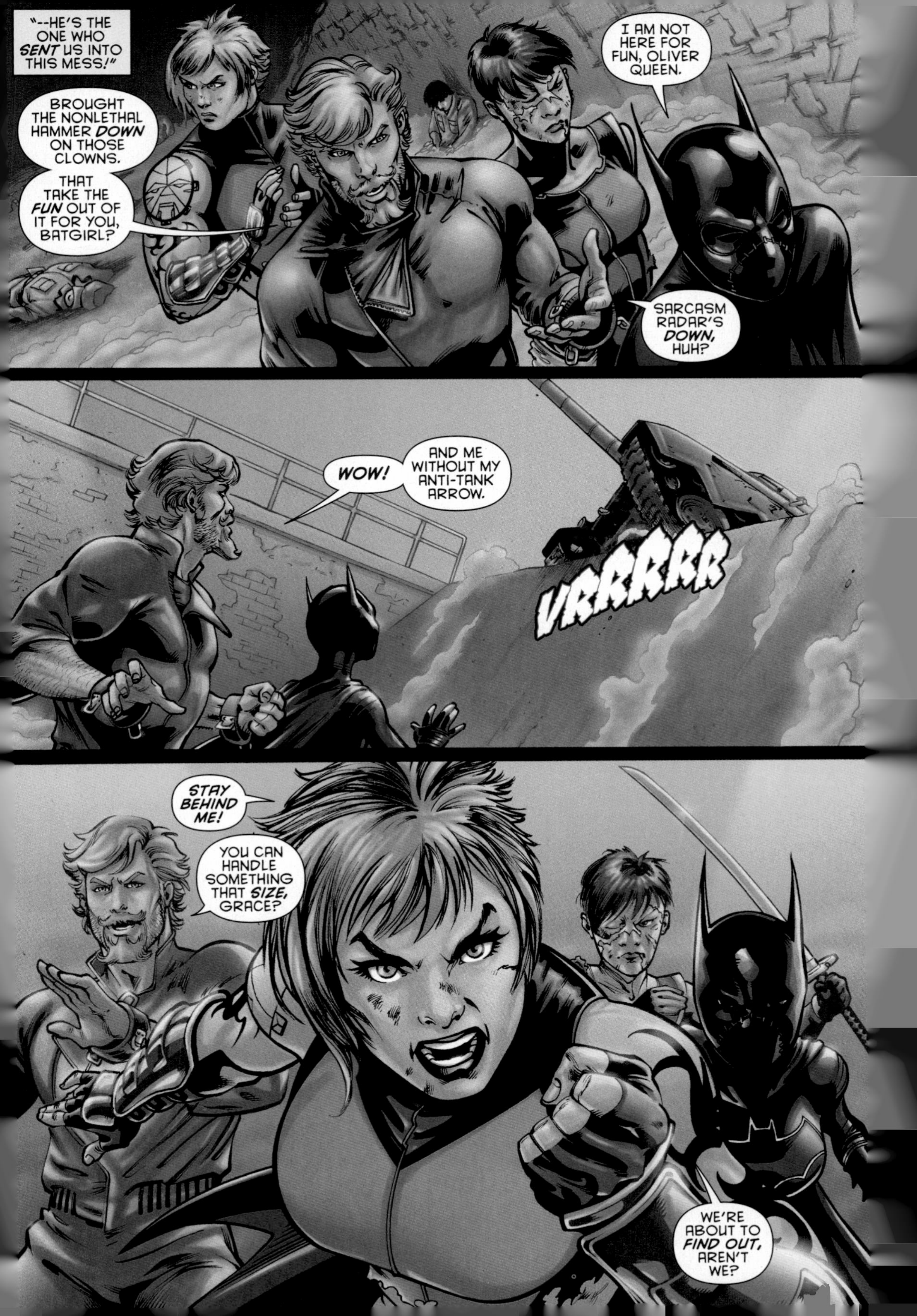
"--HE'S THE ONE WHO SENT US INTO THIS MESS!"
BROUGHT THE NONLETHAL HAMMER DOWN ON THOSE CLOWNS.
THAT TAKE THE FUN OUT OF IT FOR YOU, BATGIRL?
I AM NOT HERE FOR FUN, OLIVER QUEEN.
SARCASM RADAR'S DOWN, HUH?
WOW!
AND ME WITHOUT MY ANTI-TANK ARROW.
VRRRRR
STAY BEHIND ME!
YOU CAN HANDLE SOMETHING THAT SIZE, GRACE?
WE'RE ABOUT TO FIND OUT, AREN'T WE?

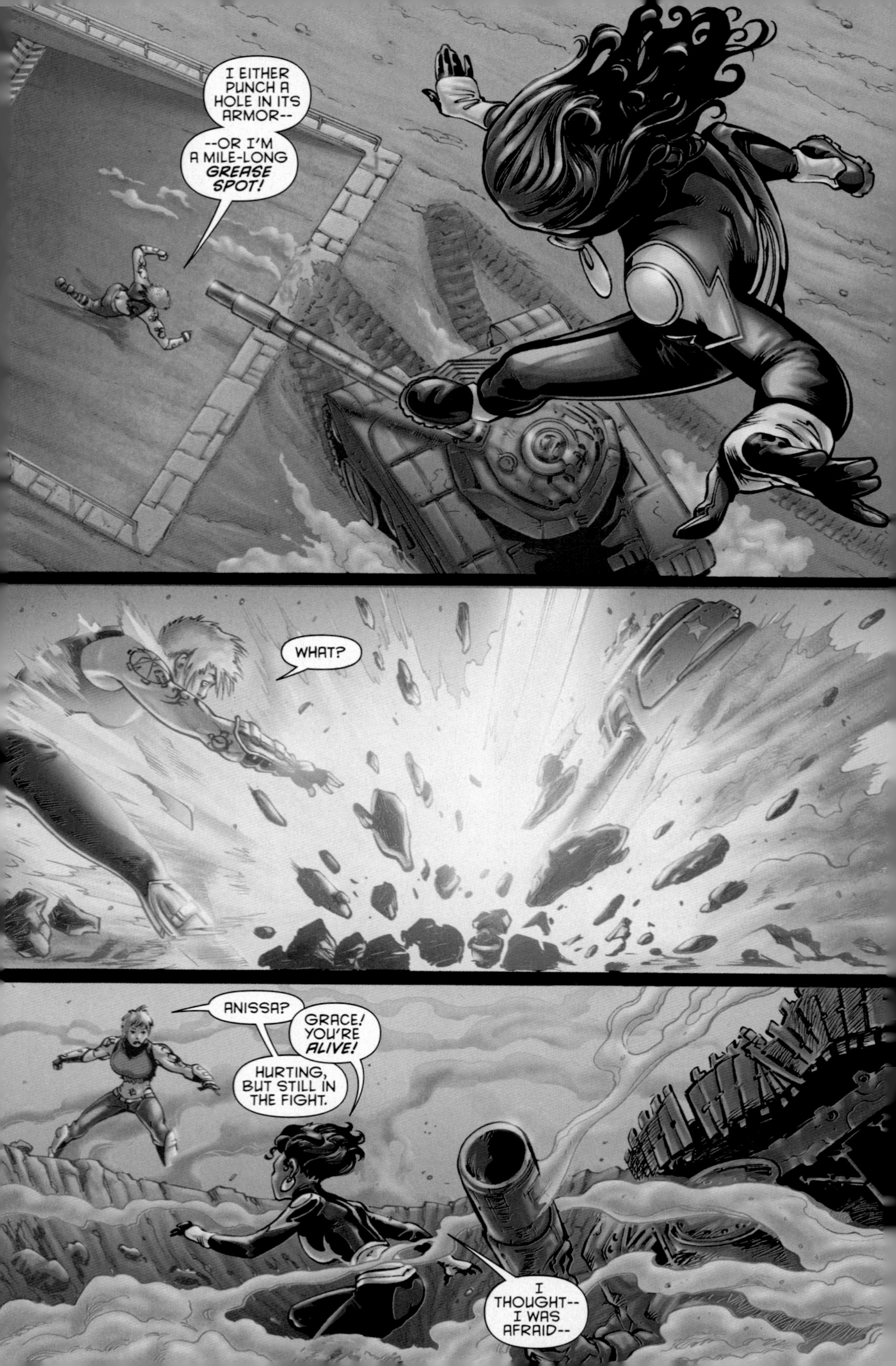
I EITHER PUNCH A HOLE IN ITS ARMOR--
--OR I'M A MILE-LONG GREASE SPOT!
WHAT?
ANISSA?
GRACE! YOU'RE ALIVE!
HURTING, BUT STILL IN THE FIGHT.
I THOUGHT-- I WAS AFRAID--

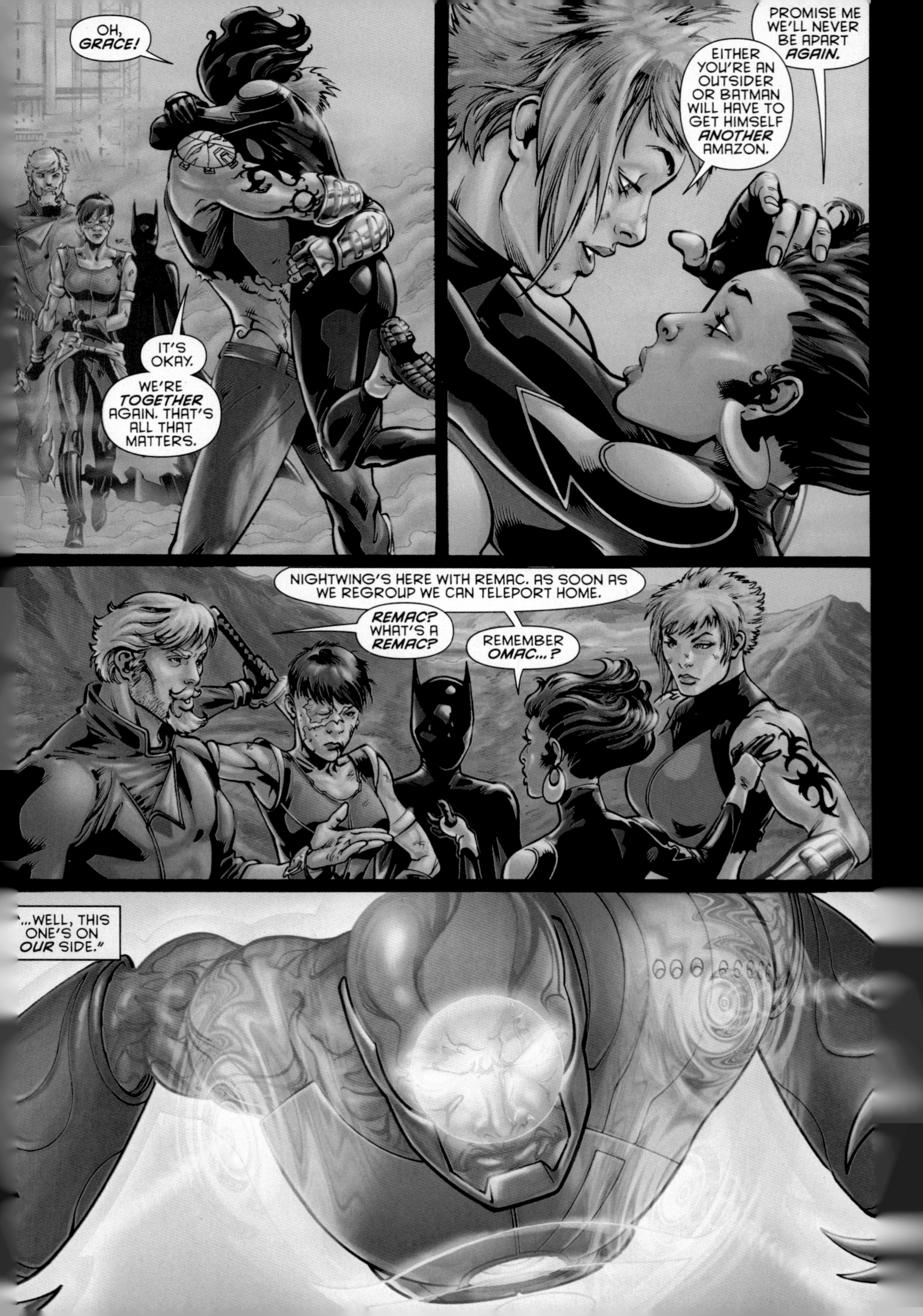

OH, GRACE!
IT'S OKAY.
WE'RE TOGETHER AGAIN. THAT'S ALL THAT MATTERS.
PROMISE ME WE'LL NEVER BE APART AGAIN.
EITHER YOU'RE AN OUTSIDER OR BATMAN WILL HAVE TO GET HIMSELF ANOTHER AMAZON.
NIGHTWING'S HERE WITH REMAC. AS SOON AS WE REGROUP WE CAN TELEPORT HOME.
REMAC? WHAT'S A REMAC?
REMEMBER OMAC...?
"...WELL, THIS ONE'S ON OUR SIDE."

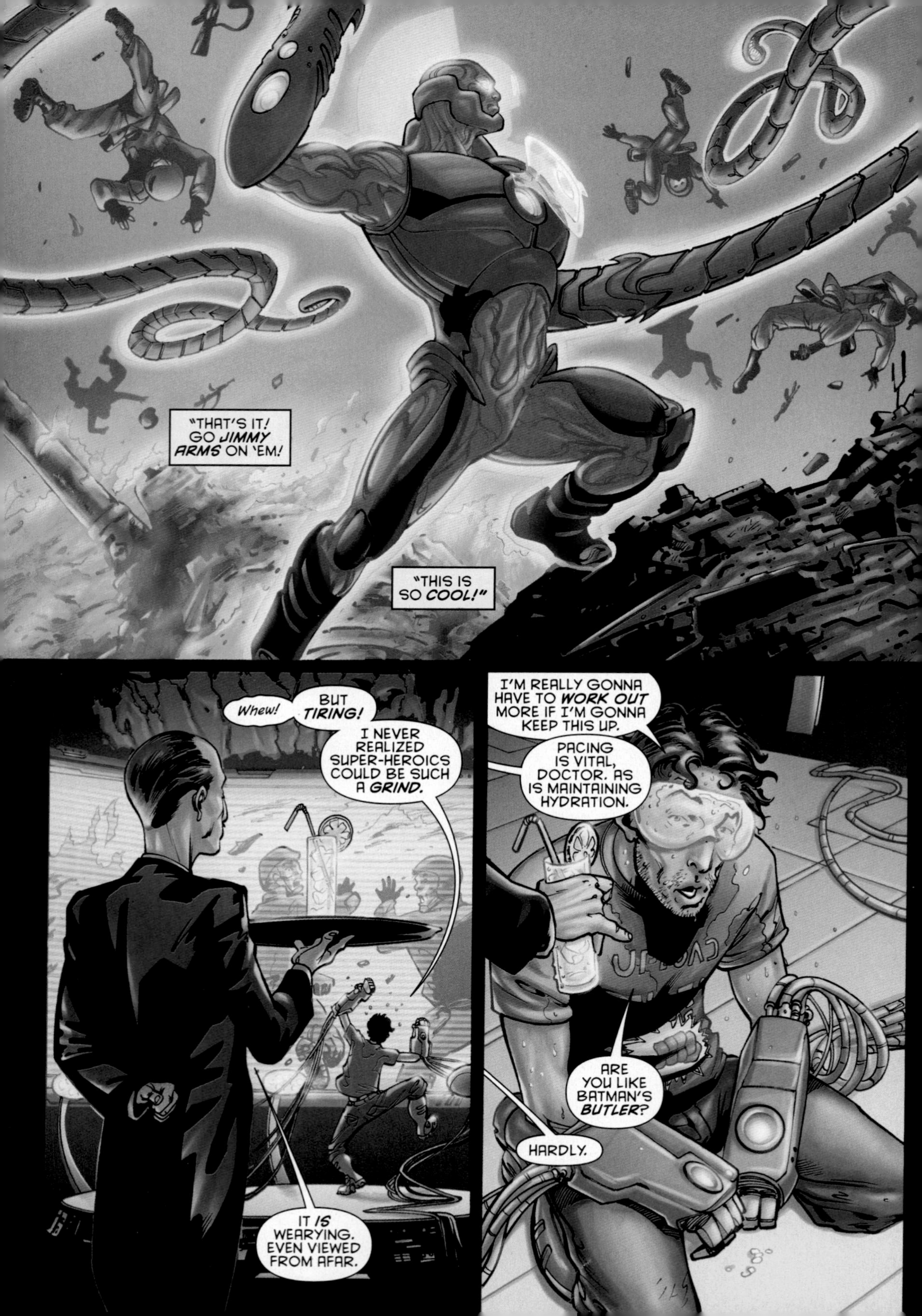
"THAT'S IT! GO JIMMY ARMS ON 'EM!
"THIS IS SO COOL!"
Whew!
BUT TIRING!
I NEVER REALIZED SUPER-HEROICS COULD BE SUCH A GRIND.
IT IS WEARYING. EVEN VIEWED FROM AFAR.
I'M REALLY GONNA HAVE TO WORK OUT MORE IF I'M GONNA KEEP THIS UP.
PACING IS VITAL, DOCTOR. AS IS MAINTAINING HYDRATION.
ARE YOU LIKE BATMAN'S BUTLER?
HARDLY.

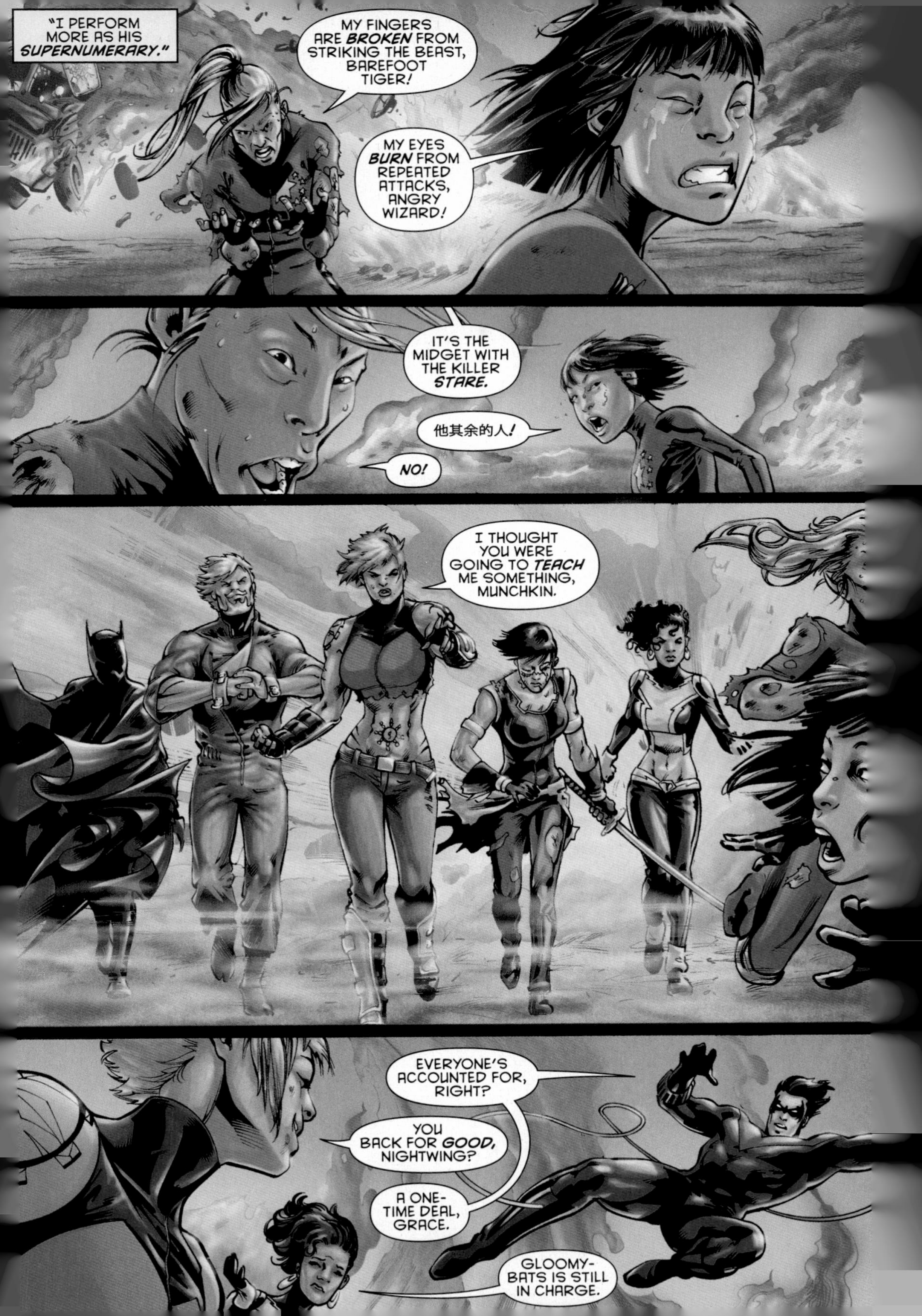
"I PERFORM MORE AS HIS SUPERNUMERARY."
MY FINGERS ARE BROKEN FROM STRIKING THE BEAST, BAREFOOT TIGER!
MY EYES BURN FROM REPEATED ATTACKS, ANGRY WIZARD!
IT'S THE MIDGET WITH THE KILLER STARE.
他其余的人!
NO!
I THOUGHT YOU WERE GOING TO TEACH ME SOMETHING, MUNCHKIN.
EVERYONE'S ACCOUNTED FOR, RIGHT?
YOU BACK FOR GOOD, NIGHTWING?
A ONE-TIME DEAL, GRACE.
GLOOMY-BATS IS STILL IN CHARGE.

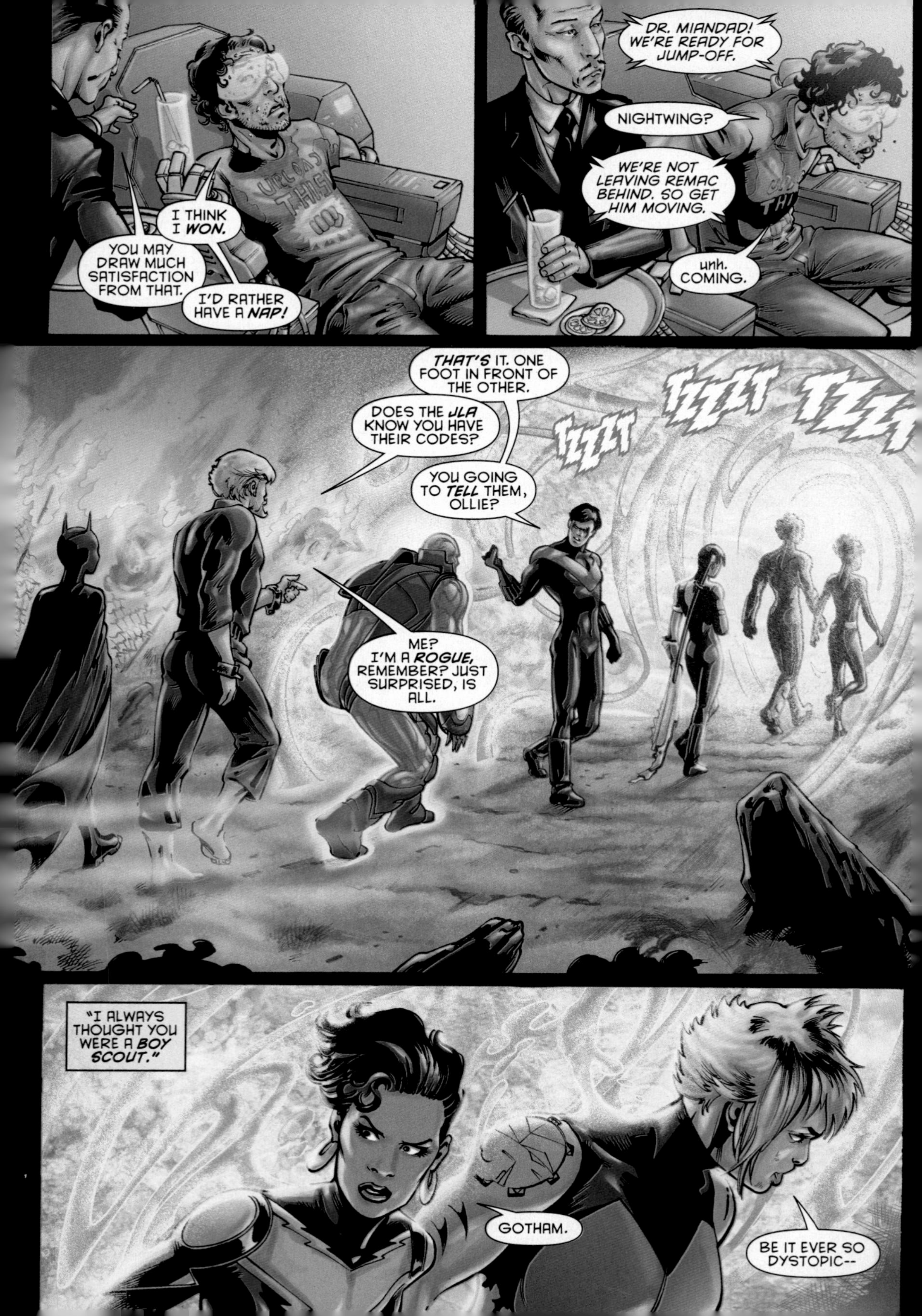
I THINK I WON.
YOU MAY DRAW MUCH SATISFACTION FROM THAT.
I'D RATHER HAVE A NAP!
DR. MIANDAD! WE'RE READY FOR JUMP-OFF.
NIGHTWING?
WE'RE NOT LEAVING REMAC BEHIND. SO GET HIM MOVING.
unh. COMING.
THAT'S IT. ONE FOOT IN FRONT OF THE OTHER.
DOES THE JLA KNOW YOU HAVE THEIR CODES?
YOU GOING TO TELL THEM, OLLIE?
TZZZT
TZZZT
TZZZT
ME? I'M A ROGUE, REMEMBER? JUST SURPRISED, IS ALL.
"I ALWAYS THOUGHT YOU WERE A BOY SCOUT."
GOTHAM.
BE IT EVER SO DYSTOPIC--

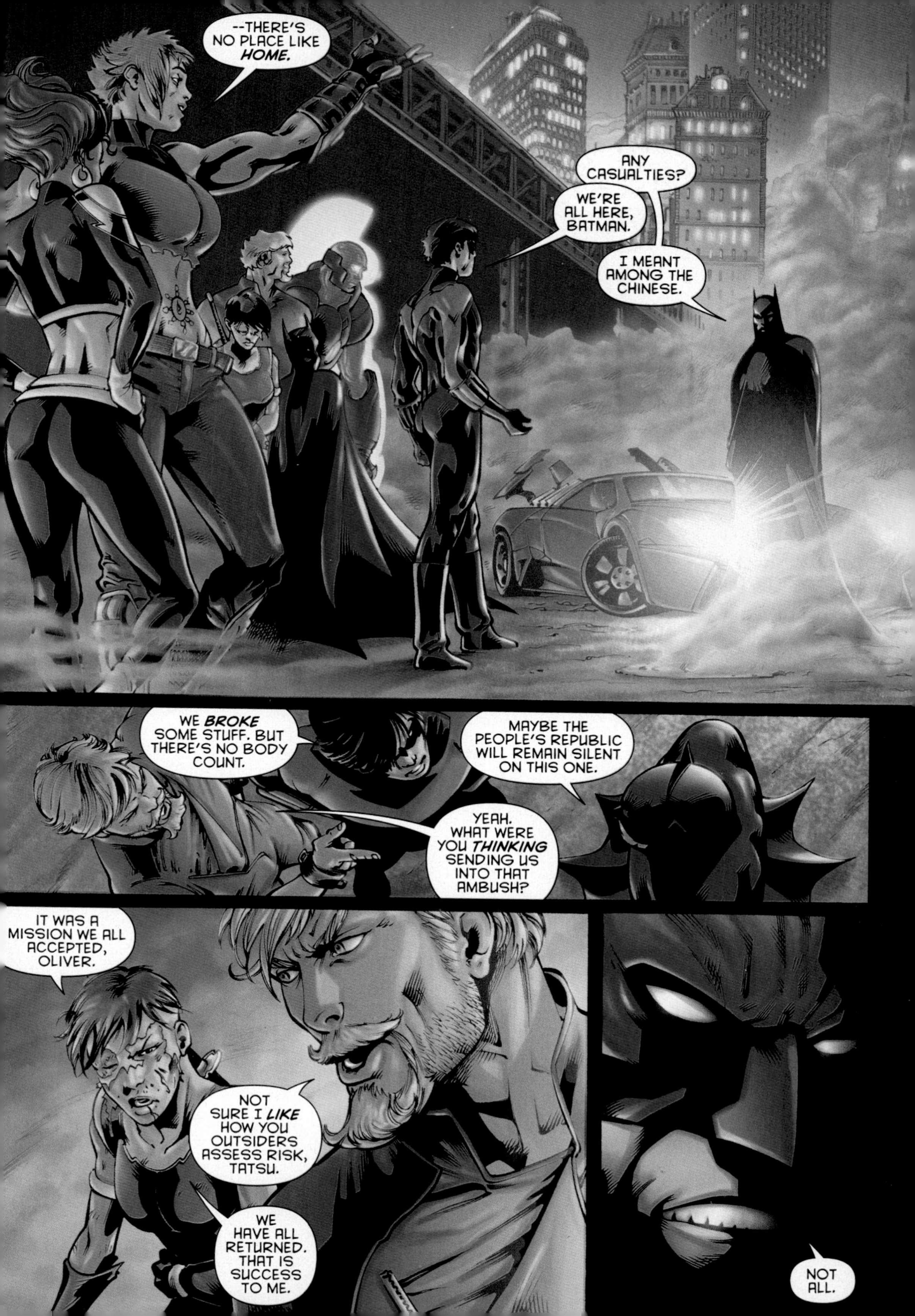
--THERE'S NO PLACE LIKE *HOME.*
ANY CASUALTIES?
WE'RE ALL HERE, BATMAN.
I MEANT AMONG THE CHINESE.
WE *BROKE* SOME STUFF. BUT THERE'S NO BODY COUNT.
MAYBE THE PEOPLE'S REPUBLIC WILL REMAIN SILENT ON THIS ONE.
YEAH. WHAT WERE YOU *THINKING* SENDING US INTO THAT AMBUSH?
IT WAS A MISSION WE ALL ACCEPTED, OLIVER.
NOT SURE I *LIKE* HOW YOU OUTSIDERS ASSESS RISK, TATSU.
WE HAVE ALL RETURNED. THAT IS SUCCESS TO ME.
NOT ALL.

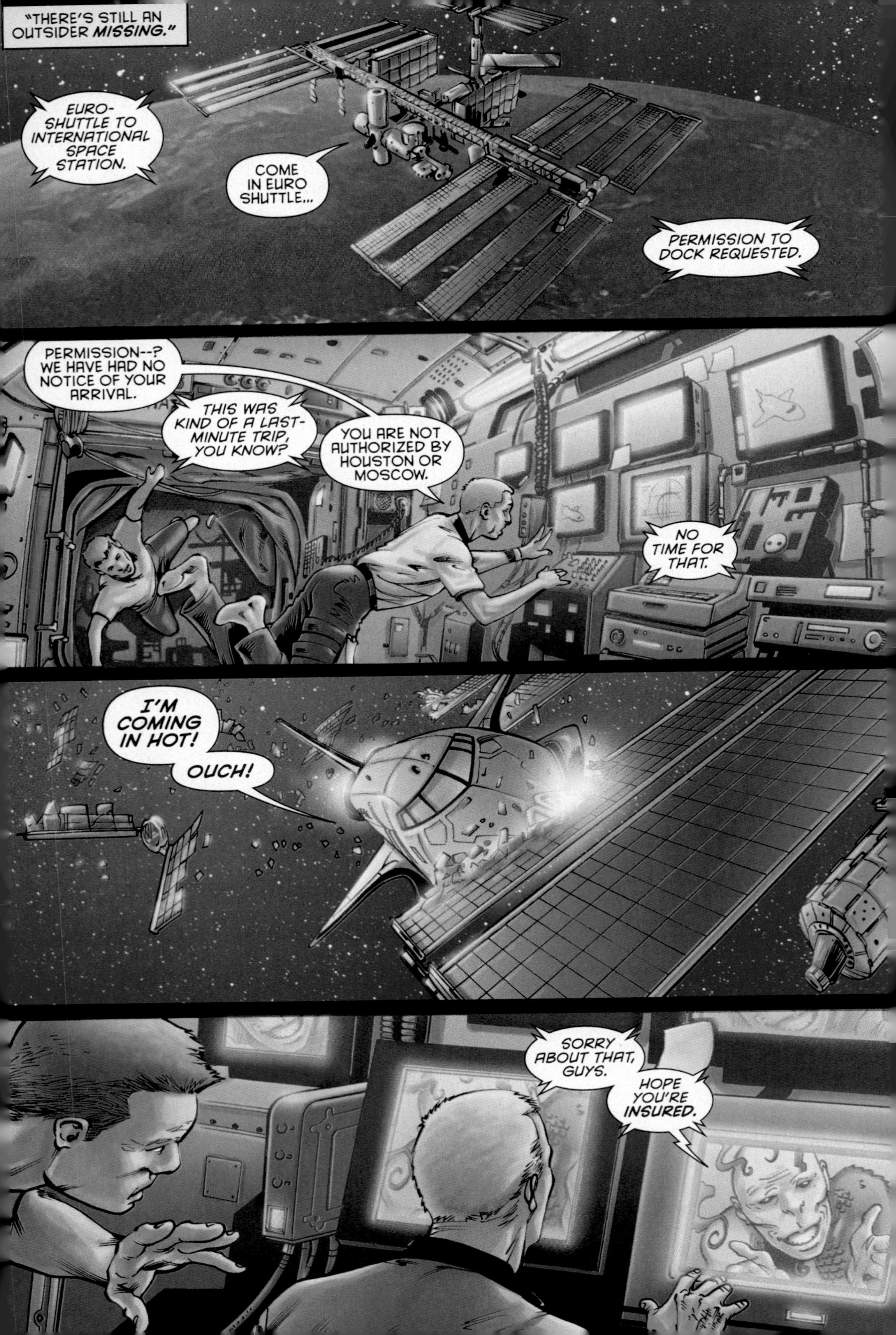
"THERE'S STILL AN OUTSIDER MISSING."
EURO-SHUTTLE TO INTERNATIONAL SPACE STATION.
COME IN EURO SHUTTLE...
PERMISSION TO DOCK REQUESTED.
PERMISSION--? WE HAVE HAD NO NOTICE OF YOUR ARRIVAL.
THIS WAS KIND OF A LAST-MINUTE TRIP, YOU KNOW?
YOU ARE NOT AUTHORIZED BY HOUSTON OR MOSCOW.
NO TIME FOR THAT.
I'M COMING IN HOT!
OUCH!
SORRY ABOUT THAT, GUYS.
HOPE YOU'RE INSURED.

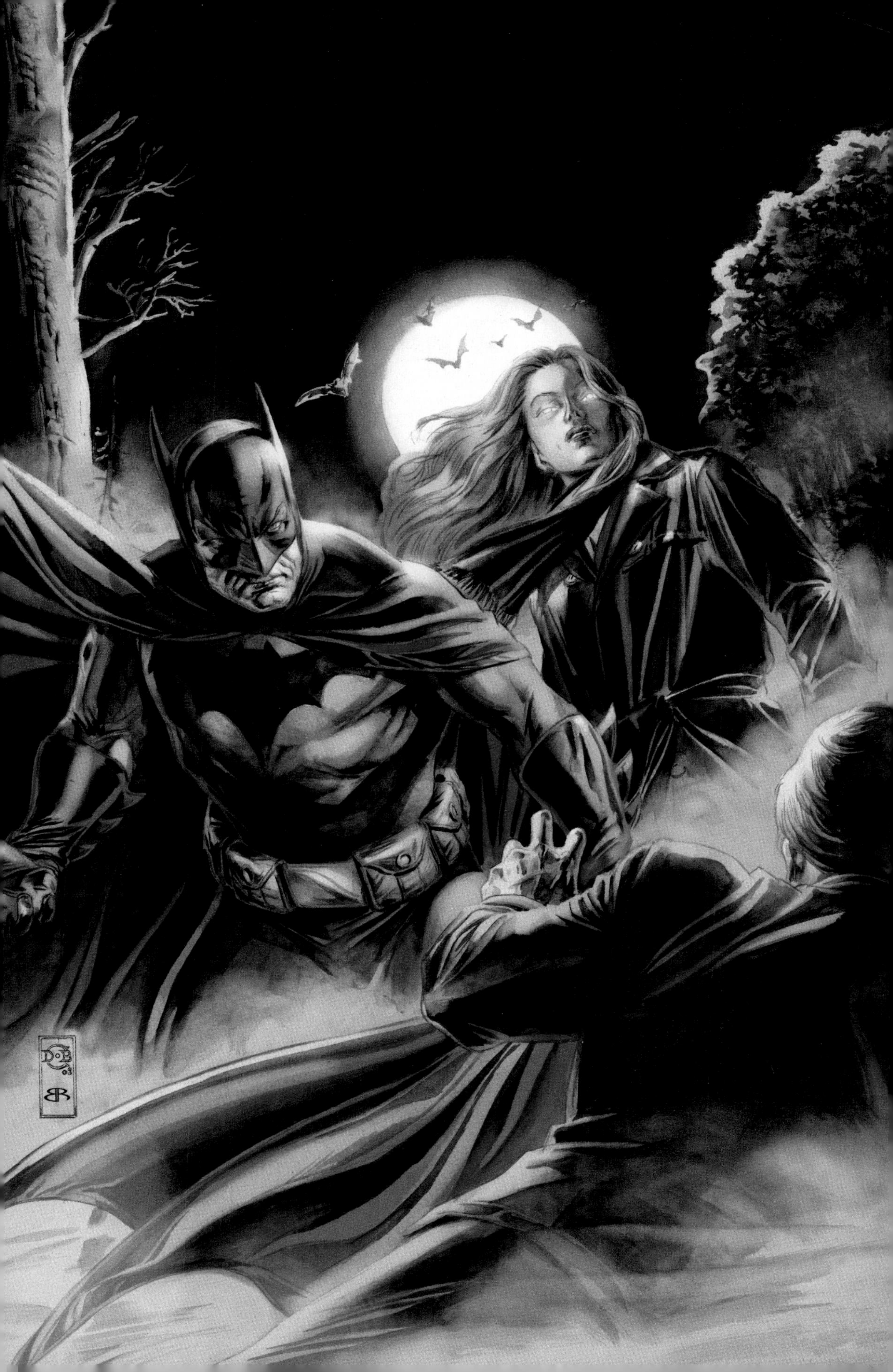

part FOUR

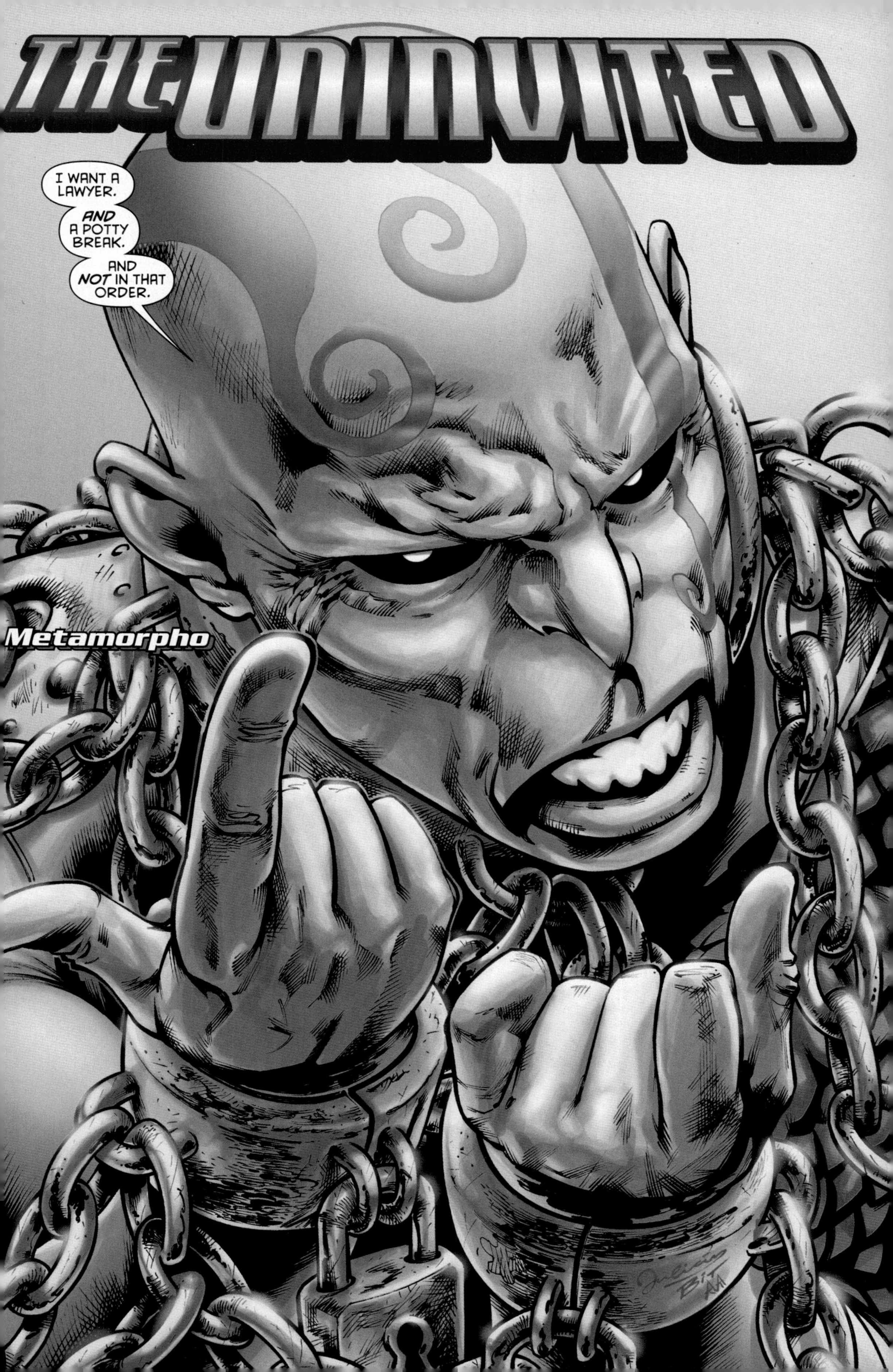
THE UNINVITED
I WANT A LAWYER.
AND A POTTY BREAK.
AND NOT IN THAT ORDER.
Metamorpho

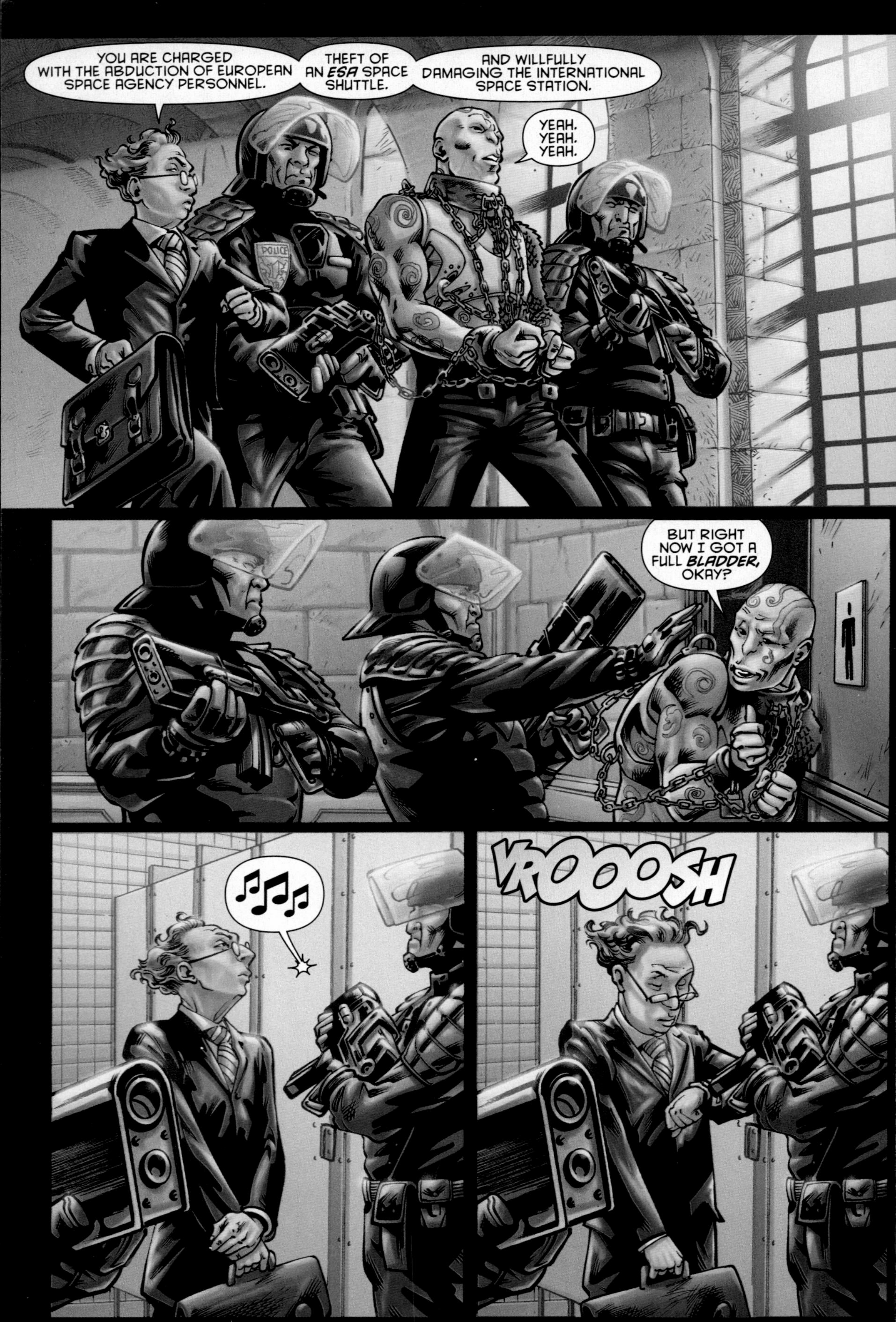
YOU ARE CHARGED WITH THE ABDUCTION OF EUROPEAN SPACE AGENCY PERSONNEL.
THEFT OF AN ESA SPACE SHUTTLE.
AND WILLFULLY DAMAGING THE INTERNATIONAL SPACE STATION.
YEAH. YEAH. YEAH.
POLICE
BUT RIGHT NOW I GOT A FULL BLADDER, OKAY?
♫♫♫
VROOOSH

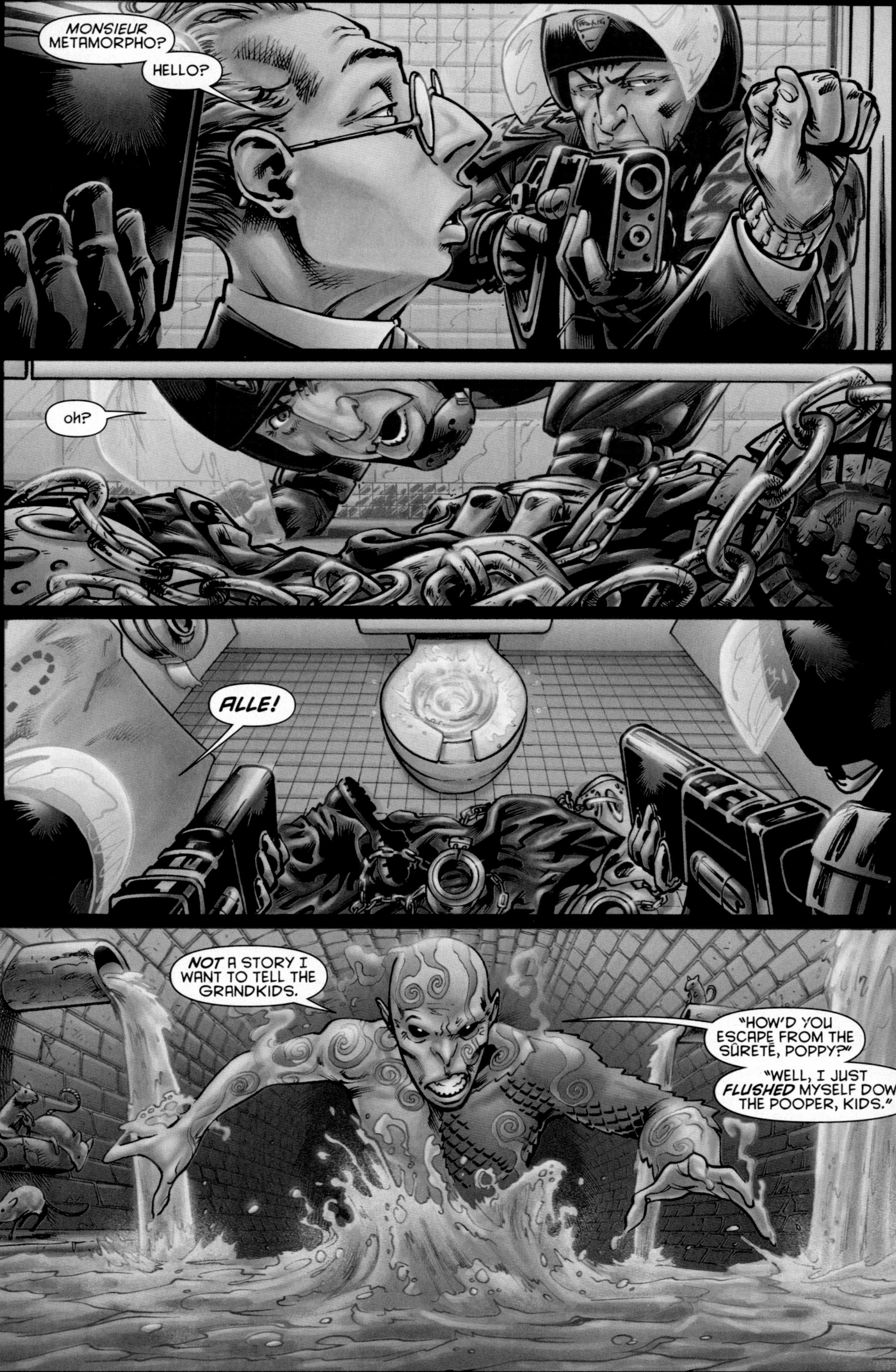
MONSIEUR METAMORPHO?
HELLO?
oh?
ALLE!
NOT A STORY I WANT TO TELL THE GRANDKIDS.
"HOW'D YOU ESCAPE FROM THE SÛRETÉ, POPPY?"
"WELL, I JUST FLUSHED MYSELF DOWN THE POOPER, KIDS."

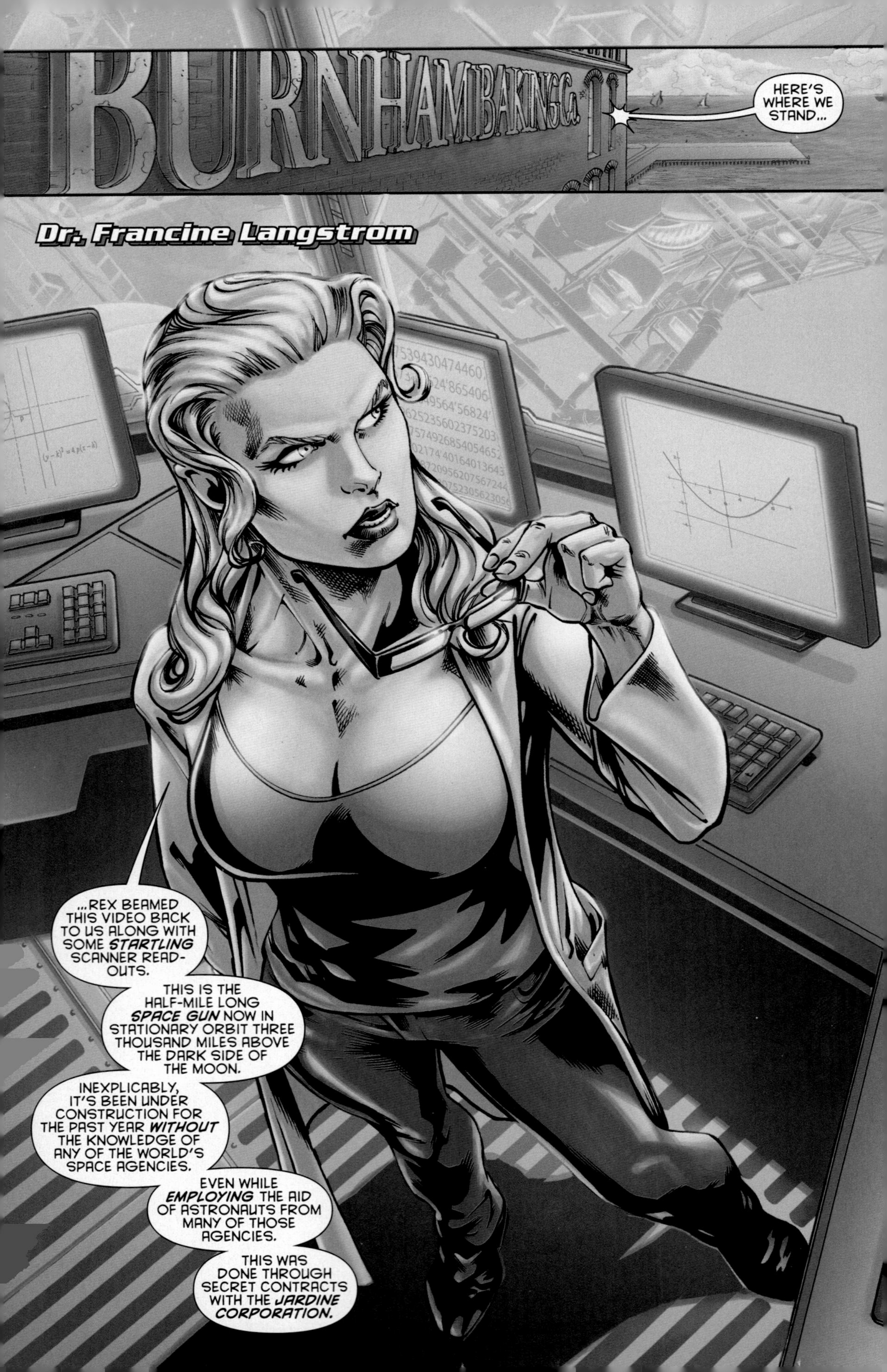

BURNHAM BAKING CO.
HERE'S WHERE WE STAND...
Dr. Francine Langstrom
...REX BEAMED THIS VIDEO BACK TO US ALONG WITH SOME STARTLING SCANNER READ-OUTS.
THIS IS THE HALF-MILE LONG SPACE GUN NOW IN STATIONARY ORBIT THREE THOUSAND MILES ABOVE THE DARK SIDE OF THE MOON.
INEXPLICABLY, IT'S BEEN UNDER CONSTRUCTION FOR THE PAST YEAR WITHOUT THE KNOWLEDGE OF ANY OF THE WORLD'S SPACE AGENCIES.
EVEN WHILE EMPLOYING THE AID OF ASTRONAUTS FROM MANY OF THOSE AGENCIES.
THIS WAS DONE THROUGH SECRET CONTRACTS WITH THE JARDINE CORPORATION.

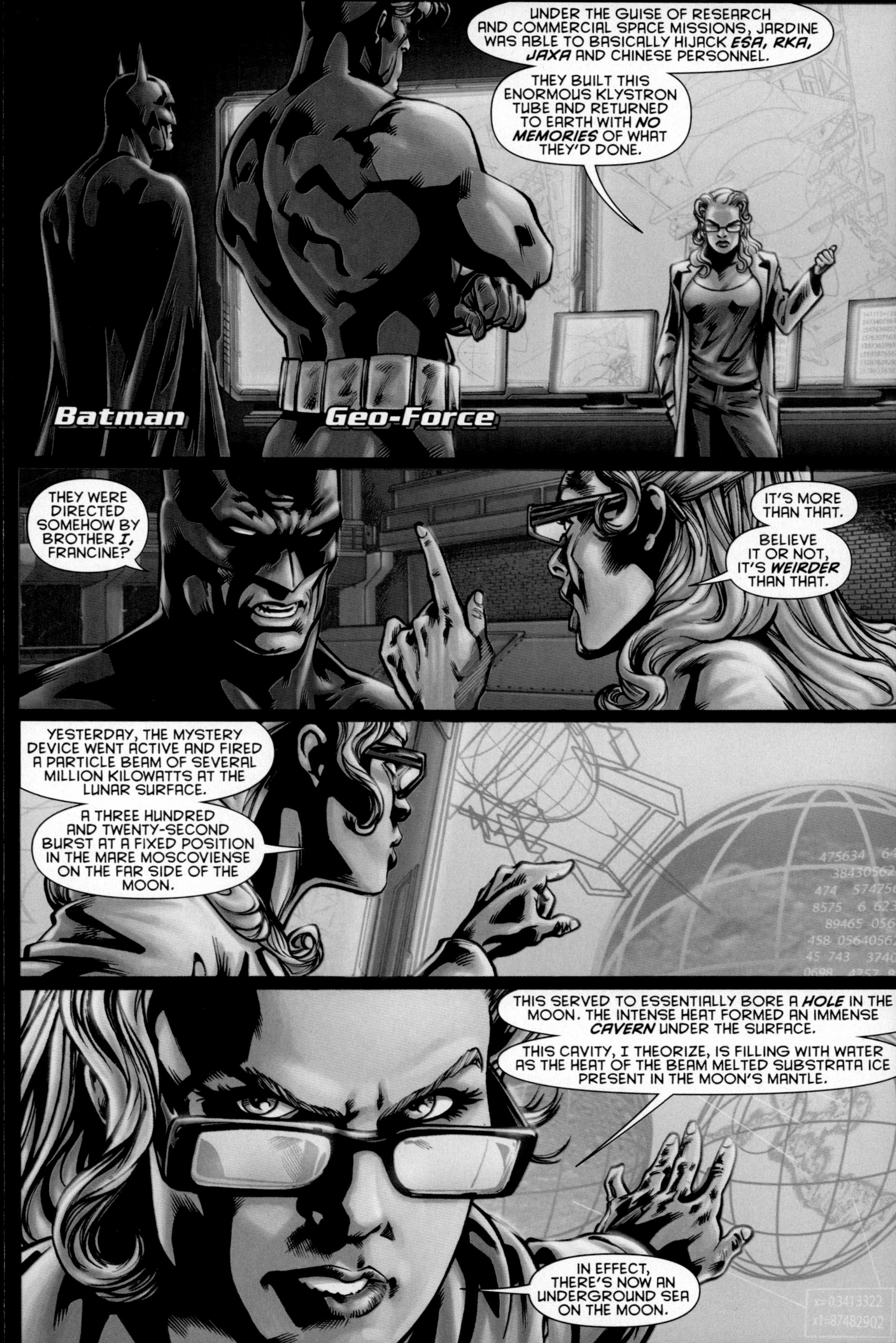
UNDER THE GUISE OF RESEARCH AND COMMERCIAL SPACE MISSIONS, JARDINE WAS ABLE TO BASICALLY HIJACK *ESA, RKA, JAXA* AND CHINESE PERSONNEL.
THEY BUILT THIS ENORMOUS KLYSTRON TUBE AND RETURNED TO EARTH WITH *NO MEMORIES* OF WHAT THEY'D DONE.
Batman
Geo-Force
THEY WERE DIRECTED SOMEHOW BY BROTHER *I*, FRANCINE?
IT'S MORE THAN THAT.
BELIEVE IT OR NOT, IT'S *WEIRDER* THAN THAT.
YESTERDAY, THE MYSTERY DEVICE WENT ACTIVE AND FIRED A PARTICLE BEAM OF SEVERAL MILLION KILOWATTS AT THE LUNAR SURFACE.
A THREE HUNDRED AND TWENTY-SECOND BURST AT A FIXED POSITION IN THE MARE MOSCOVIENSE ON THE FAR SIDE OF THE MOON.
THIS SERVED TO ESSENTIALLY BORE A *HOLE* IN THE MOON. THE INTENSE HEAT FORMED AN IMMENSE *CAVERN* UNDER THE SURFACE.
THIS CAVITY, I THEORIZE, IS FILLING WITH WATER AS THE HEAT OF THE BEAM MELTED SUBSTRATA ICE PRESENT IN THE MOON'S MANTLE.
IN EFFECT, THERE'S NOW AN UNDERGROUND SEA ON THE MOON.

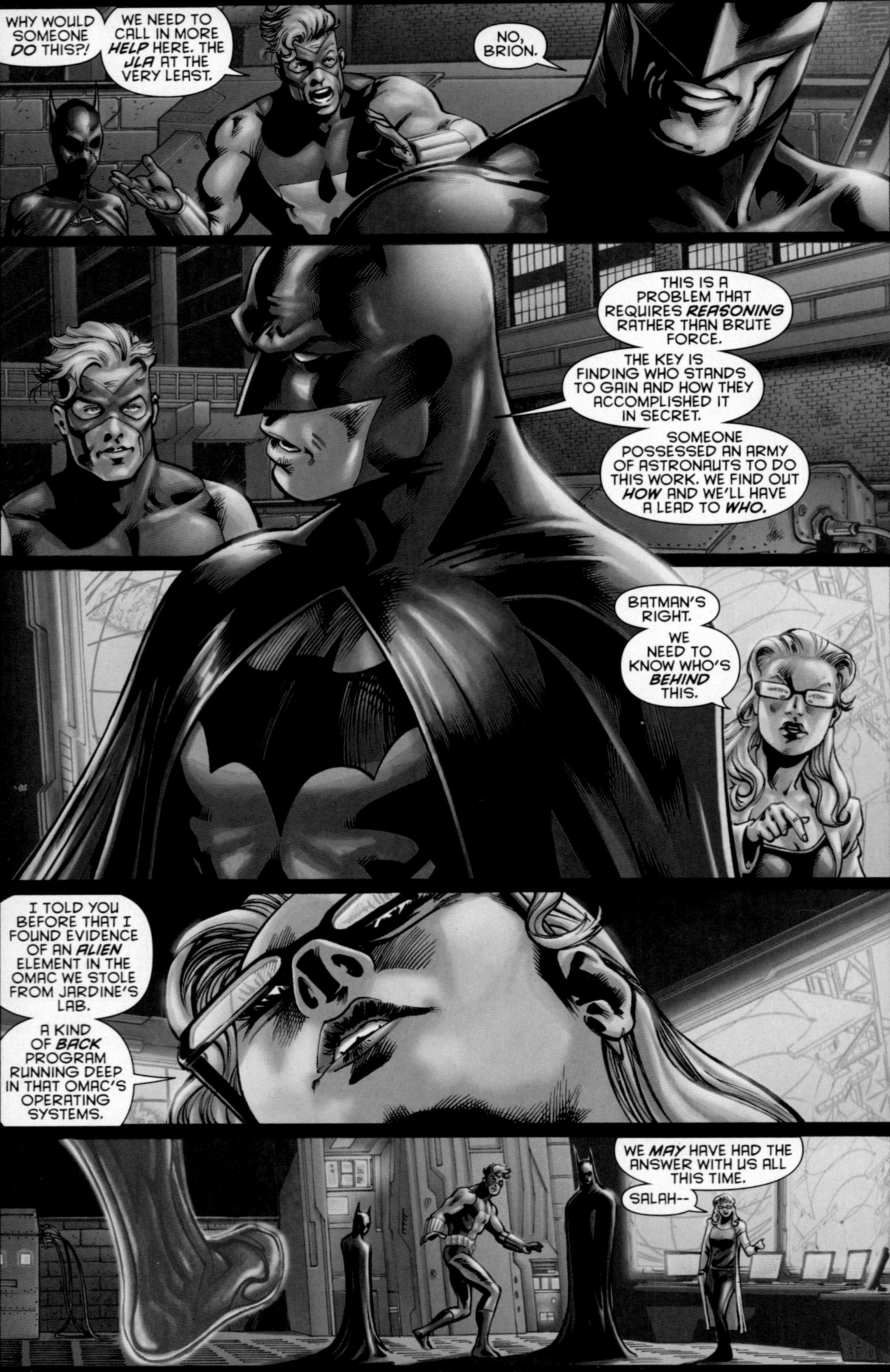
WHY WOULD SOMEONE DO THIS?!
WE NEED TO CALL IN MORE HELP HERE. THE JLA AT THE VERY LEAST.
NO, BRION.
THIS IS A PROBLEM THAT REQUIRES REASONING RATHER THAN BRUTE FORCE.
THE KEY IS FINDING WHO STANDS TO GAIN AND HOW THEY ACCOMPLISHED IT IN SECRET.
SOMEONE POSSESSED AN ARMY OF ASTRONAUTS TO DO THIS WORK. WE FIND OUT HOW AND WE'LL HAVE A LEAD TO WHO.
BATMAN'S RIGHT.
WE NEED TO KNOW WHO'S BEHIND THIS.
I TOLD YOU BEFORE THAT I FOUND EVIDENCE OF AN ALIEN ELEMENT IN THE OMAC WE STOLE FROM JARDINE'S LAB.
A KIND OF BACK PROGRAM RUNNING DEEP IN THAT OMAC'S OPERATING SYSTEMS.
WE MAY HAVE HAD THE ANSWER WITH US ALL THIS TIME.
SALAH--

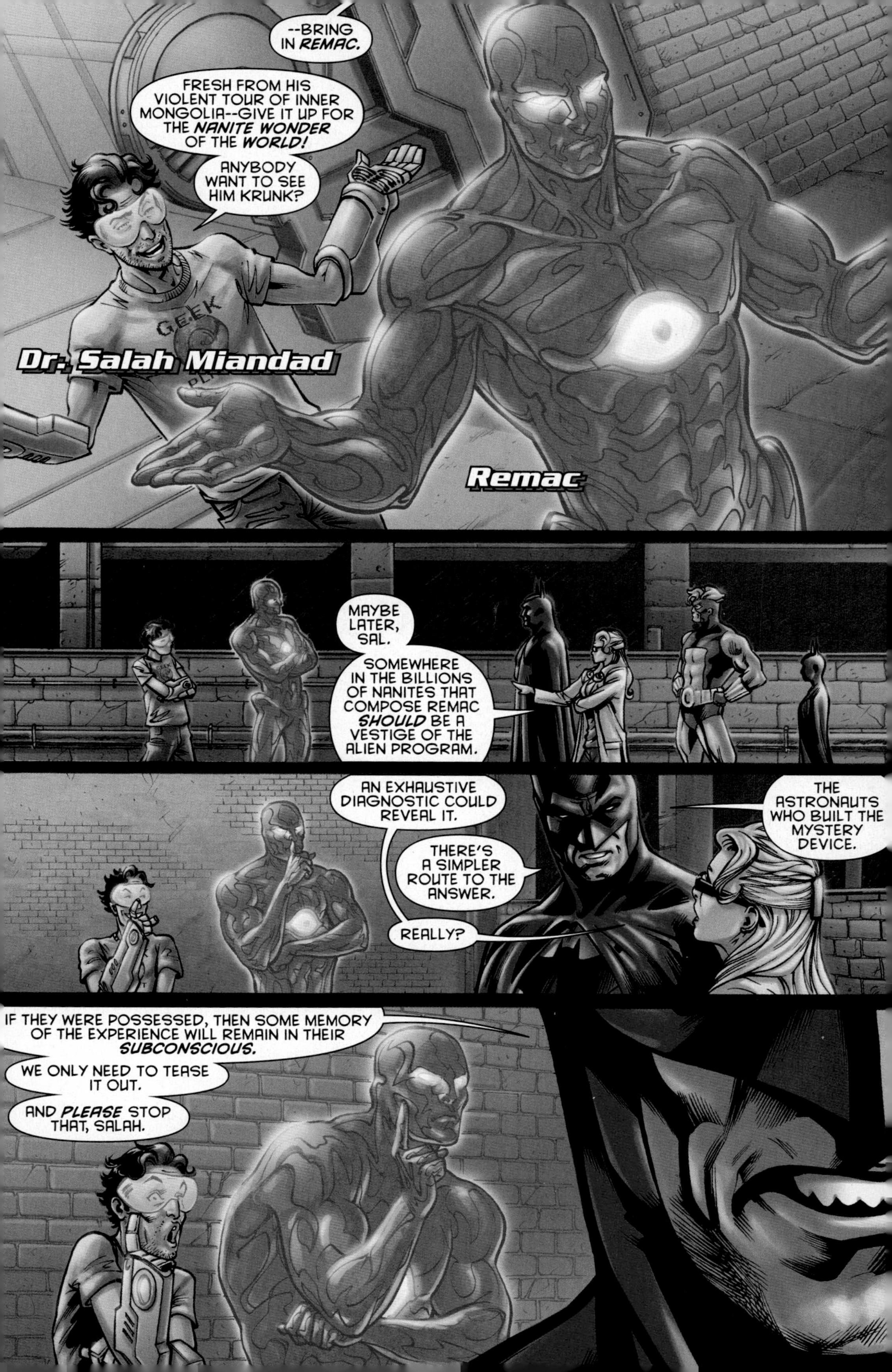
--BRING IN REMAC.
FRESH FROM HIS VIOLENT TOUR OF INNER MONGOLIA--GIVE IT UP FOR THE NANITE WONDER OF THE WORLD!
ANYBODY WANT TO SEE HIM KRUNK?
Dr. Salah Miandad
Remac
MAYBE LATER, SAL.
SOMEWHERE IN THE BILLIONS OF NANITES THAT COMPOSE REMAC SHOULD BE A VESTIGE OF THE ALIEN PROGRAM.
AN EXHAUSTIVE DIAGNOSTIC COULD REVEAL IT.
THERE'S A SIMPLER ROUTE TO THE ANSWER.
REALLY?
THE ASTRONAUTS WHO BUILT THE MYSTERY DEVICE.
IF THEY WERE POSSESSED, THEN SOME MEMORY OF THE EXPERIENCE WILL REMAIN IN THEIR SUBCONSCIOUS.
WE ONLY NEED TO TEASE IT OUT.
AND PLEASE STOP THAT, SALAH.

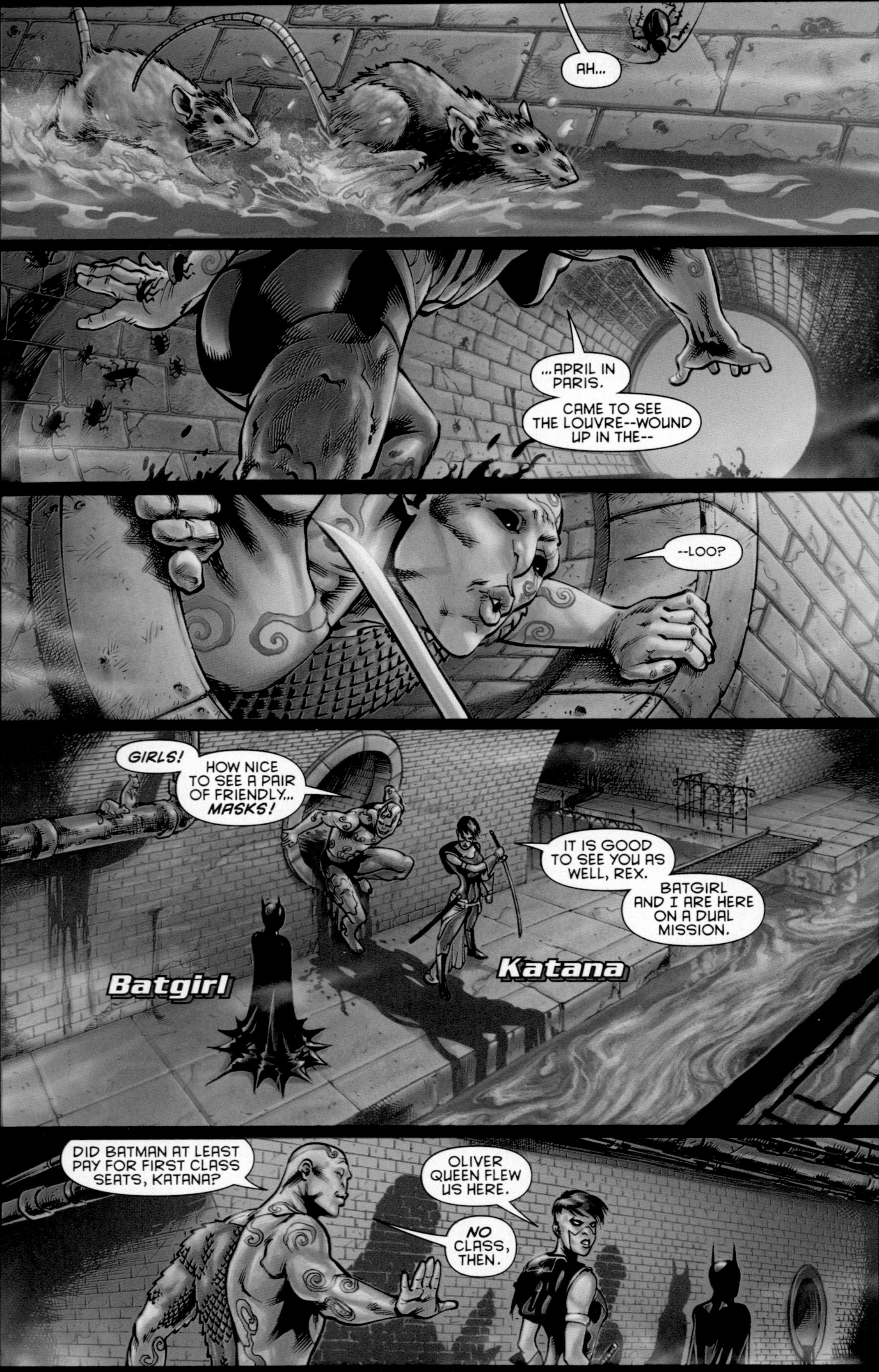
AH...
...APRIL IN PARIS.
CAME TO SEE THE LOUVRE--WOUND UP IN THE--
--LOO?
GIRLS!
HOW NICE TO SEE A PAIR OF FRIENDLY... MASKS!
IT IS GOOD TO SEE YOU AS WELL, REX.
BATGIRL AND I ARE HERE ON A DUAL MISSION.
Batgirl
Katana
DID BATMAN AT LEAST PAY FOR FIRST CLASS SEATS, KATANA?
OLIVER QUEEN FLEW US HERE.
NO CLASS, THEN.

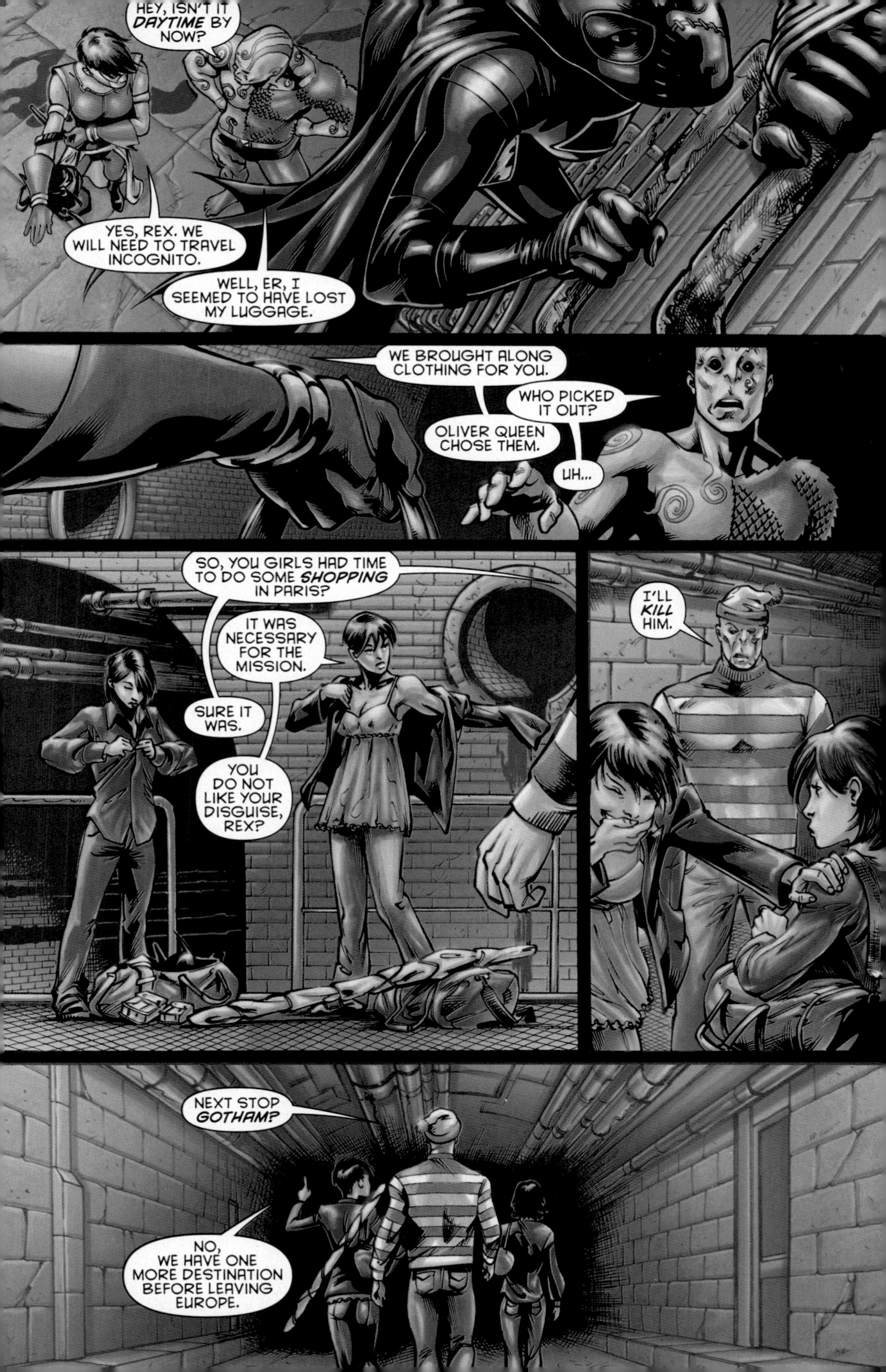

HEY, ISN'T IT DAYTIME BY NOW?
YES, REX. WE WILL NEED TO TRAVEL INCOGNITO.
WELL, ER, I SEEMED TO HAVE LOST MY LUGGAGE.
WE BROUGHT ALONG CLOTHING FOR YOU.
WHO PICKED IT OUT?
OLIVER QUEEN CHOSE THEM.
UH...
SO, YOU GIRLS HAD TIME TO DO SOME SHOPPING IN PARIS?
IT WAS NECESSARY FOR THE MISSION.
SURE IT WAS.
YOU DO NOT LIKE YOUR DISGUISE, REX?
I'LL KILL HIM.
NEXT STOP GOTHAM?
NO, WE HAVE ONE MORE DESTINATION BEFORE LEAVING EUROPE.

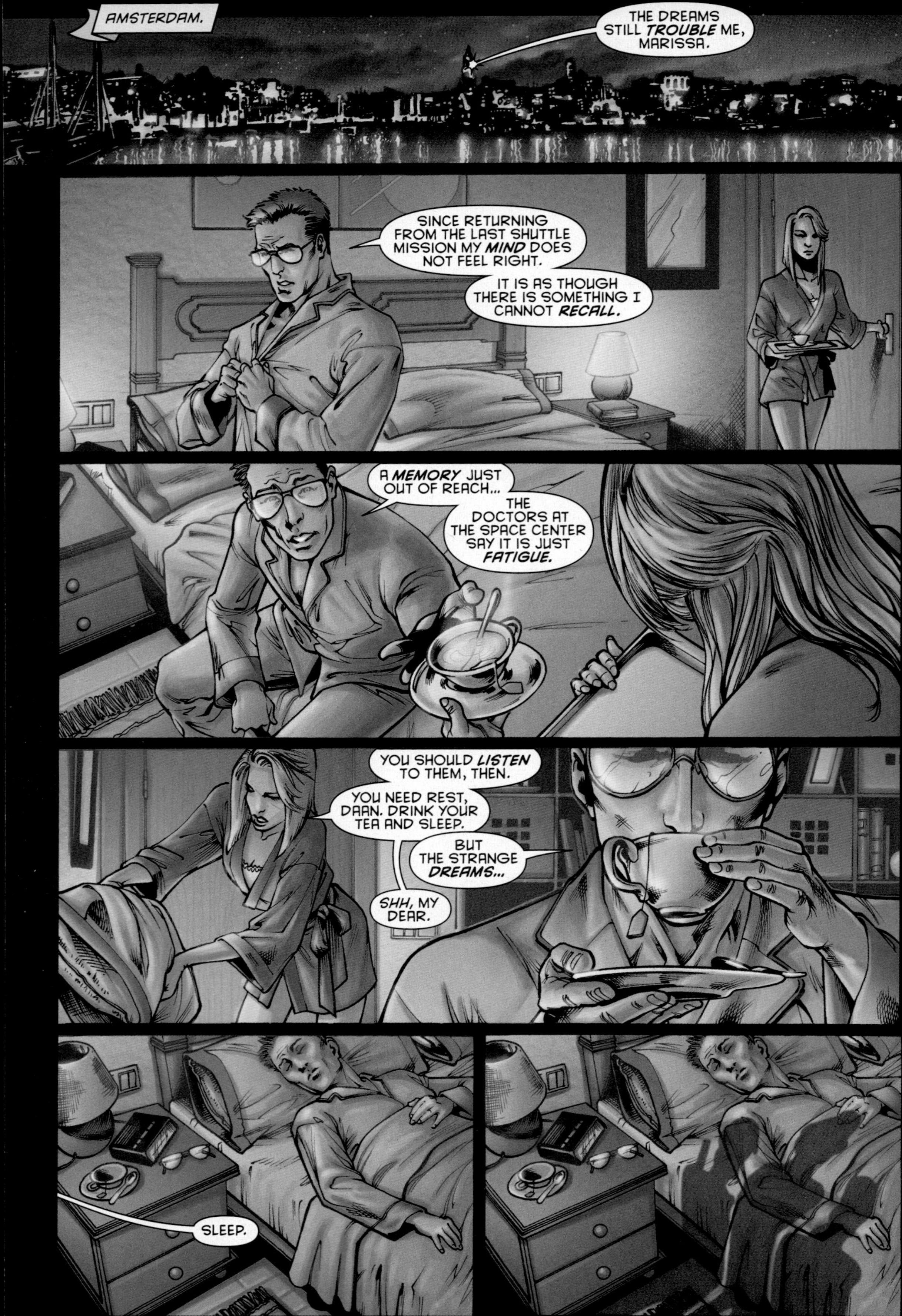
AMSTERDAM.
THE DREAMS STILL TROUBLE ME, MARISSA.
SINCE RETURNING FROM THE LAST SHUTTLE MISSION MY MIND DOES NOT FEEL RIGHT.
IT IS AS THOUGH THERE IS SOMETHING I CANNOT RECALL.
A MEMORY JUST OUT OF REACH...
THE DOCTORS AT THE SPACE CENTER SAY IT IS JUST FATIGUE.
YOU SHOULD LISTEN TO THEM, THEN.
YOU NEED REST, DAAN. DRINK YOUR TEA AND SLEEP.
BUT THE STRANGE DREAMS...
SHH, MY DEAR.
SLEEP.

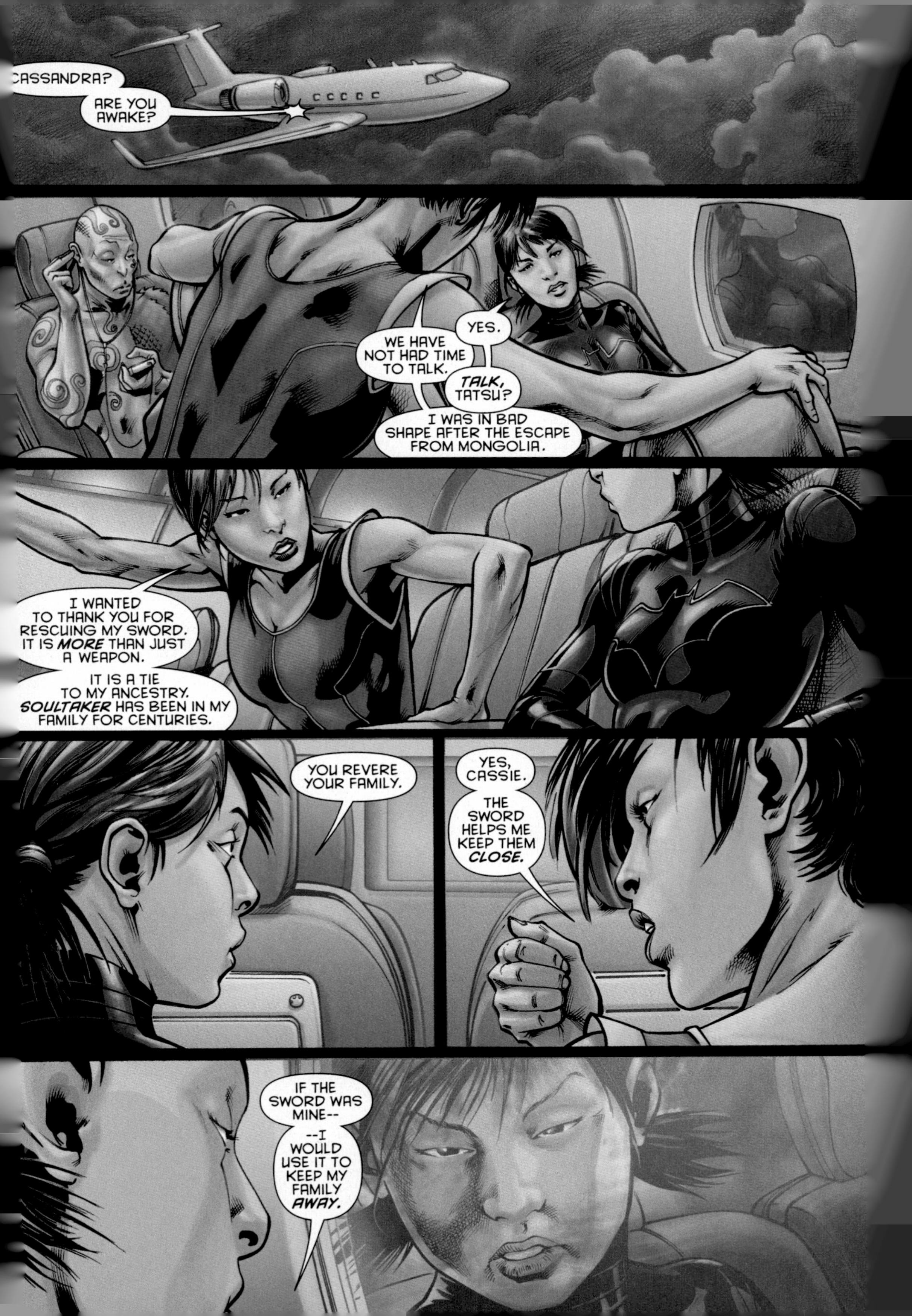
CASSANDRA?
ARE YOU AWAKE?
YES.
WE HAVE NOT HAD TIME TO TALK.
*TALK,* TATSU?
I WAS IN BAD SHAPE AFTER THE ESCAPE FROM MONGOLIA.
I WANTED TO THANK YOU FOR RESCUING MY SWORD. IT IS *MORE* THAN JUST A WEAPON.
IT IS A TIE TO MY ANCESTRY. *SOULTAKER* HAS BEEN IN MY FAMILY FOR CENTURIES.
YOU REVERE YOUR FAMILY.
YES, CASSIE.
THE SWORD HELPS ME KEEP THEM *CLOSE.*
IF THE SWORD WAS MINE--
--I WOULD USE IT TO KEEP MY FAMILY *AWAY.*

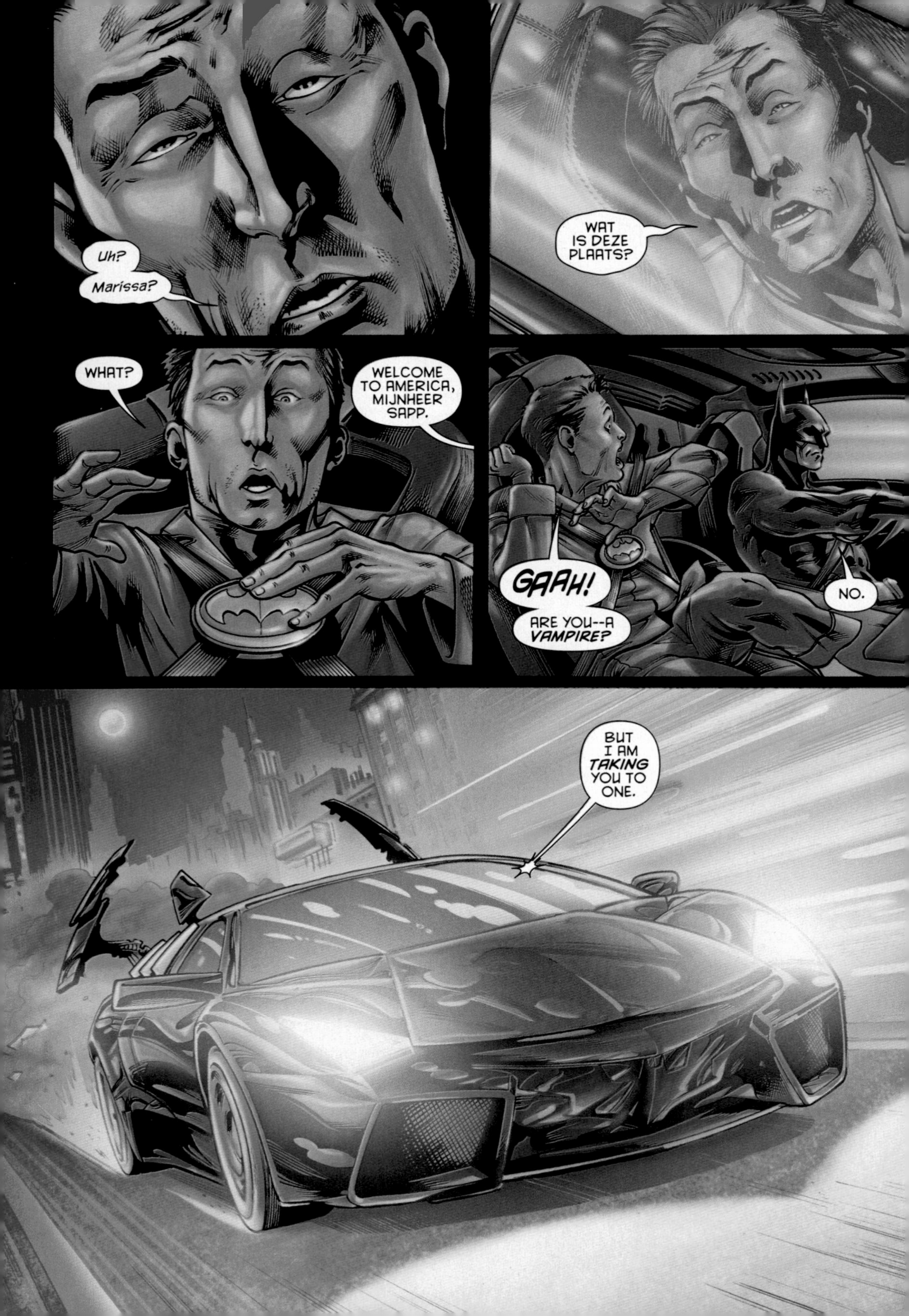
Uh?
Marissa?
WAT IS DEZE PLAATS?
WHAT?
WELCOME TO AMERICA, MIJNHEER SAPP.
GAAH!
ARE YOU--A VAMPIRE?
NO.
BUT I AM TAKING YOU TO ONE.

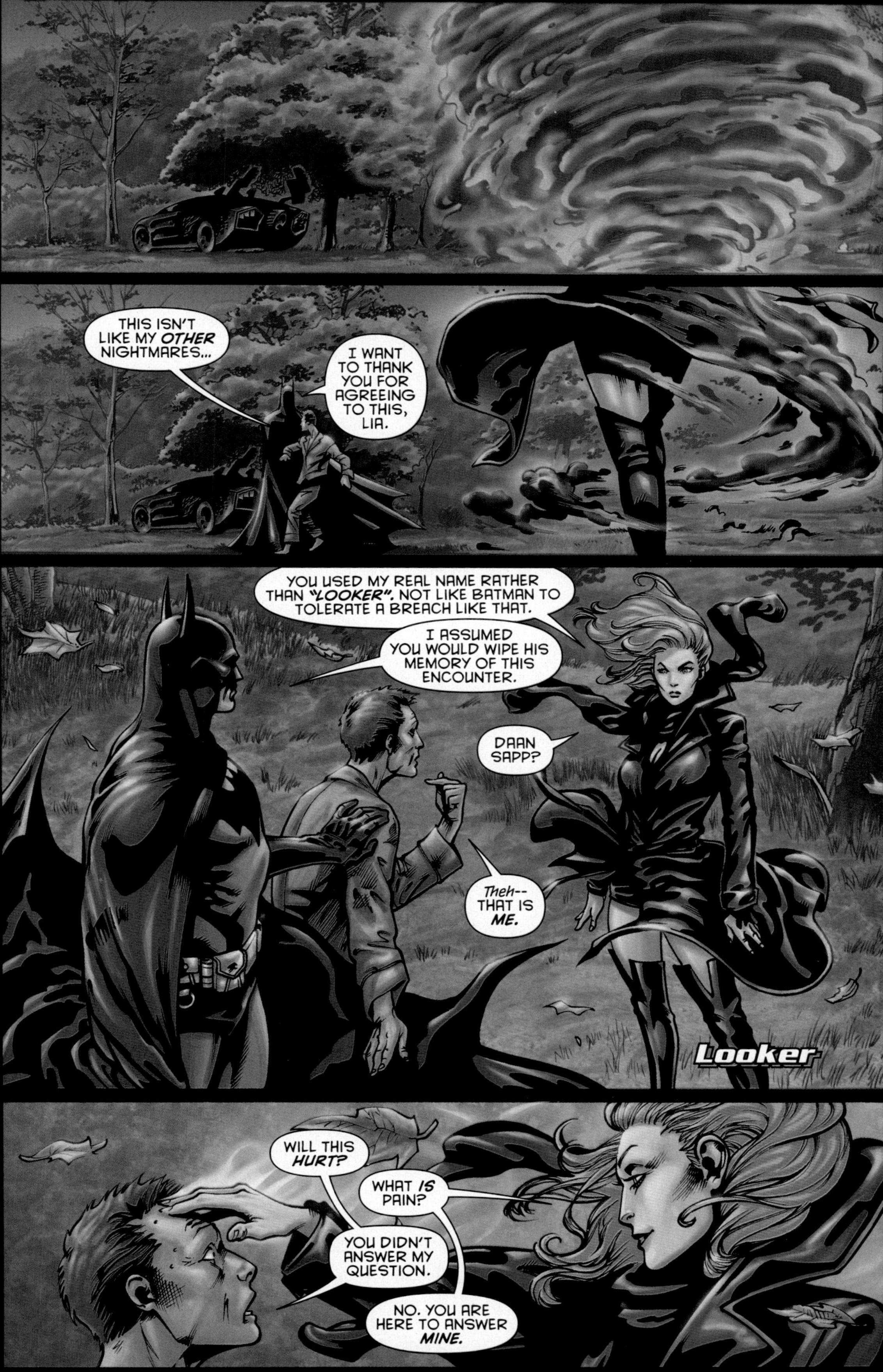

THIS ISN'T LIKE MY *OTHER* NIGHTMARES...
I WANT TO THANK YOU FOR AGREEING TO THIS, LIA.
YOU USED MY REAL NAME RATHER THAN *"LOOKER"*. NOT LIKE BATMAN TO TOLERATE A BREACH LIKE THAT.
I ASSUMED YOU WOULD WIPE HIS MEMORY OF THIS ENCOUNTER.
DAAN SAPP?
*Theh--* THAT IS *ME.*
Looker
WILL THIS *HURT?*
WHAT *IS* PAIN?
YOU DIDN'T ANSWER MY QUESTION.
NO. YOU ARE HERE TO ANSWER *MINE.*

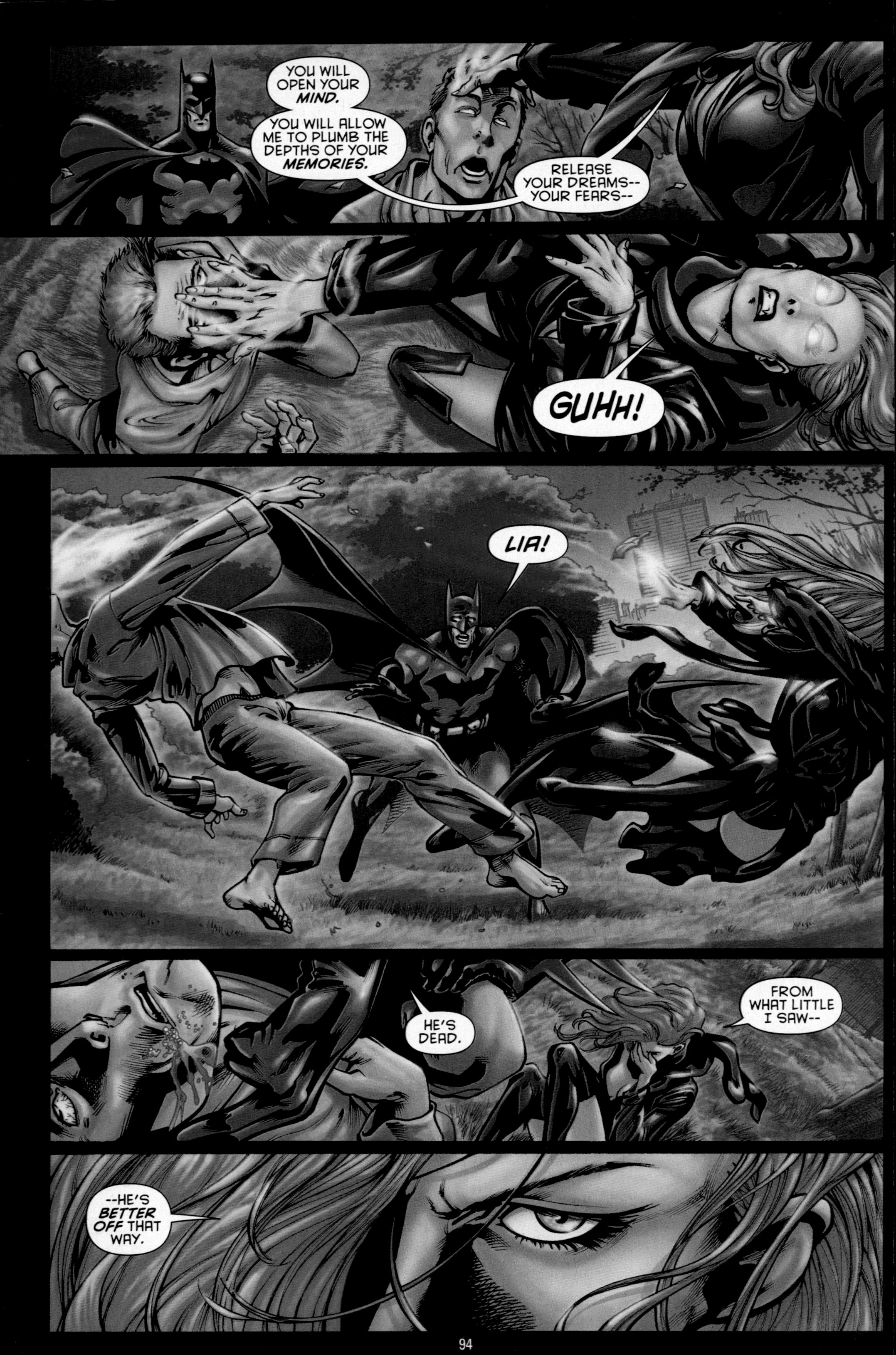
YOU WILL OPEN YOUR MIND.
YOU WILL ALLOW ME TO PLUMB THE DEPTHS OF YOUR MEMORIES.
RELEASE YOUR DREAMS-- YOUR FEARS--
GUHH!
LIA!
HE'S DEAD.
FROM WHAT LITTLE I SAW--
--HE'S BETTER OFF THAT WAY.

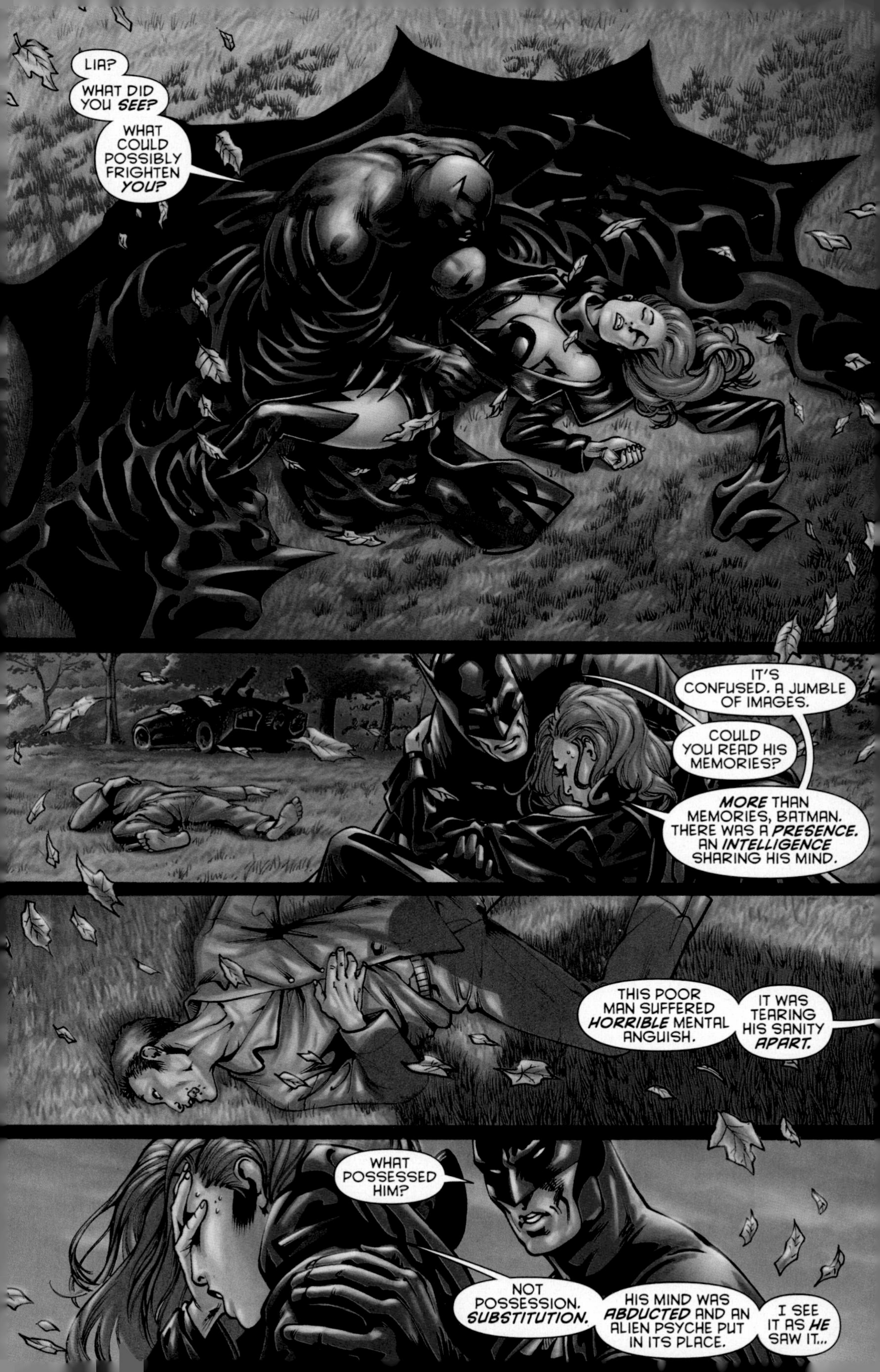
LIA?
WHAT DID YOU SEE?
WHAT COULD POSSIBLY FRIGHTEN YOU?
IT'S CONFUSED. A JUMBLE OF IMAGES.
COULD YOU READ HIS MEMORIES?
MORE THAN MEMORIES, BATMAN. THERE WAS A PRESENCE. AN INTELLIGENCE SHARING HIS MIND.
THIS POOR MAN SUFFERED HORRIBLE MENTAL ANGUISH.
IT WAS TEARING HIS SANITY APART.
WHAT POSSESSED HIM?
NOT POSSESSION. SUBSTITUTION.
HIS MIND WAS ABDUCTED AND AN ALIEN PSYCHE PUT IN ITS PLACE.
I SEE IT AS HE SAW IT...

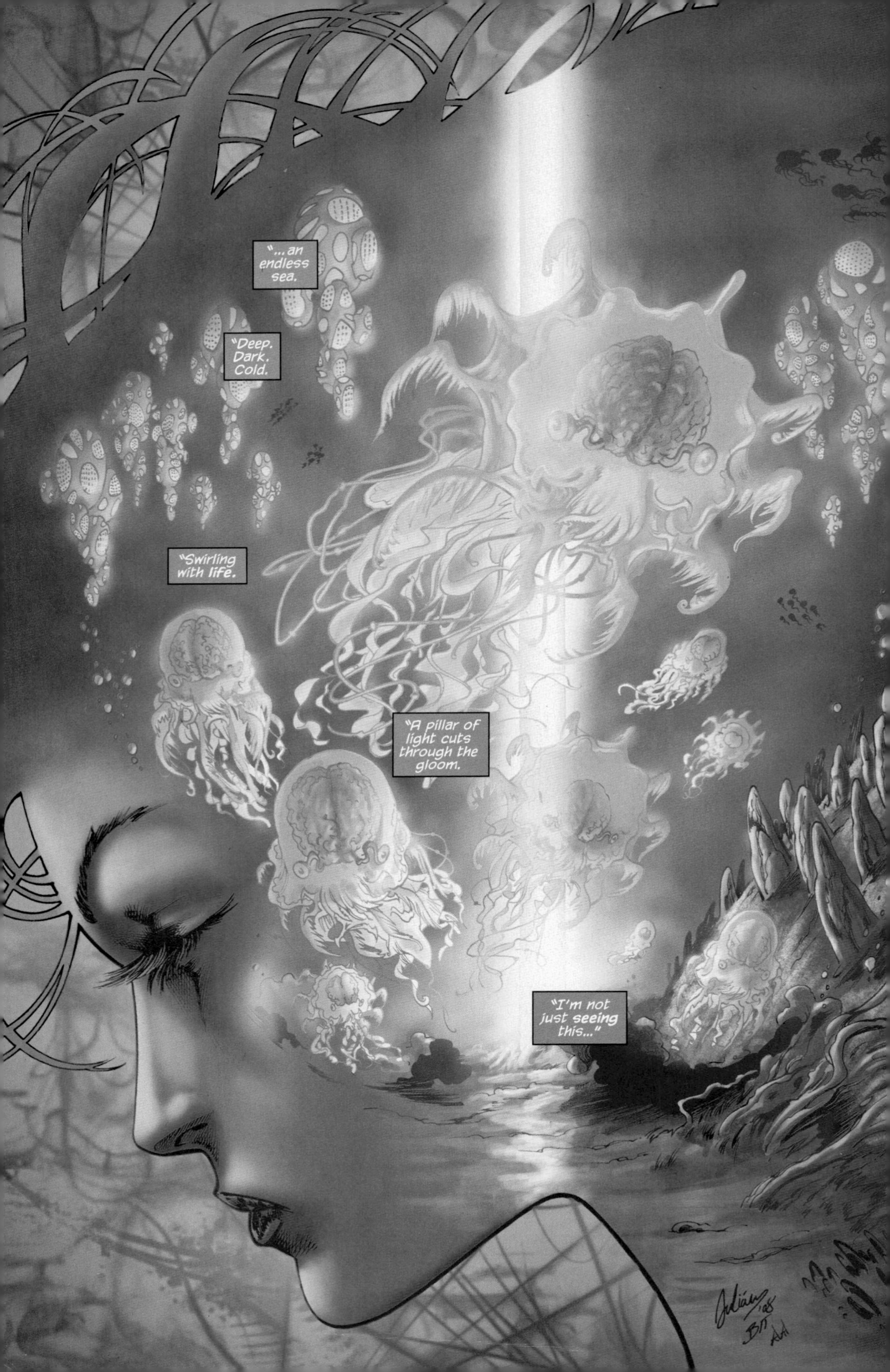
"...an endless sea.
"Deep. Dark. Cold.
"Swirling with life.
"A pillar of light cuts through the gloom.
"I'm not just seeing this..."

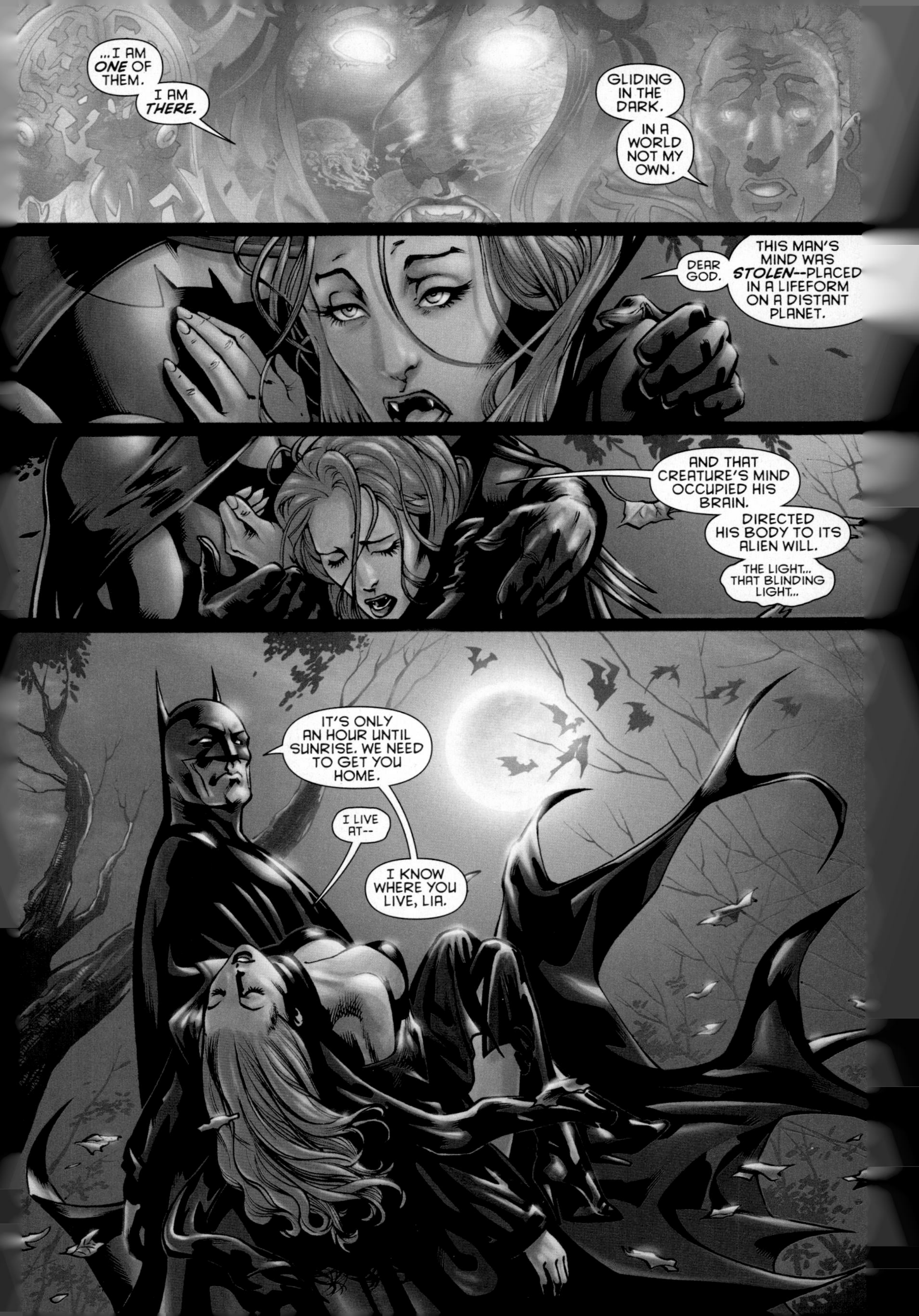
...I AM ONE OF THEM.
I AM THERE.
GLIDING IN THE DARK.
IN A WORLD NOT MY OWN.
DEAR GOD.
THIS MAN'S MIND WAS STOLEN--PLACED IN A LIFEFORM ON A DISTANT PLANET.
AND THAT CREATURE'S MIND OCCUPIED HIS BRAIN.
DIRECTED HIS BODY TO ITS ALIEN WILL.
THE LIGHT... THAT BLINDING LIGHT...
IT'S ONLY AN HOUR UNTIL SUNRISE. WE NEED TO GET YOU HOME.
I LIVE AT--
I KNOW WHERE YOU LIVE, LIA.

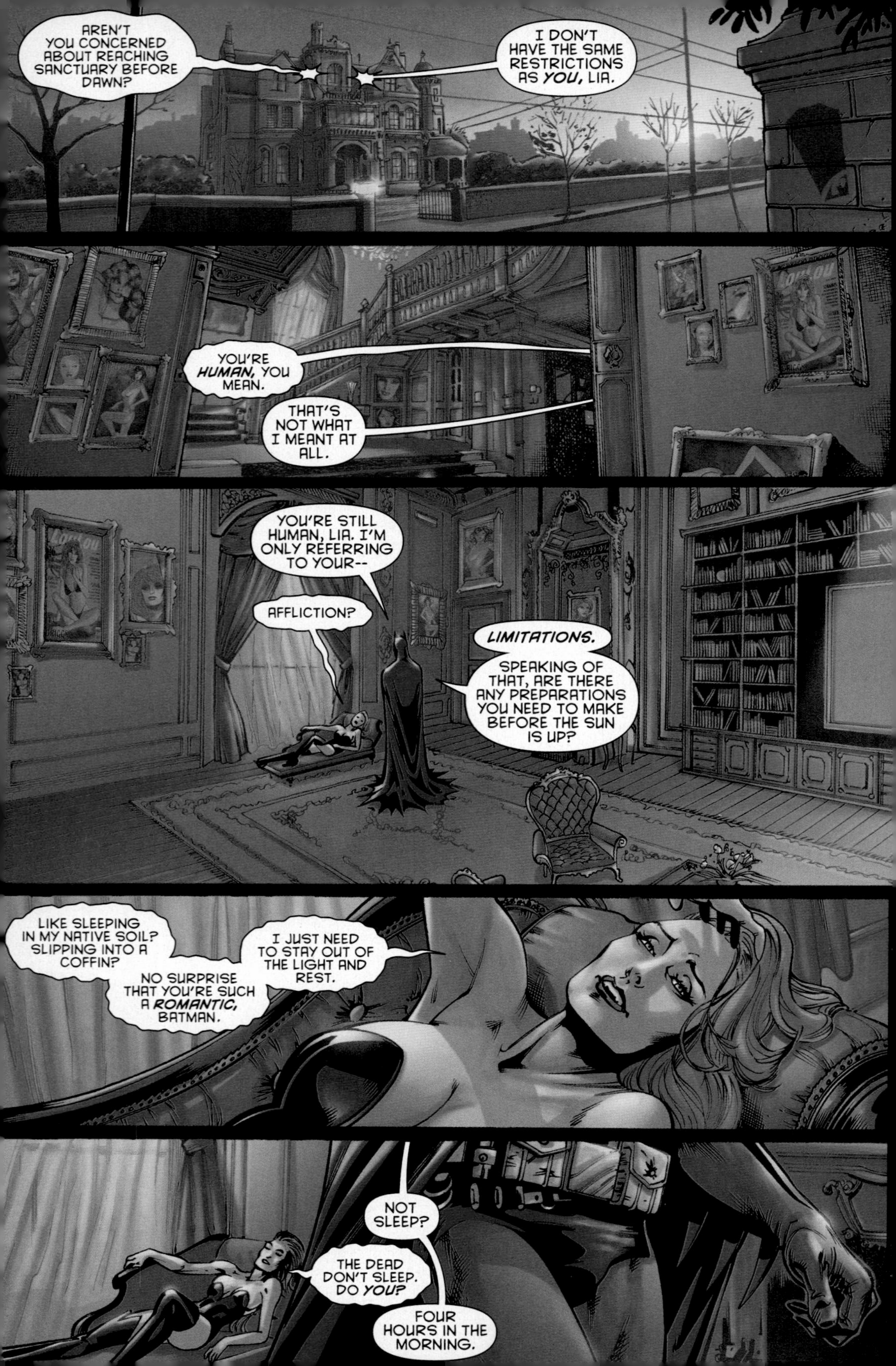
AREN'T YOU CONCERNED ABOUT REACHING SANCTUARY BEFORE DAWN?
I DON'T HAVE THE SAME RESTRICTIONS AS *YOU*, LIA.
YOU'RE *HUMAN,* YOU MEAN.
THAT'S NOT WHAT I MEANT AT ALL.
YOU'RE STILL HUMAN, LIA. I'M ONLY REFERRING TO YOUR--
AFFLICTION?
*LIMITATIONS.*
SPEAKING OF THAT, ARE THERE ANY PREPARATIONS YOU NEED TO MAKE BEFORE THE SUN IS UP?
LIKE SLEEPING IN MY NATIVE SOIL? SLIPPING INTO A COFFIN?
NO SURPRISE THAT YOU'RE SUCH A *ROMANTIC,* BATMAN.
I JUST NEED TO STAY OUT OF THE LIGHT AND REST.
NOT SLEEP?
THE DEAD DON'T SLEEP. DO *YOU?*
FOUR HOURS IN THE MORNING.

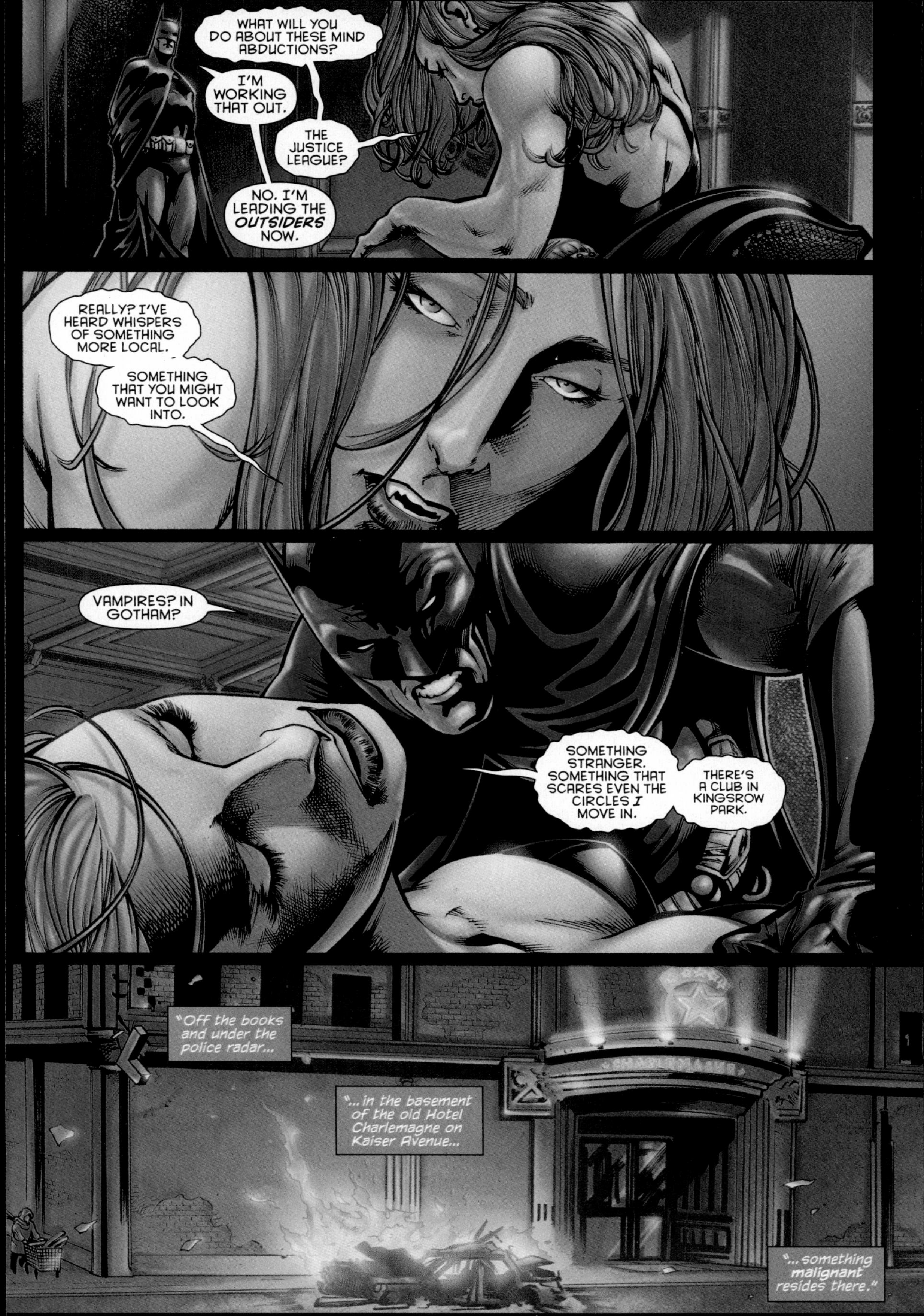

WHAT WILL YOU DO ABOUT THESE MIND ABDUCTIONS?
I'M WORKING THAT OUT.
THE JUSTICE LEAGUE?
NO. I'M LEADING THE OUTSIDERS NOW.
REALLY? I'VE HEARD WHISPERS OF SOMETHING MORE LOCAL.
SOMETHING THAT YOU MIGHT WANT TO LOOK INTO.
VAMPIRES? IN GOTHAM?
SOMETHING STRANGER. SOMETHING THAT SCARES EVEN THE CIRCLES I MOVE IN.
THERE'S A CLUB IN KINGSROW PARK.
"Off the books and under the police radar...
"...in the basement of the old Hotel Charlemagne on Kaiser Avenue...
"...something malignant resides there."

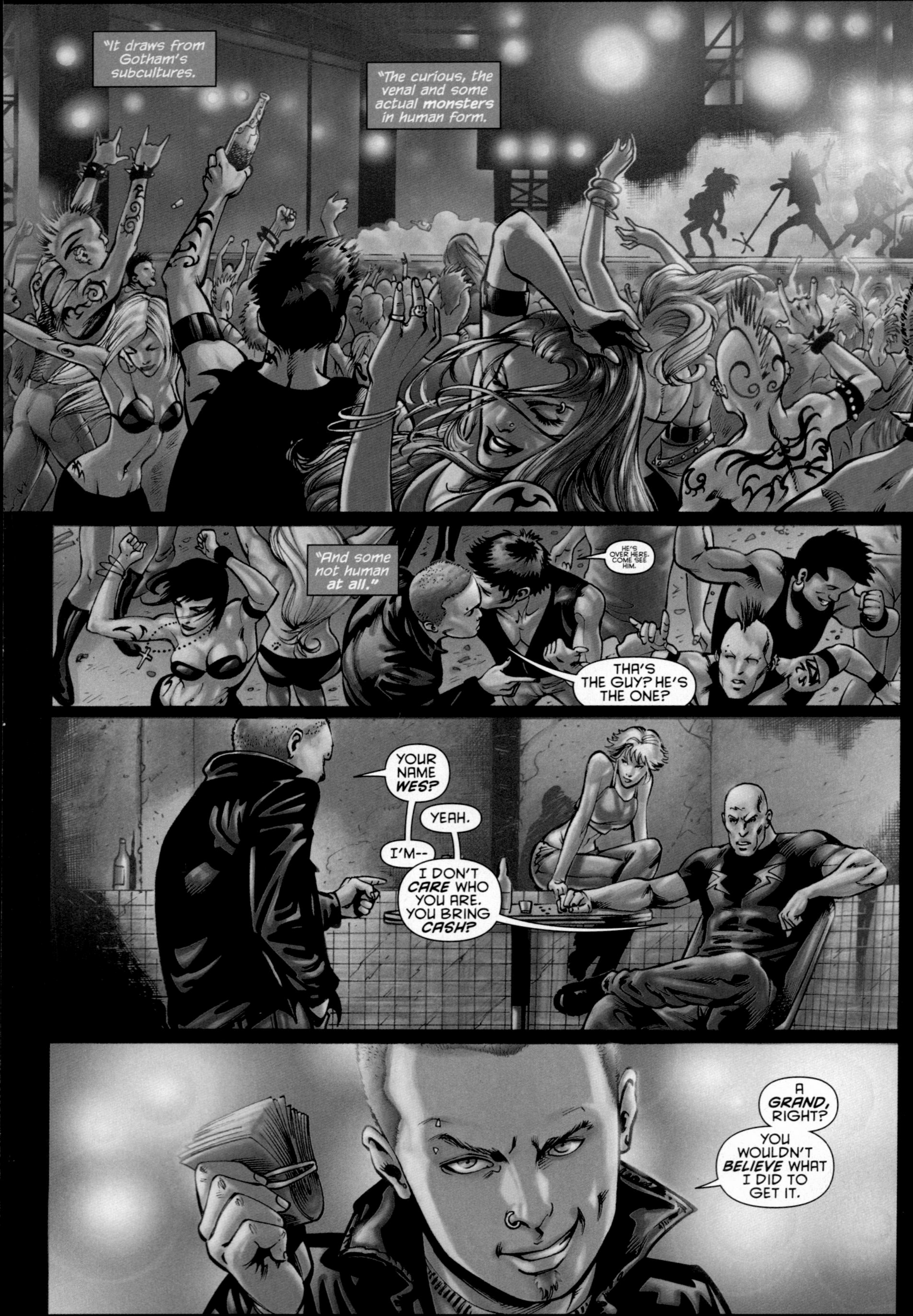
"It draws from Gotham's subcultures.
"The curious, the venal and some actual monsters in human form.
"And some not human at all."
HE'S OVER HERE. COME SEE HIM.
THA'S THE GUY? HE'S THE ONE?
YOUR NAME WES?
YEAH.
I'M--
I DON'T CARE WHO YOU ARE. YOU BRING CASH?
A GRAND, RIGHT?
YOU WOULDN'T BELIEVE WHAT I DID TO GET IT.

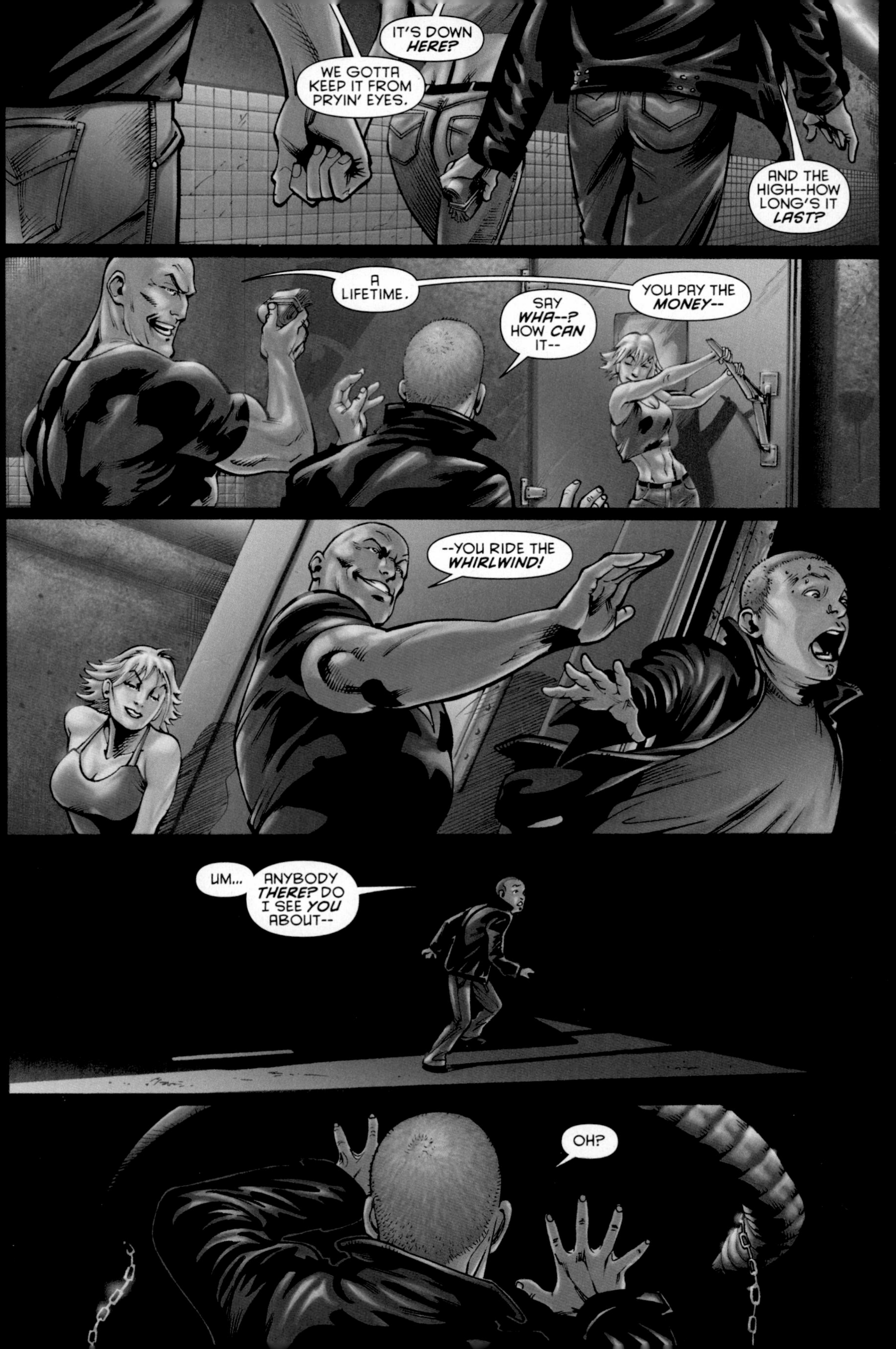

IT'S DOWN *HERE?*
WE GOTTA KEEP IT FROM PRYIN' EYES.
AND THE HIGH--HOW LONG'S IT *LAST?*
A LIFETIME.
SAY *WHA--?* HOW *CAN* IT--
YOU PAY THE *MONEY--*
--YOU RIDE THE *WHIRLWIND!*
UM...
ANYBODY *THERE?* DO I SEE *YOU* ABOUT--
OH?

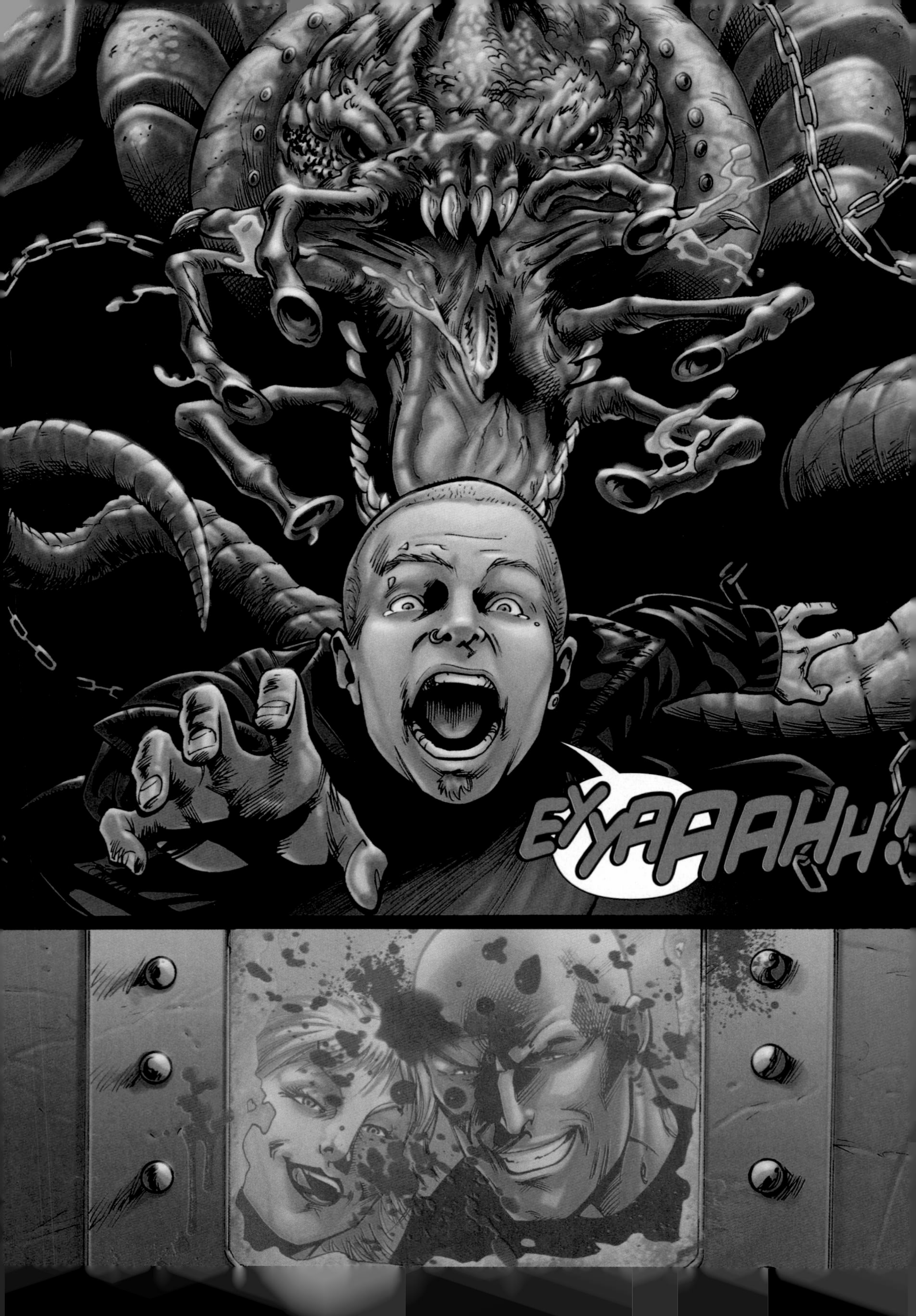
EYYAAAHH!

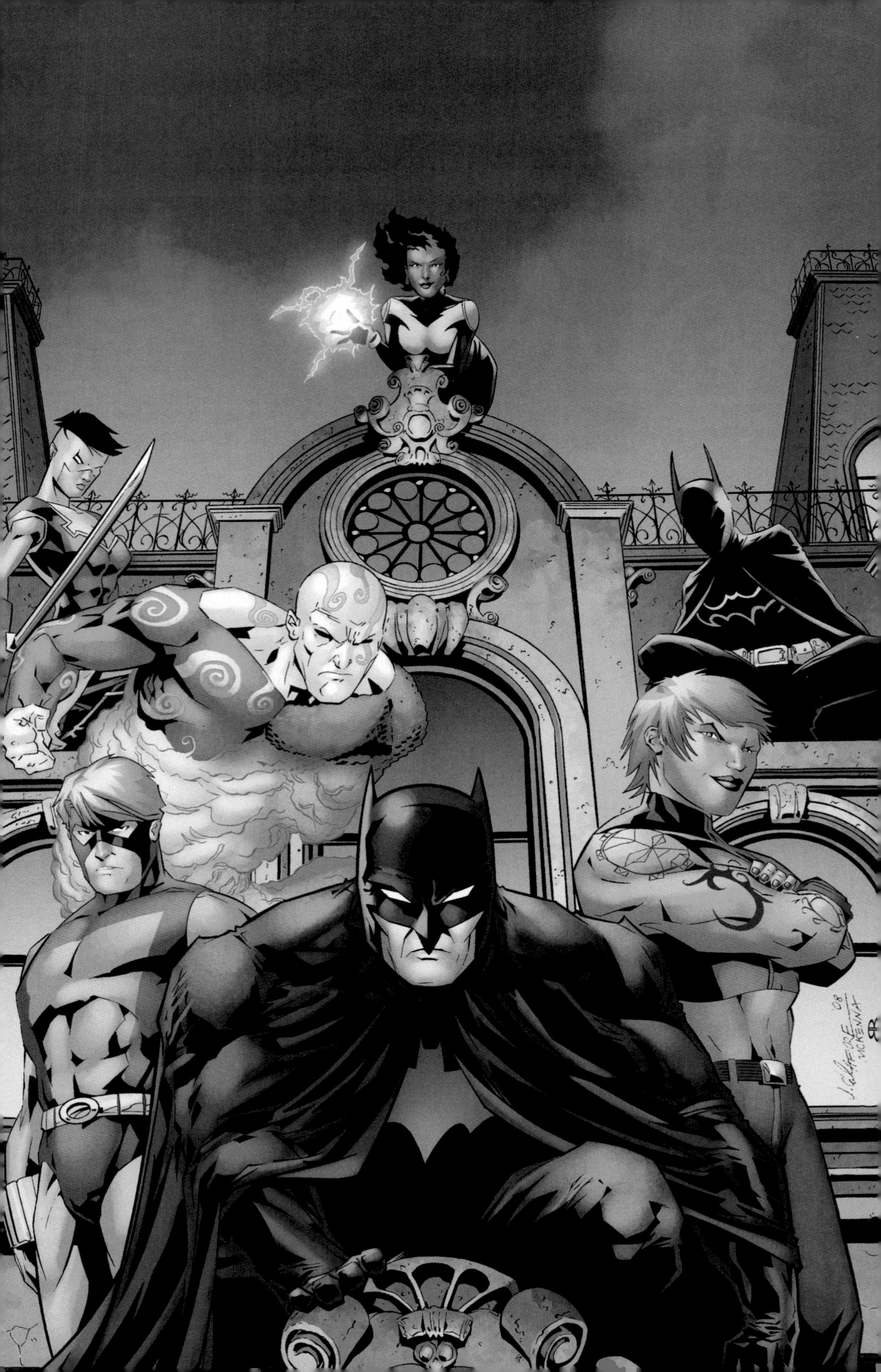

part FIVE

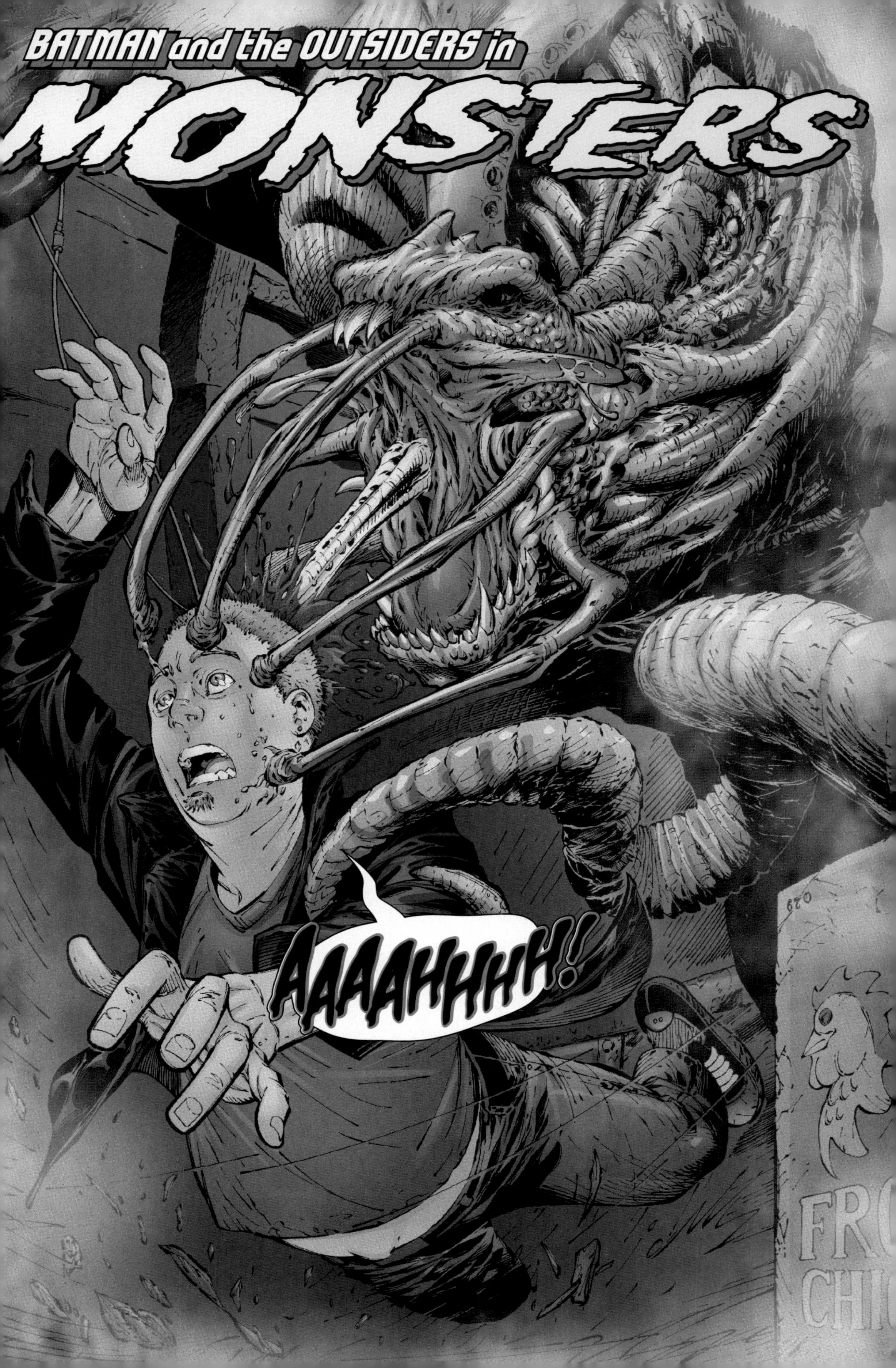
BATMAN and the OUTSIDERS in
MONSTERS
AAAAHHHH!
FRO
CHIC

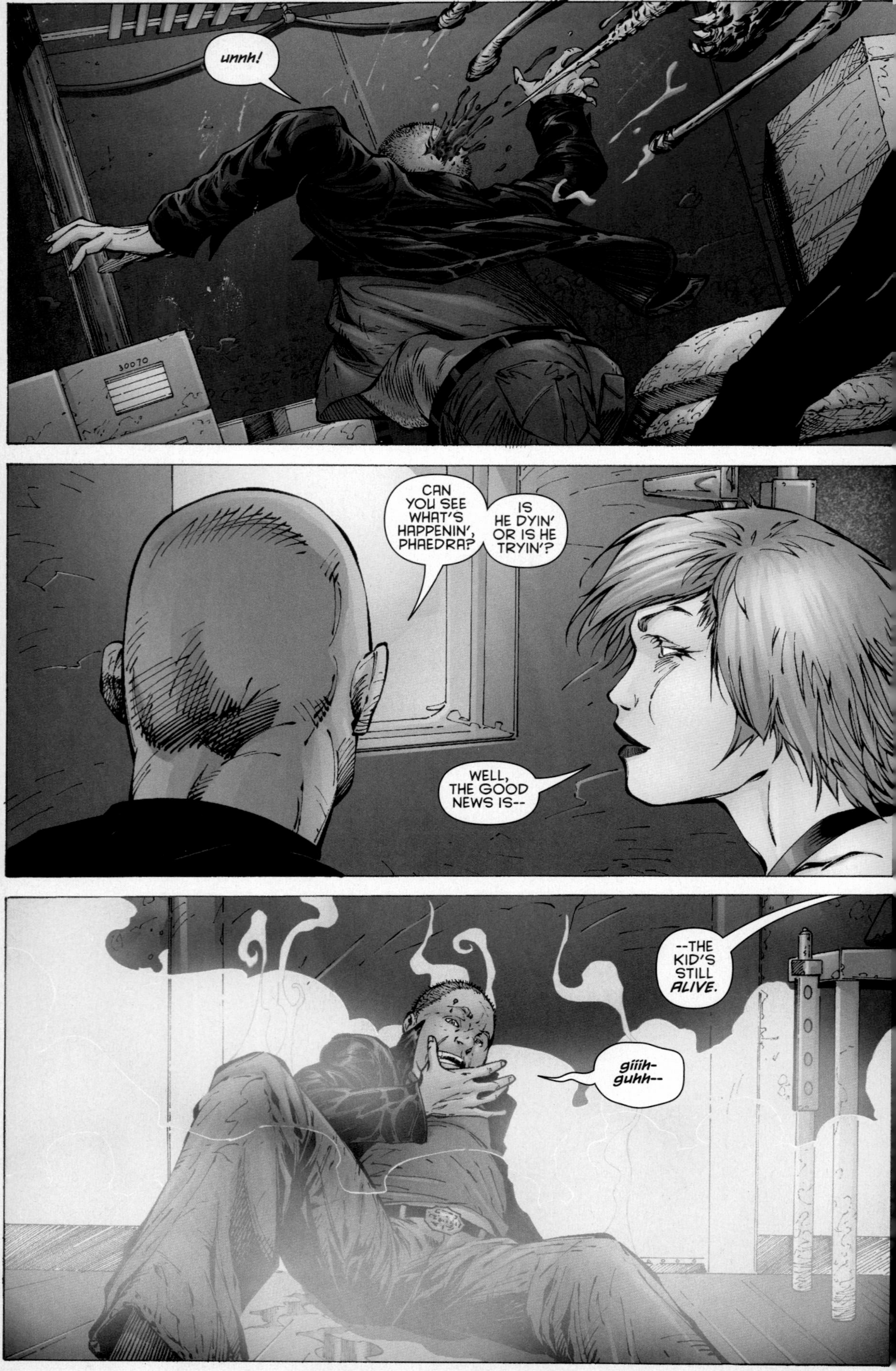
unnh!
CAN YOU SEE WHAT'S HAPPENIN', PHAEDRA?
IS HE DYIN' OR IS HE TRYIN'?
WELL, THE GOOD NEWS IS--
--THE KID'S STILL *ALIVE*.
*giiih-guhh--*

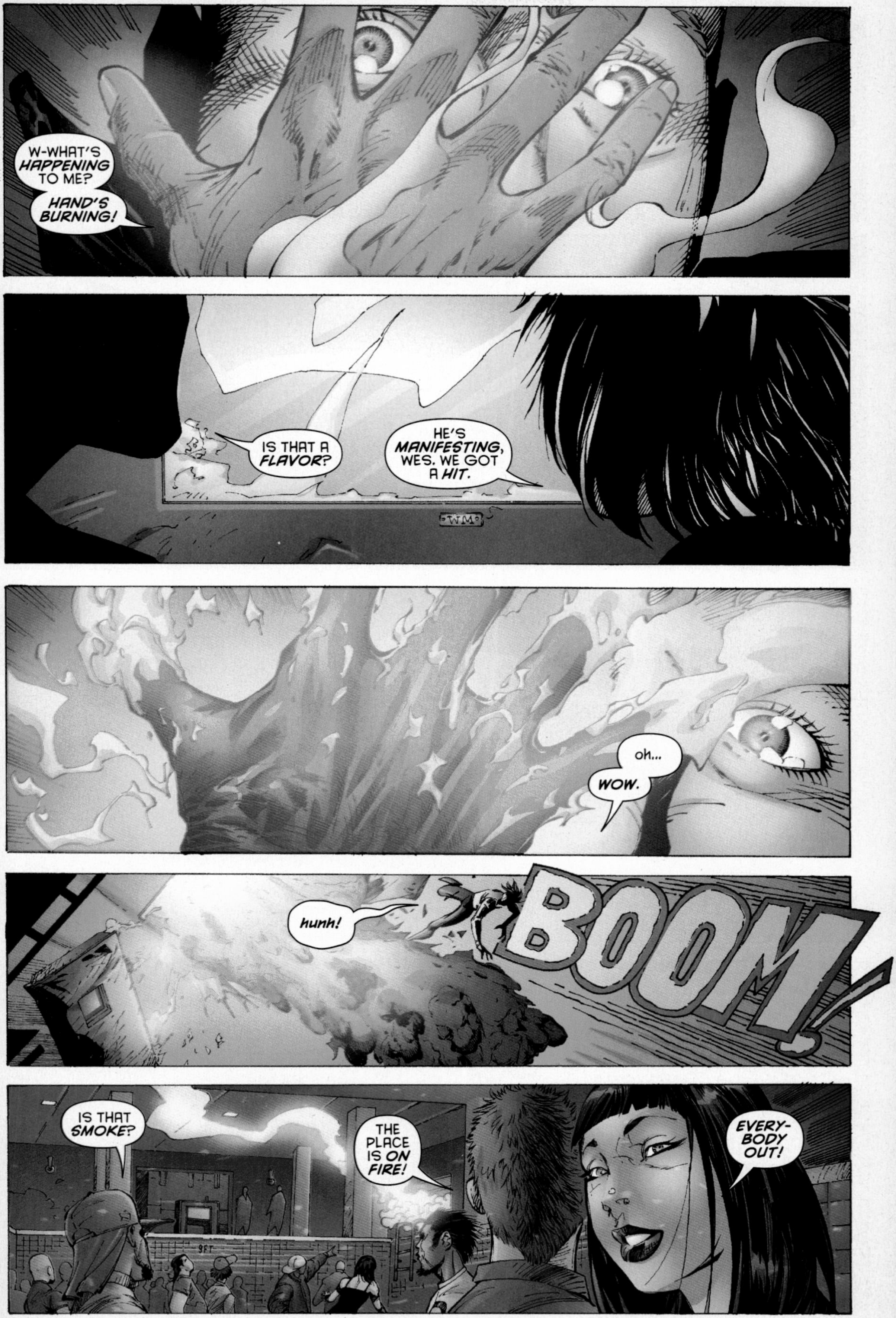
W-WHAT'S *HAPPENING* TO ME?
*HAND'S BURNING!*
IS THAT A *FLAVOR?*
HE'S *MANIFESTING,* WES. WE GOT A *HIT.*
oh...
*WOW.*
*hunh!*
BOOM!
IS THAT *SMOKE?*
THE PLACE IS *ON FIRE!*
*EVERY-BODY OUT!*

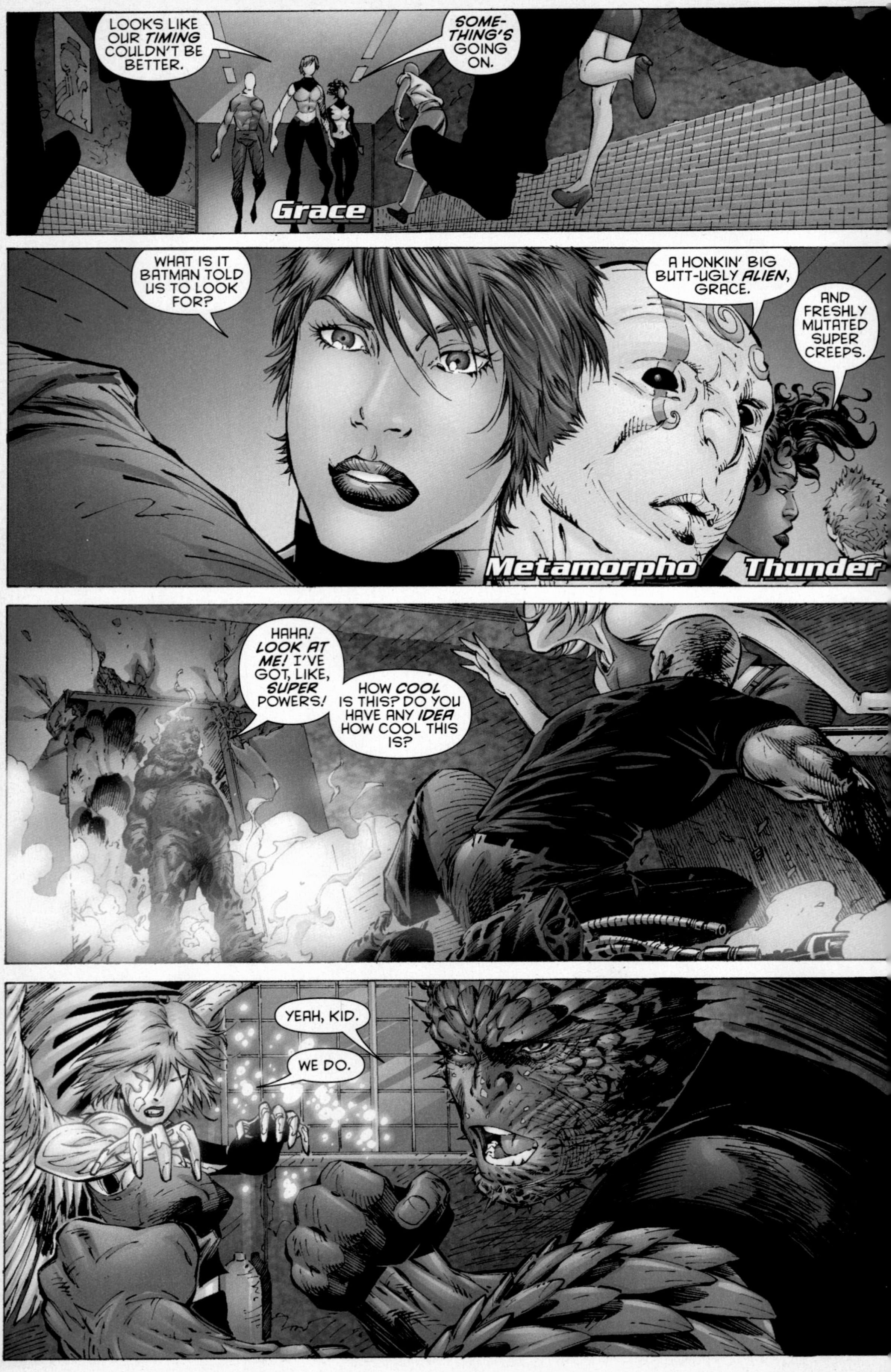
LOOKS LIKE OUR *TIMING* COULDN'T BE BETTER.
*SOME-THING'S* GOING ON.
Grace
WHAT IS IT BATMAN TOLD US TO LOOK FOR?
A HONKIN' BIG BUTT-UGLY *ALIEN*, GRACE.
AND FRESHLY MUTATED SUPER CREEPS.
Metamorpho
Thunder
HAHA! ***LOOK AT ME!*** I'VE GOT, LIKE, ***SUPER*** POWERS!
HOW ***COOL*** IS THIS? DO YOU HAVE ANY ***IDEA*** HOW COOL THIS IS?
YEAH, KID.
WE DO.

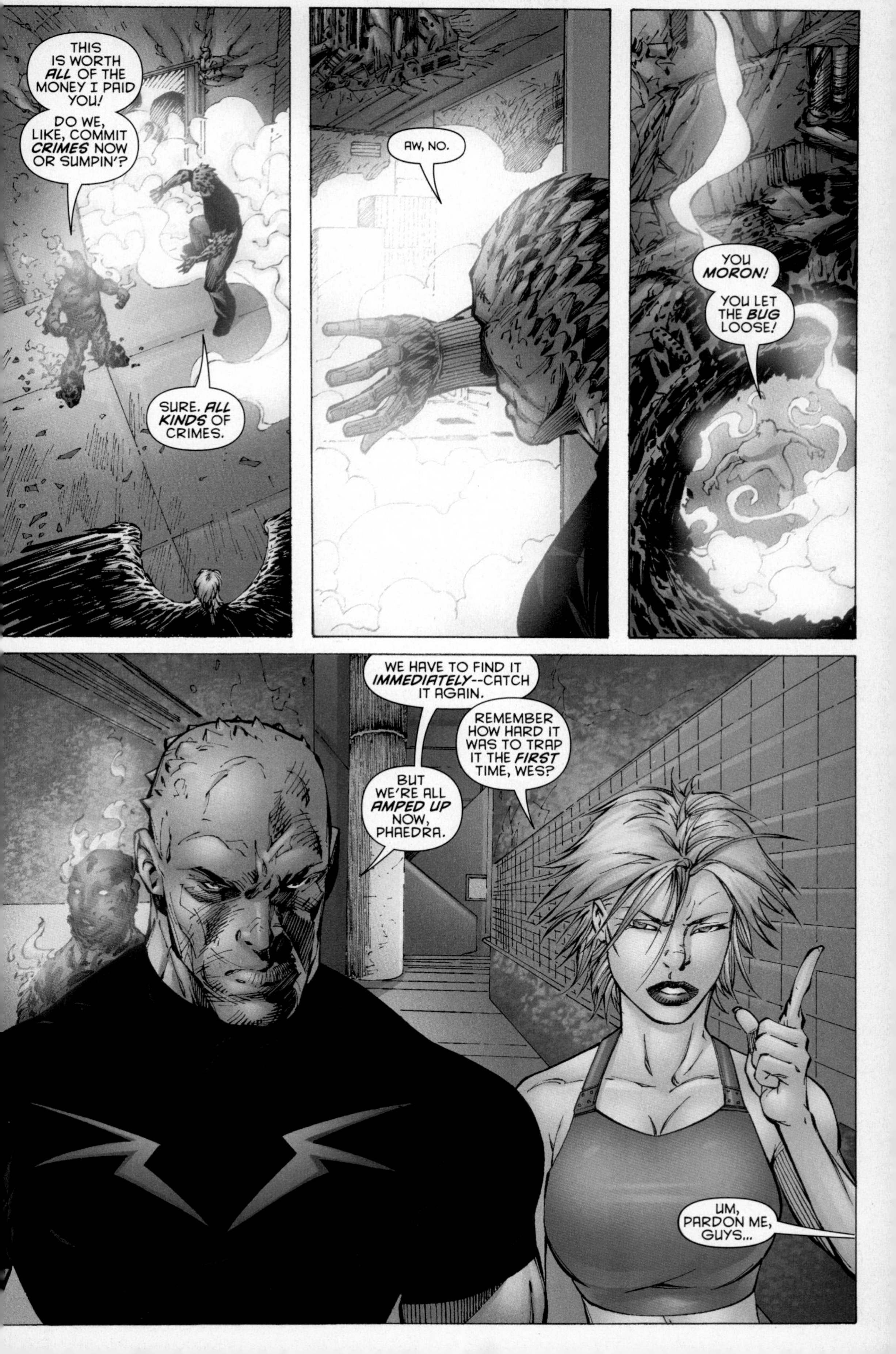
THIS IS WORTH ALL OF THE MONEY I PAID YOU!
DO WE, LIKE, COMMIT CRIMES NOW OR SUMPIN'?
SURE. ALL KINDS OF CRIMES.
AW, NO.
YOU MORON!
YOU LET THE BUG LOOSE!
WE HAVE TO FIND IT IMMEDIATELY--CATCH IT AGAIN.
BUT WE'RE ALL AMPED UP NOW, PHAEDRA.
REMEMBER HOW HARD IT WAS TO TRAP IT THE FIRST TIME, WES?
UM, PARDON ME, GUYS...

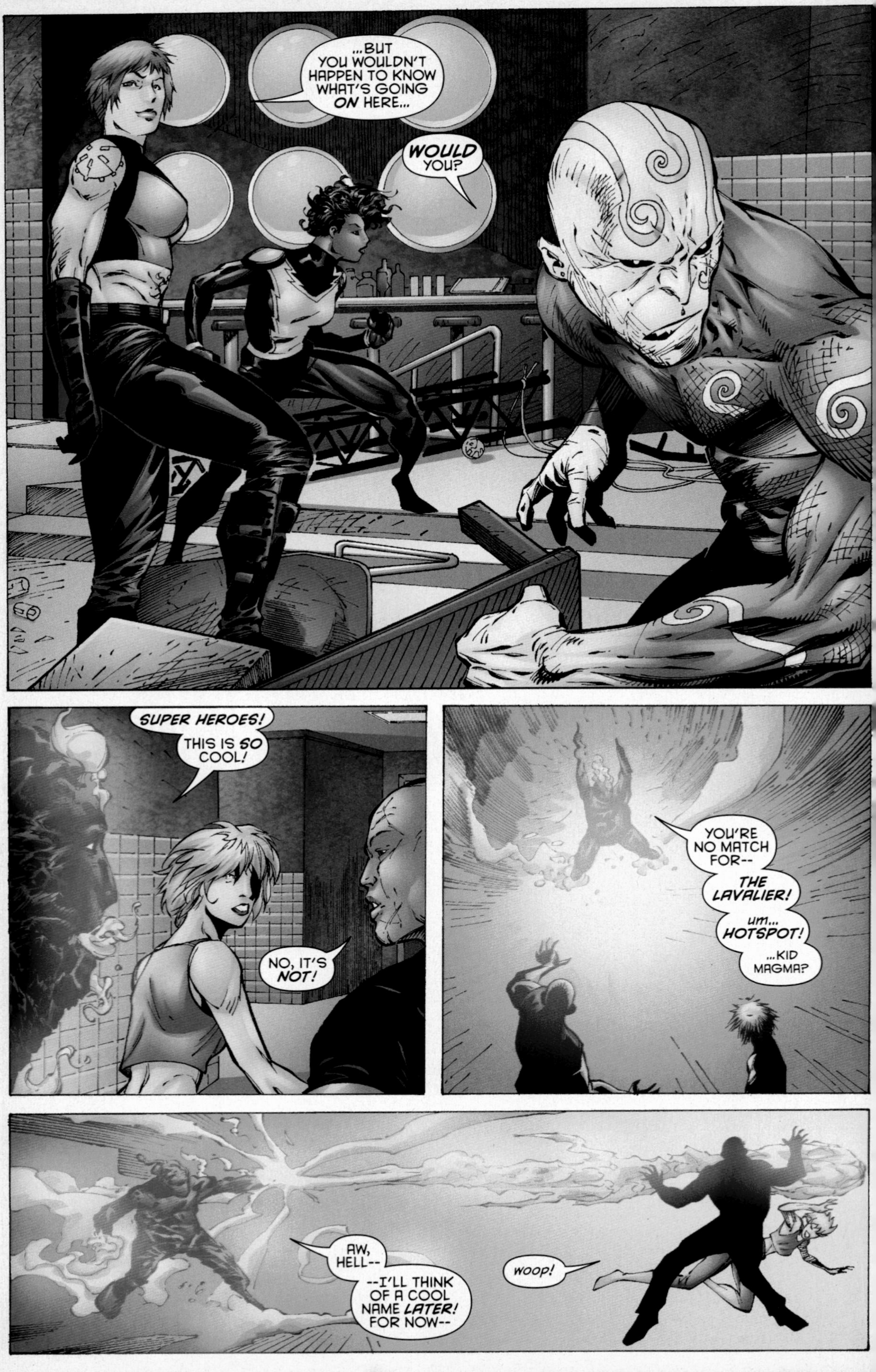
...BUT YOU WOULDN'T HAPPEN TO KNOW WHAT'S GOING ON HERE...
WOULD YOU?
SUPER HEROES!
THIS IS SO COOL!
NO, IT'S NOT!
YOU'RE NO MATCH FOR--
THE LAVALIER!
um... HOTSPOT!
...KID MAGMA?
AW, HELL--
--I'LL THINK OF A COOL NAME LATER! FOR NOW--
woop!

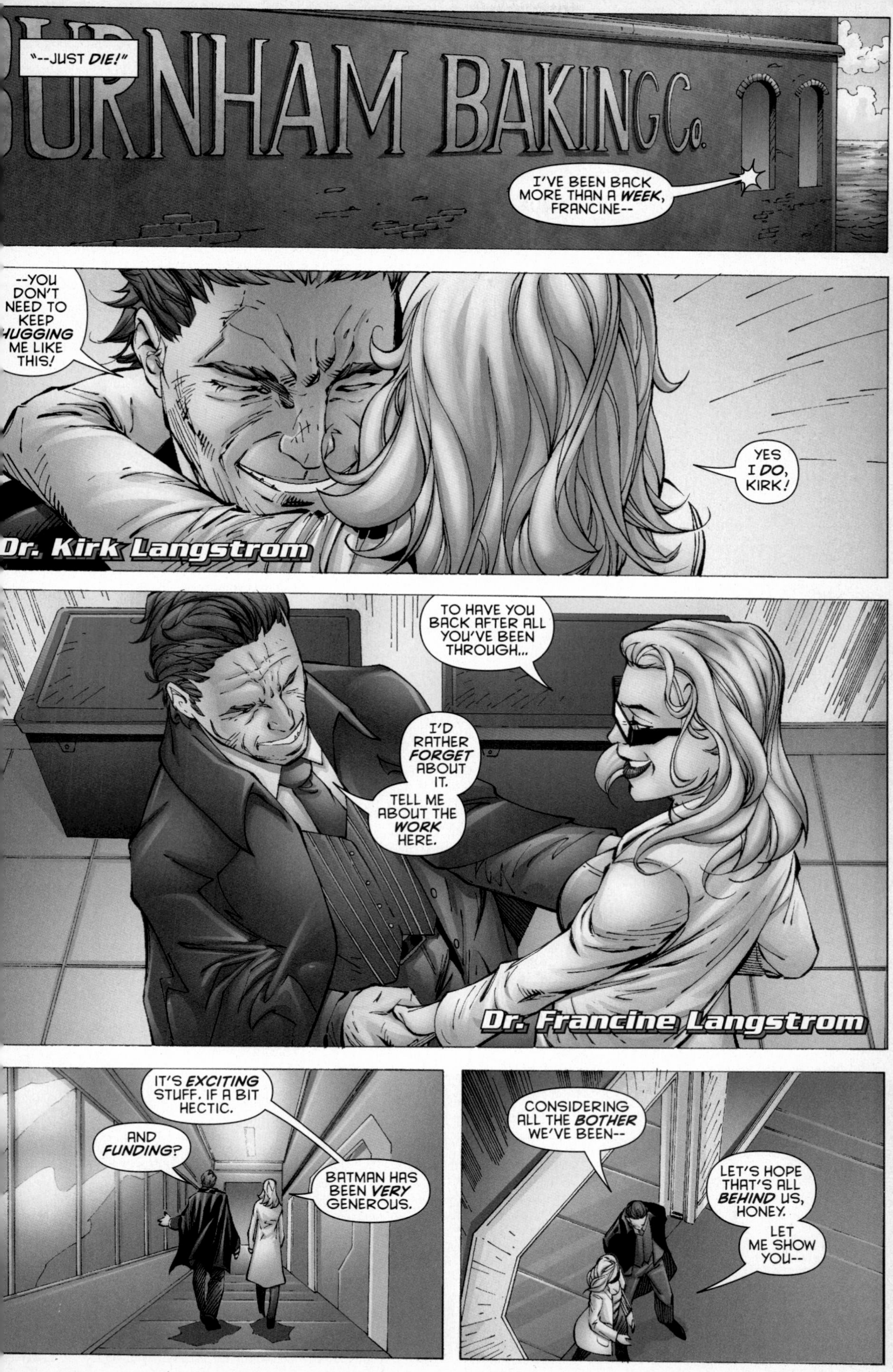
"--JUST DIE!"
BURNHAM BAKING Co.
I'VE BEEN BACK MORE THAN A WEEK, FRANCINE--
--YOU DON'T NEED TO KEEP HUGGING ME LIKE THIS!
YES I DO, KIRK!
Dr. Kirk Langstrom
TO HAVE YOU BACK AFTER ALL YOU'VE BEEN THROUGH...
I'D RATHER FORGET ABOUT IT.
TELL ME ABOUT THE WORK HERE.
Dr. Francine Langstrom
IT'S EXCITING STUFF. IF A BIT HECTIC.
AND FUNDING?
BATMAN HAS BEEN VERY GENEROUS.
CONSIDERING ALL THE BOTHER WE'VE BEEN--
LET'S HOPE THAT'S ALL BEHIND US, HONEY.
LET ME SHOW YOU--

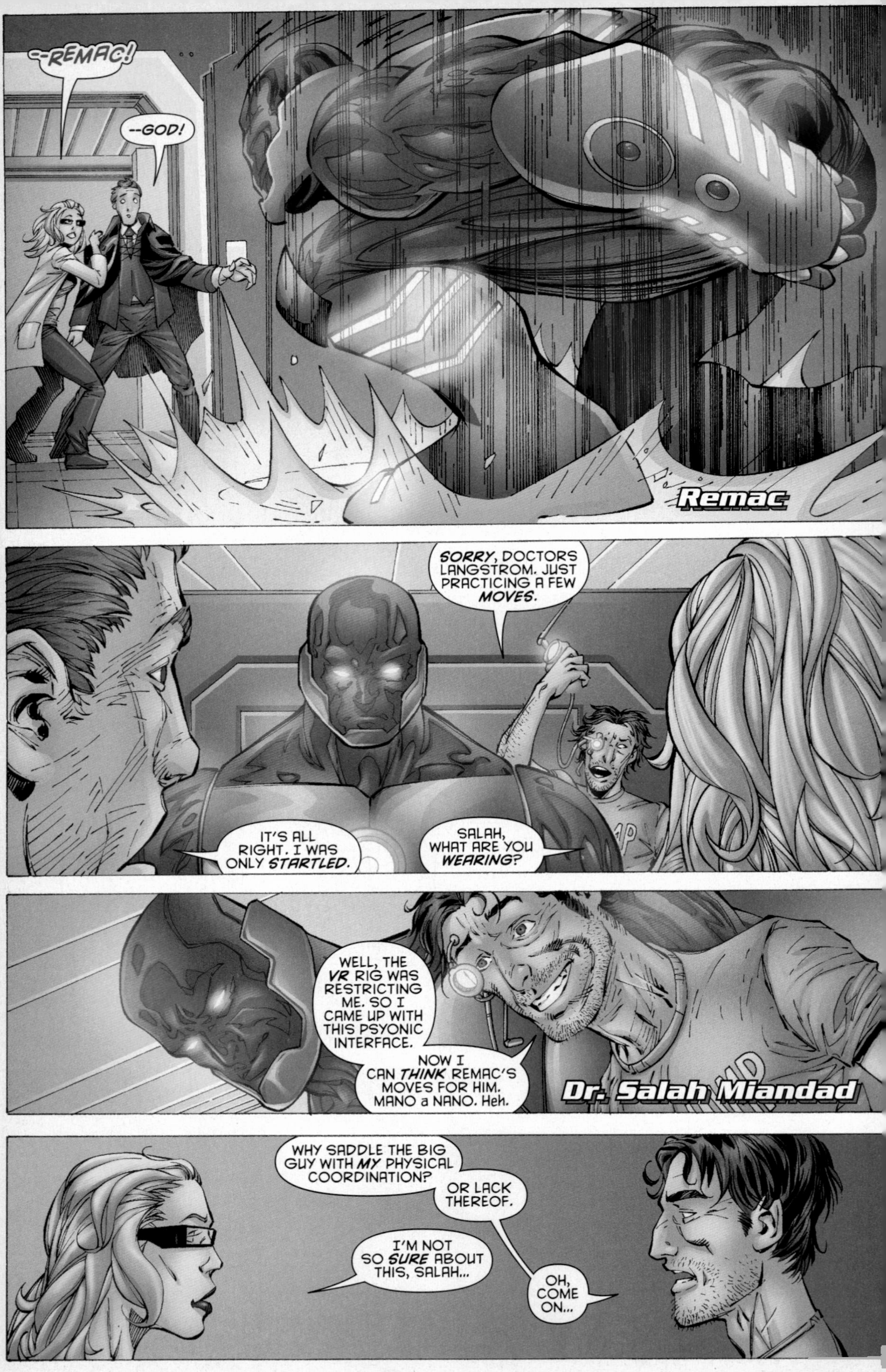
--REMAC!
--GOD!
Remac
SORRY, DOCTORS LANGSTROM. JUST PRACTICING A FEW MOVES.
IT'S ALL RIGHT. I WAS ONLY STARTLED.
SALAH, WHAT ARE YOU WEARING?
WELL, THE VR RIG WAS RESTRICTING ME. SO I CAME UP WITH THIS PSYONIC INTERFACE.
NOW I CAN THINK REMAC'S MOVES FOR HIM. MANO a NANO. Heh.
Dr. Salah Miandad
WHY SADDLE THE BIG GUY WITH MY PHYSICAL COORDINATION?
OR LACK THEREOF.
I'M NOT SO SURE ABOUT THIS, SALAH...
OH, COME ON...

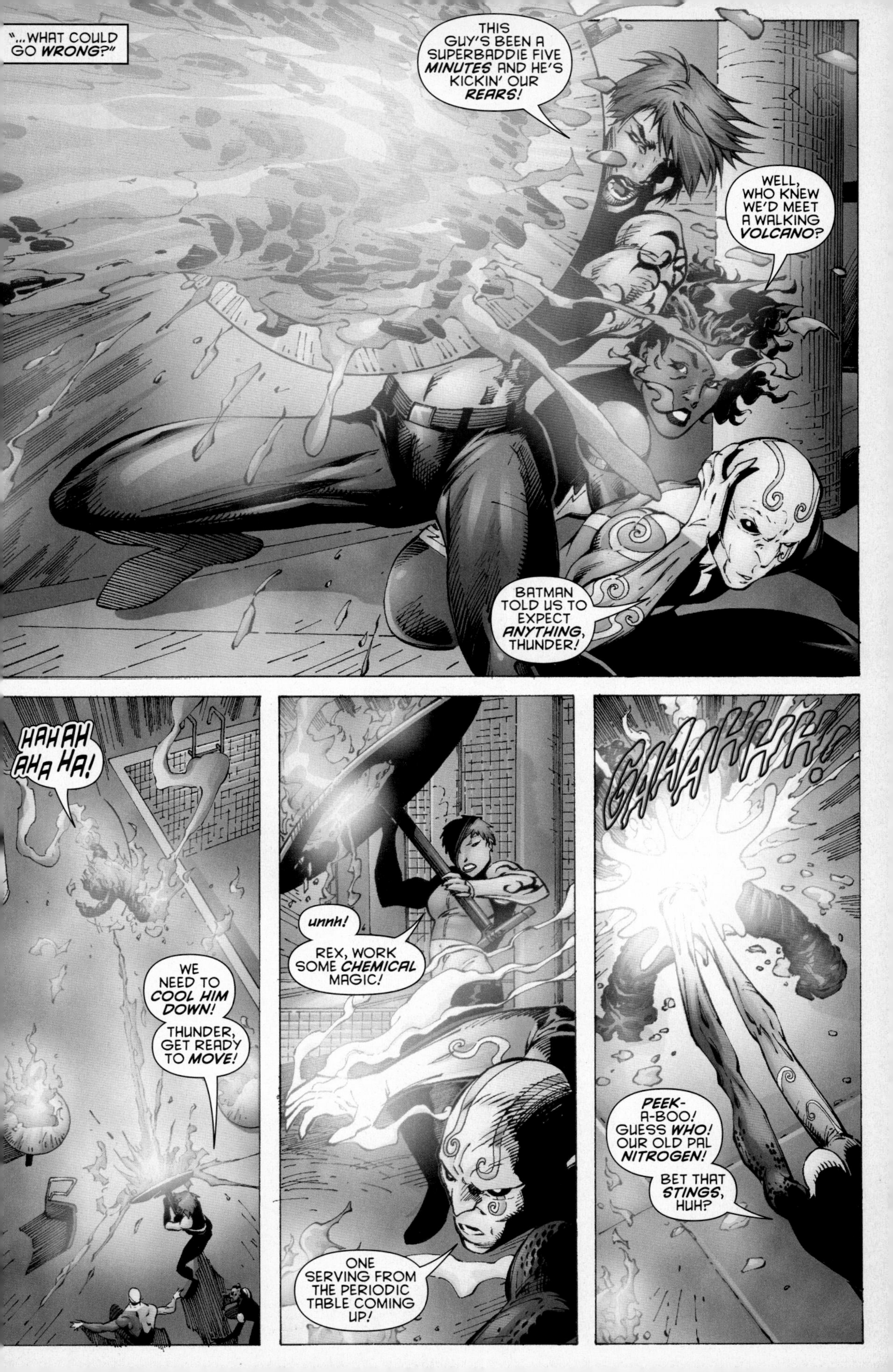
"...WHAT COULD GO WRONG?"
THIS GUY'S BEEN A SUPERBADDIE FIVE MINUTES AND HE'S KICKIN' OUR REARS!
WELL, WHO KNEW WE'D MEET A WALKING VOLCANO?
BATMAN TOLD US TO EXPECT ANYTHING, THUNDER!
HAHAH AHA HA!
WE NEED TO COOL HIM DOWN!
THUNDER, GET READY TO MOVE!
unnh!
REX, WORK SOME CHEMICAL MAGIC!
ONE SERVING FROM THE PERIODIC TABLE COMING UP!
GAAAHHH!
PEEK-A-BOO! GUESS WHO! OUR OLD PAL NITROGEN!
BET THAT STINGS, HUH?

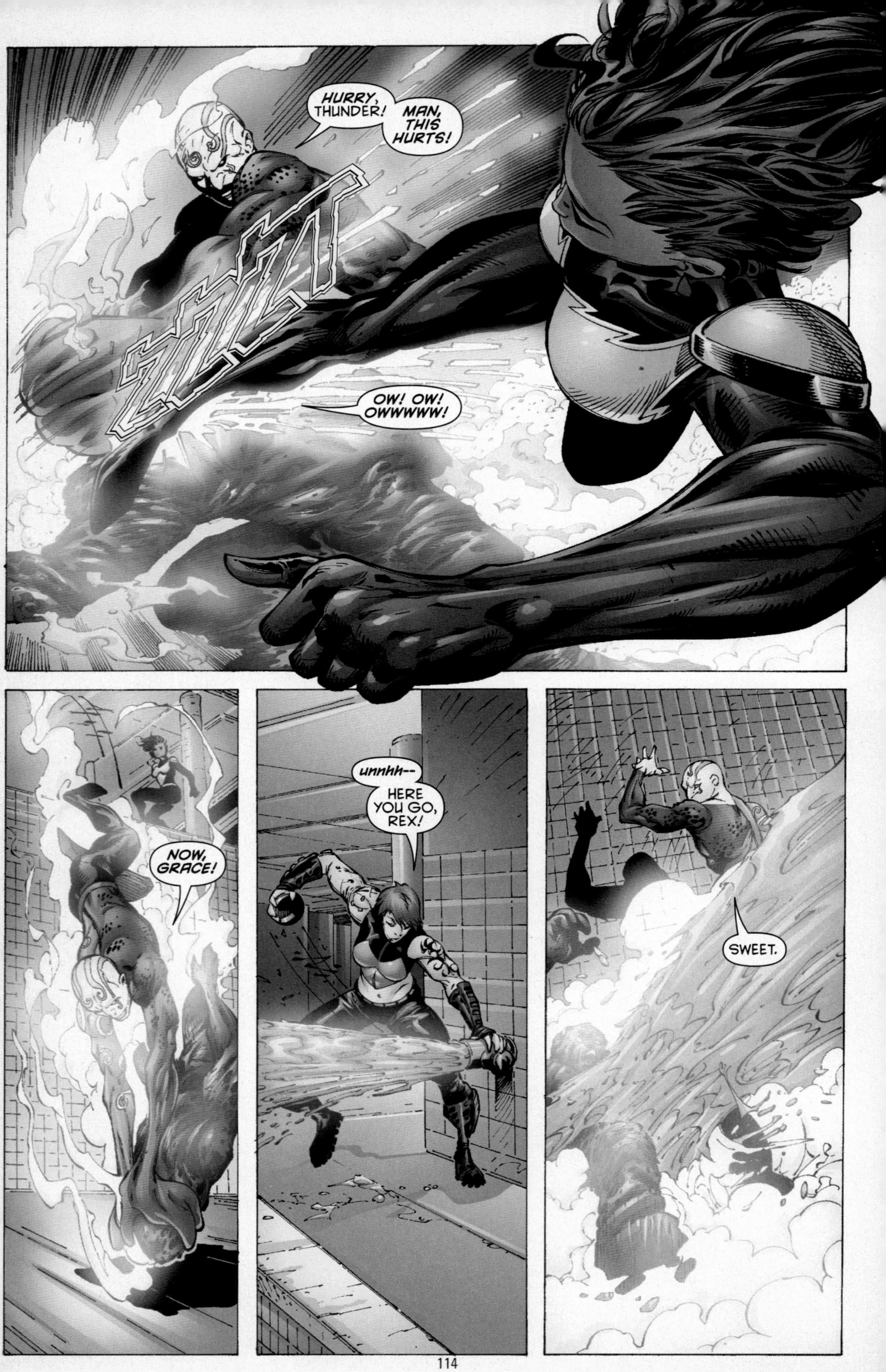
HURRY, THUNDER!
MAN, THIS HURTS!
OW! OW! OWWWWW!
NOW, GRACE!
unnhh-- HERE YOU GO, REX!
SWEET.

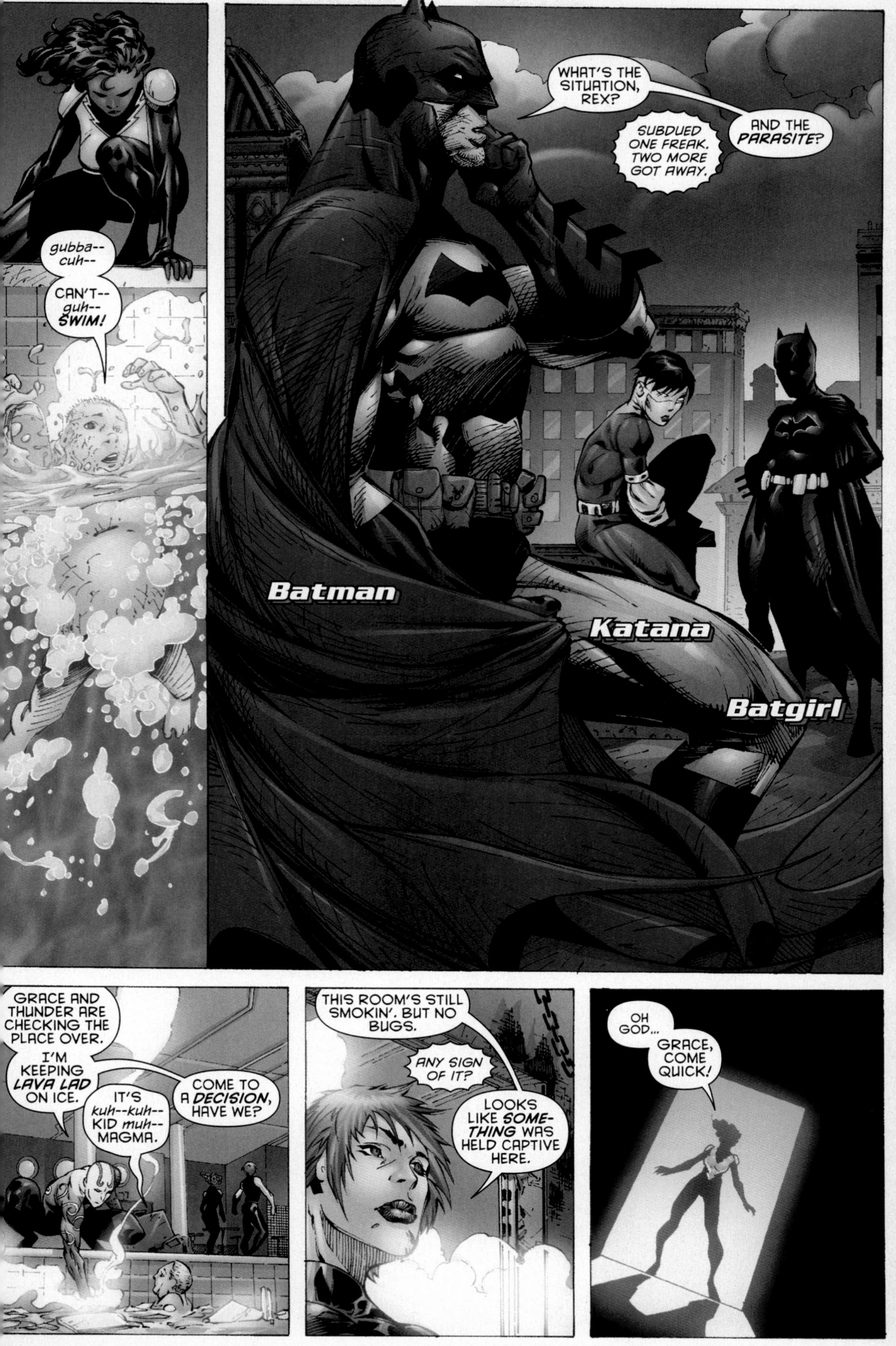
gubba-- cuh--
CAN'T-- guh-- SWIM!
WHAT'S THE SITUATION, REX?
SUBDUED ONE FREAK. TWO MORE GOT AWAY.
AND THE PARASITE?
Batman
Katana
Batgirl
GRACE AND THUNDER ARE CHECKING THE PLACE OVER.
I'M KEEPING LAVA LAD ON ICE.
IT'S kuh--kuh-- KID muh-- MAGMA.
COME TO A DECISION, HAVE WE?
THIS ROOM'S STILL SMOKIN'. BUT NO BUGS.
ANY SIGN OF IT?
LOOKS LIKE SOMETHING WAS HELD CAPTIVE HERE.
OH GOD...
GRACE, COME QUICK!

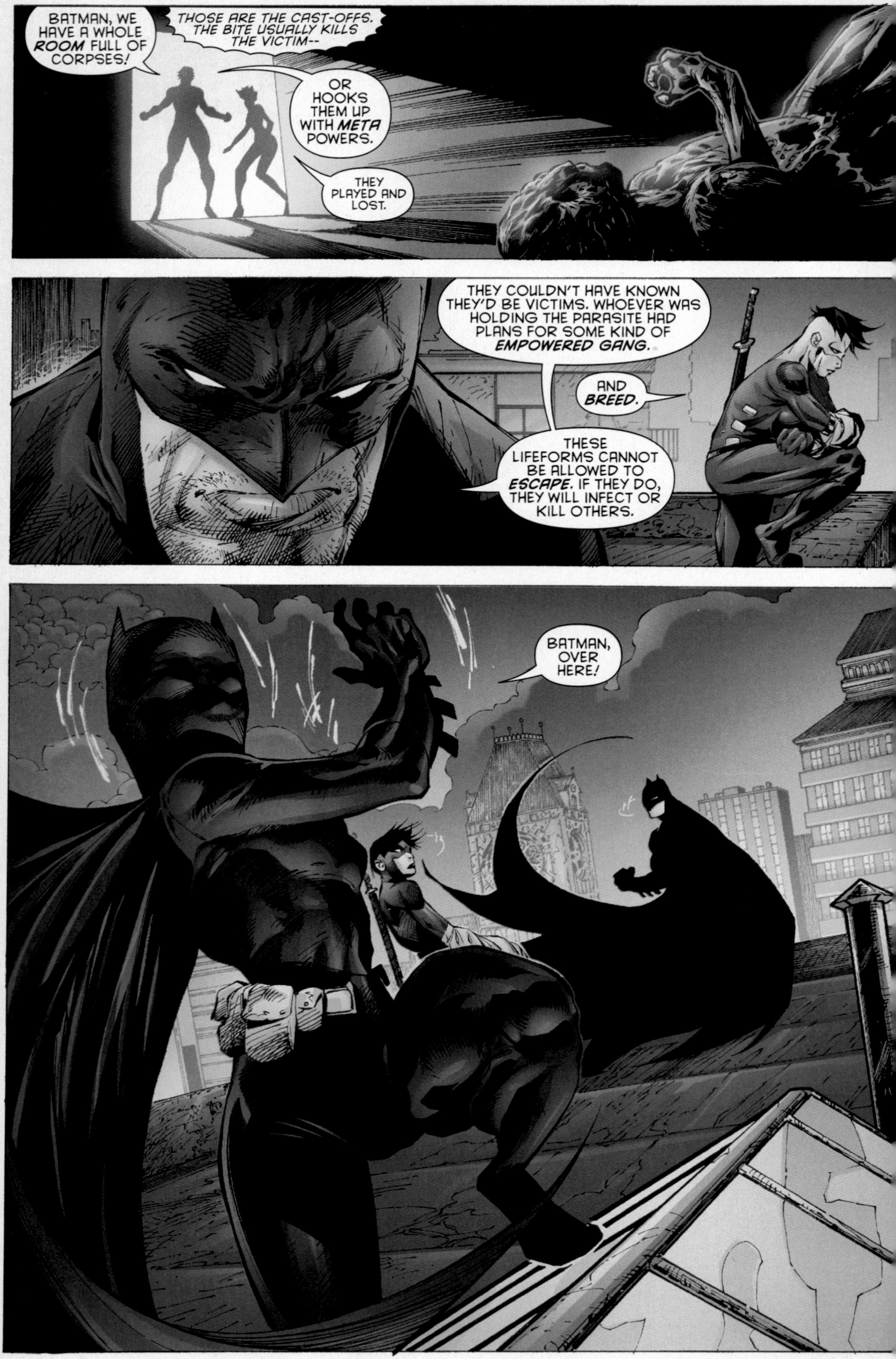

BATMAN, WE HAVE A WHOLE ROOM FULL OF CORPSES!
THOSE ARE THE CAST-OFFS. THE BITE USUALLY KILLS THE VICTIM--
OR HOOKS THEM UP WITH META POWERS.
THEY PLAYED AND LOST.
THEY COULDN'T HAVE KNOWN THEY'D BE VICTIMS. WHOEVER WAS HOLDING THE PARASITE HAD PLANS FOR SOME KIND OF EMPOWERED GANG.
AND BREED.
THESE LIFEFORMS CANNOT BE ALLOWED TO ESCAPE. IF THEY DO, THEY WILL INFECT OR KILL OTHERS.
BATMAN, OVER HERE!

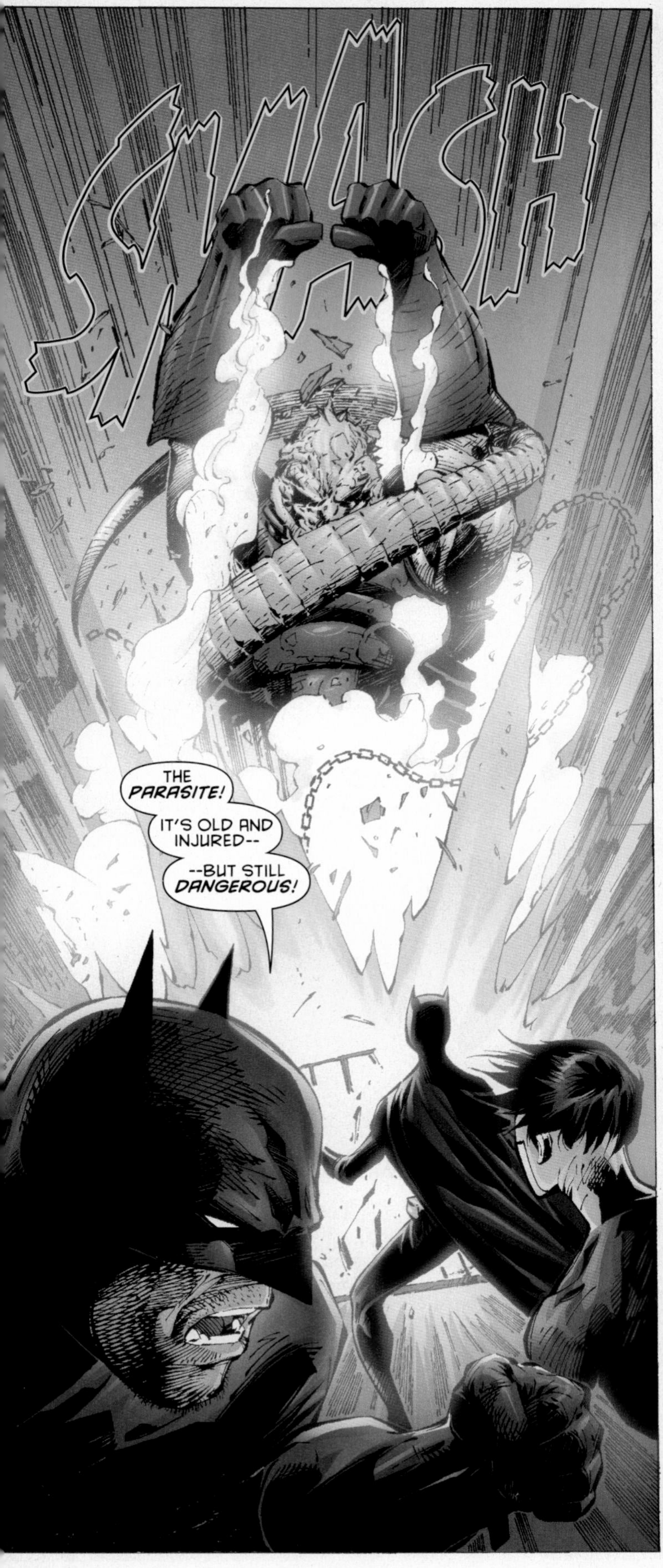
SMASH
THE PARASITE!
IT'S OLD AND INJURED--
--BUT STILL DANGEROUS!

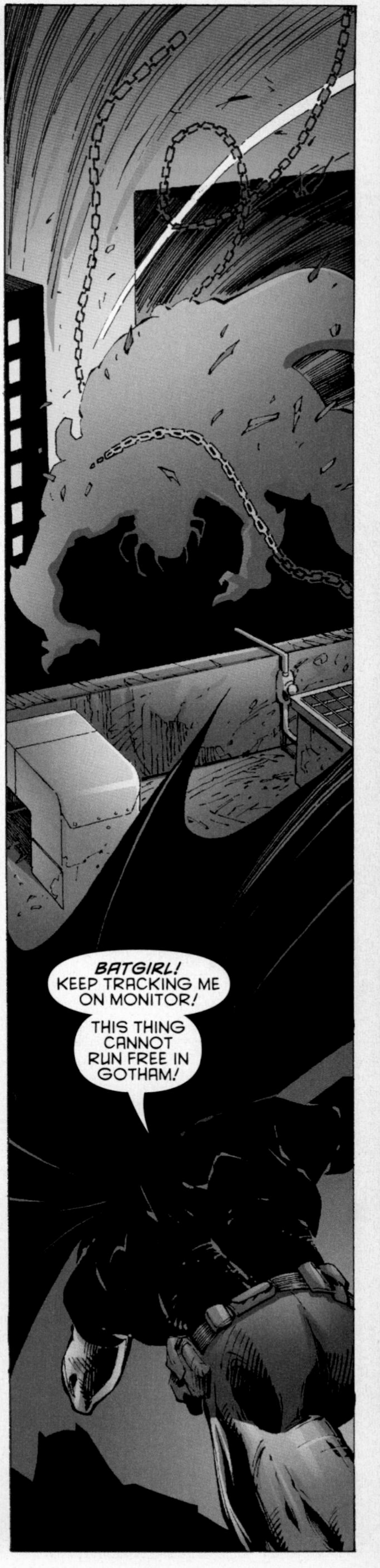
BATGIRL! KEEP TRACKING ME ON MONITOR!
THIS THING CANNOT RUN FREE IN GOTHAM!

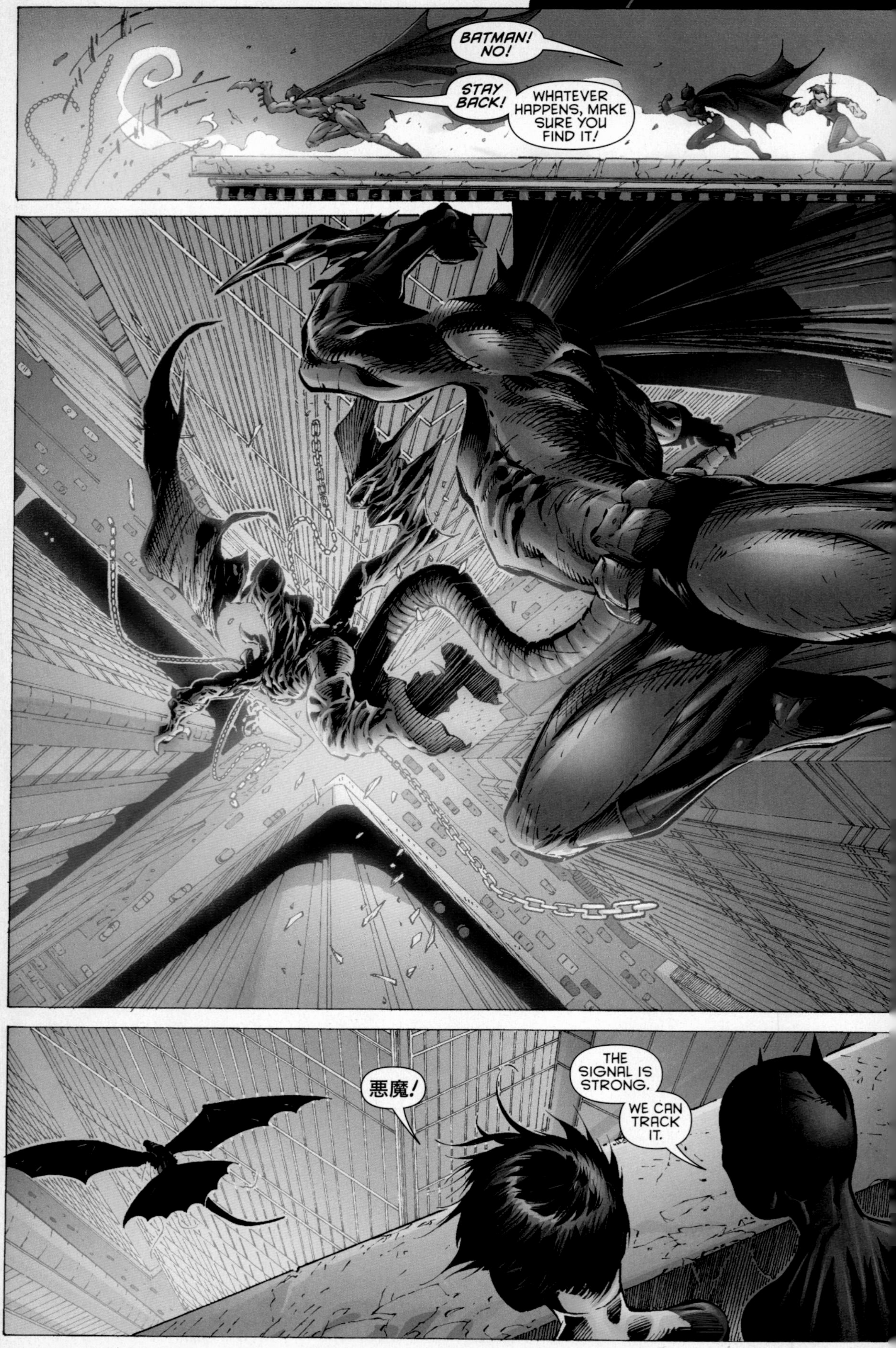
BATMAN! NO!
STAY BACK!
WHATEVER HAPPENS, MAKE SURE YOU FIND IT!
悪魔!
THE SIGNAL IS STRONG.
WE CAN TRACK IT.

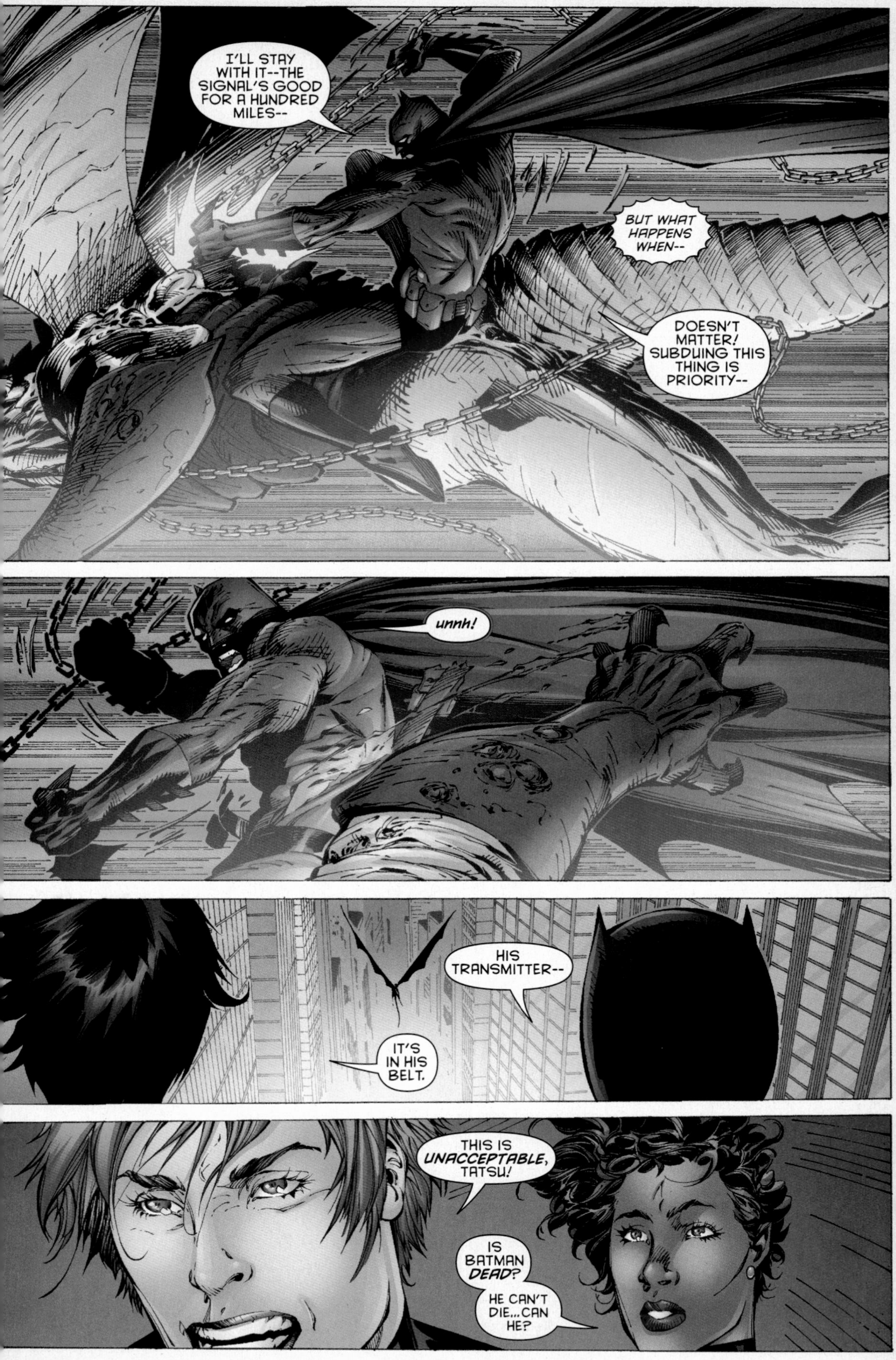
I'LL STAY WITH IT--THE SIGNAL'S GOOD FOR A HUNDRED MILES--
BUT WHAT HAPPENS WHEN--
DOESN'T MATTER! SUBDUING THIS THING IS PRIORITY--
unnh!
HIS TRANSMITTER--
IT'S IN HIS BELT.
THIS IS UNACCEPTABLE, TATSU!
IS BATMAN DEAD?
HE CAN'T DIE...CAN HE?

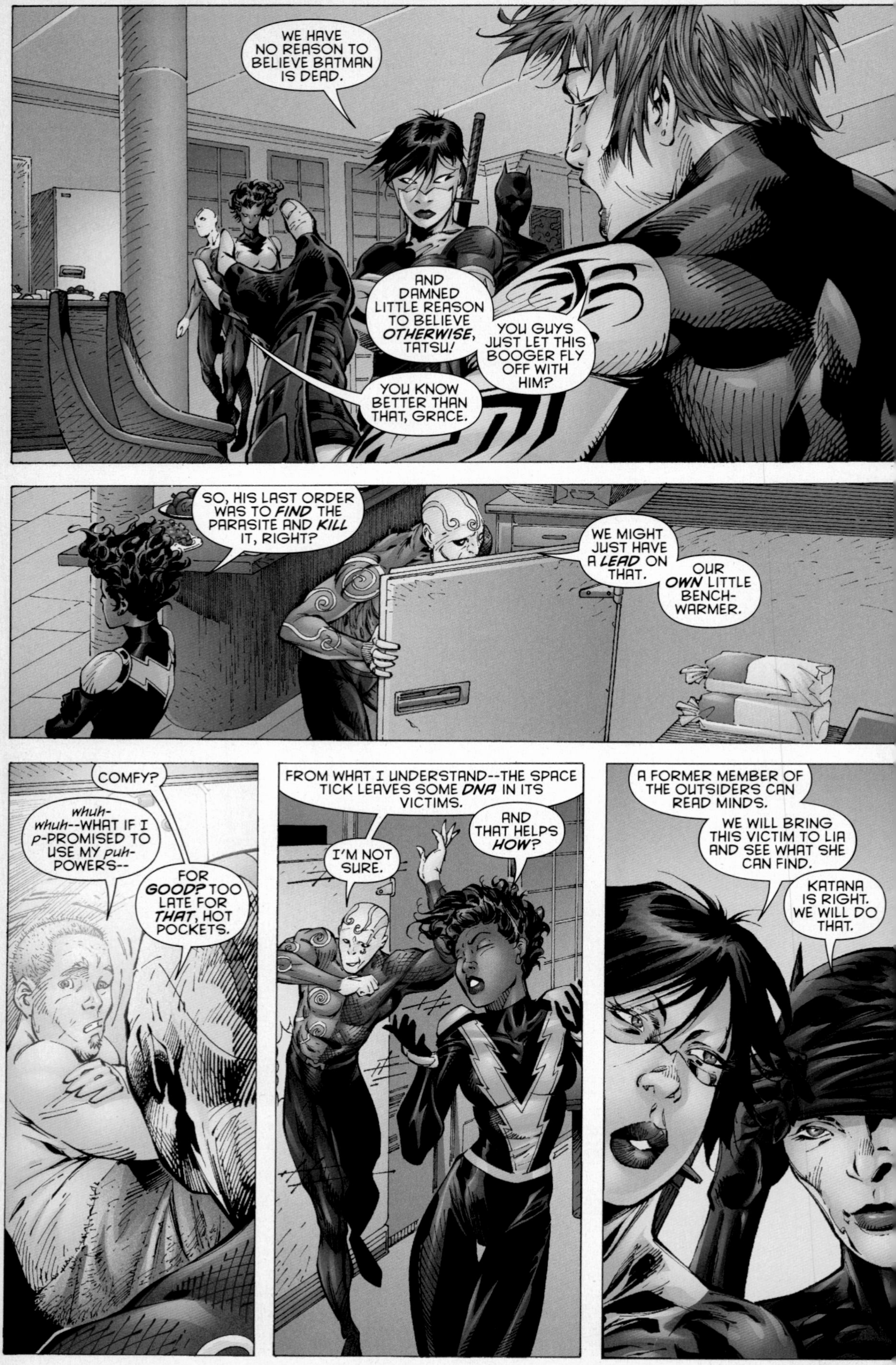

WE HAVE NO REASON TO BELIEVE BATMAN IS DEAD.
AND DAMNED LITTLE REASON TO BELIEVE *OTHERWISE*, TATSU!
YOU GUYS JUST LET THIS BOOGER FLY OFF WITH HIM?
YOU KNOW BETTER THAN THAT, GRACE.
SO, HIS LAST ORDER WAS TO *FIND* THE PARASITE AND *KILL* IT, RIGHT?
WE MIGHT JUST HAVE A *LEAD* ON THAT.
OUR *OWN* LITTLE BENCH-WARMER.
COMFY?
*whuh*-*whuh*--WHAT IF I *p*-PROMISED TO USE MY *puh*-POWERS--
FOR *GOOD?* TOO LATE FOR *THAT*, HOT POCKETS.
FROM WHAT I UNDERSTAND--THE SPACE TICK LEAVES SOME *DNA* IN ITS VICTIMS.
AND THAT HELPS *HOW*?
I'M NOT SURE.
A FORMER MEMBER OF THE OUTSIDERS CAN READ MINDS.
WE WILL BRING THIS VICTIM TO LIA AND SEE WHAT SHE CAN FIND.
KATANA IS RIGHT. WE WILL DO THAT.

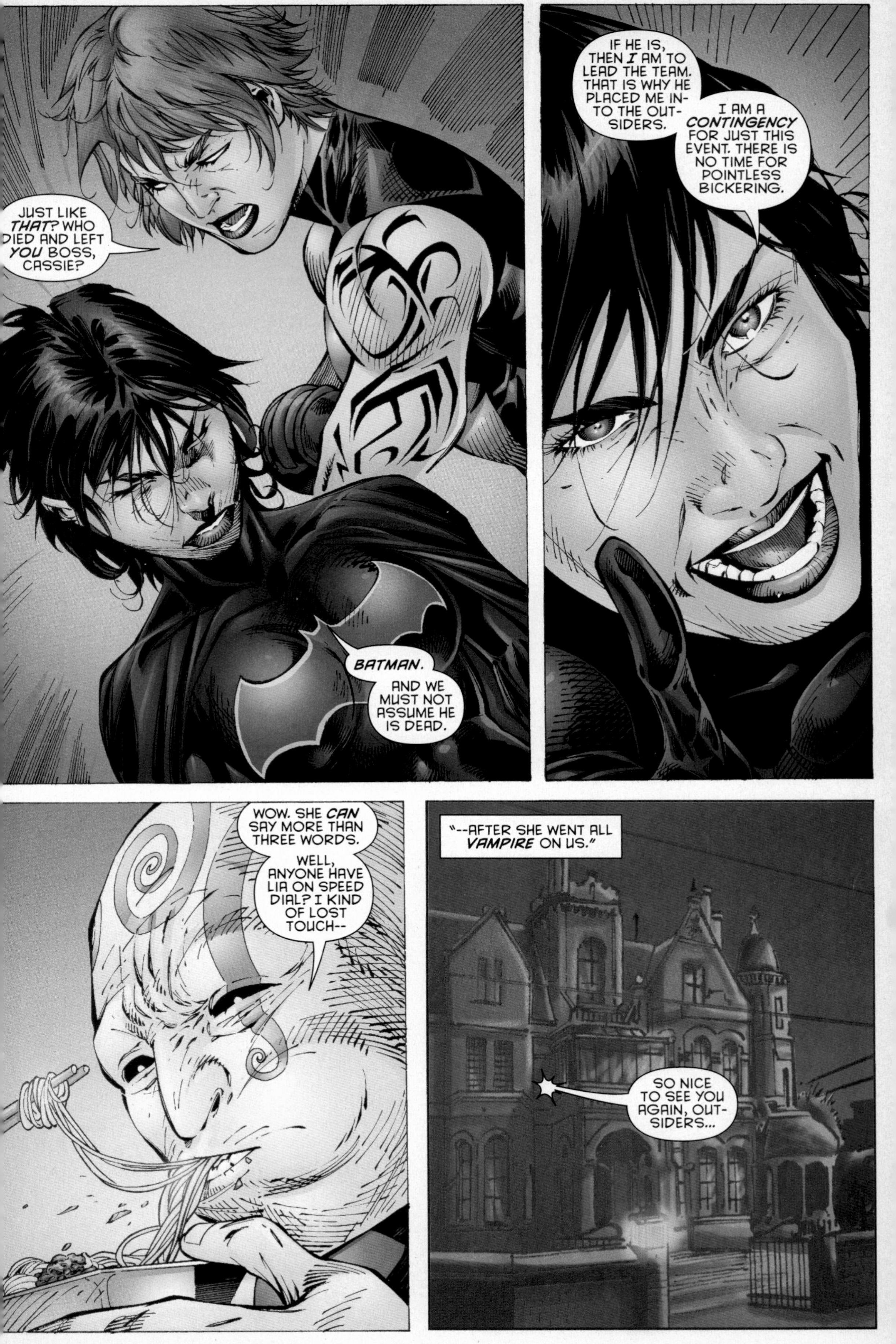

JUST LIKE THAT? WHO DIED AND LEFT YOU BOSS, CASSIE?
BATMAN.
AND WE MUST NOT ASSUME HE IS DEAD.
IF HE IS, THEN I AM TO LEAD THE TEAM. THAT IS WHY HE PLACED ME INTO THE OUT-SIDERS.
I AM A CONTINGENCY FOR JUST THIS EVENT. THERE IS NO TIME FOR POINTLESS BICKERING.
WOW. SHE CAN SAY MORE THAN THREE WORDS.
WELL, ANYONE HAVE LIA ON SPEED DIAL? I KIND OF LOST TOUCH--
"--AFTER SHE WENT ALL VAMPIRE ON US."
SO NICE TO SEE YOU AGAIN, OUT-SIDERS...

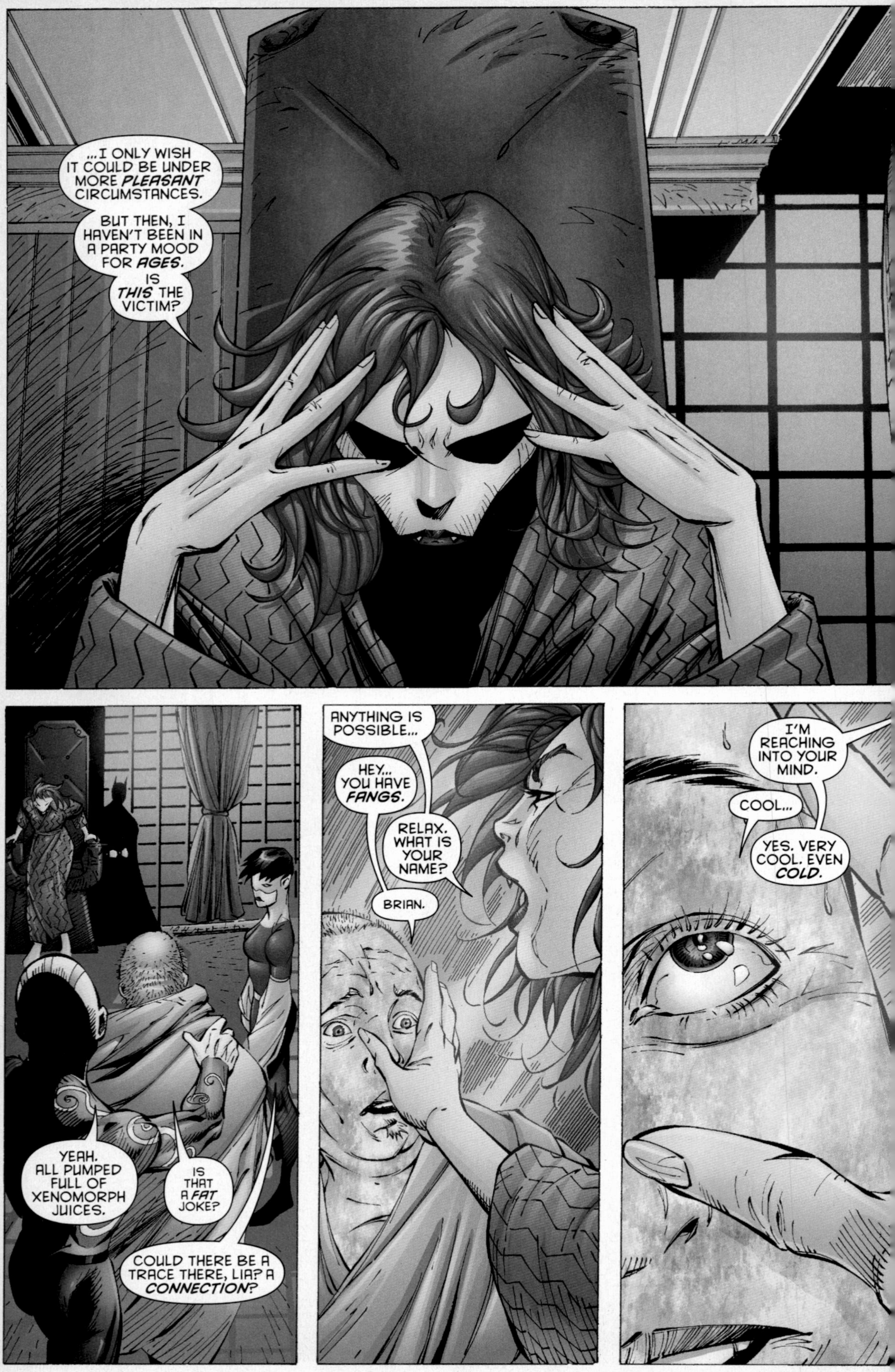
...I ONLY WISH IT COULD BE UNDER MORE PLEASANT CIRCUMSTANCES.
BUT THEN, I HAVEN'T BEEN IN A PARTY MOOD FOR AGES.
IS THIS THE VICTIM?
YEAH. ALL PUMPED FULL OF XENOMORPH JUICES.
IS THAT A FAT JOKE?
COULD THERE BE A TRACE THERE, LIA? A CONNECTION?
ANYTHING IS POSSIBLE...
HEY... YOU HAVE FANGS.
RELAX. WHAT IS YOUR NAME?
BRIAN.
I'M REACHING INTO YOUR MIND.
COOL...
YES. VERY COOL. EVEN COLD.

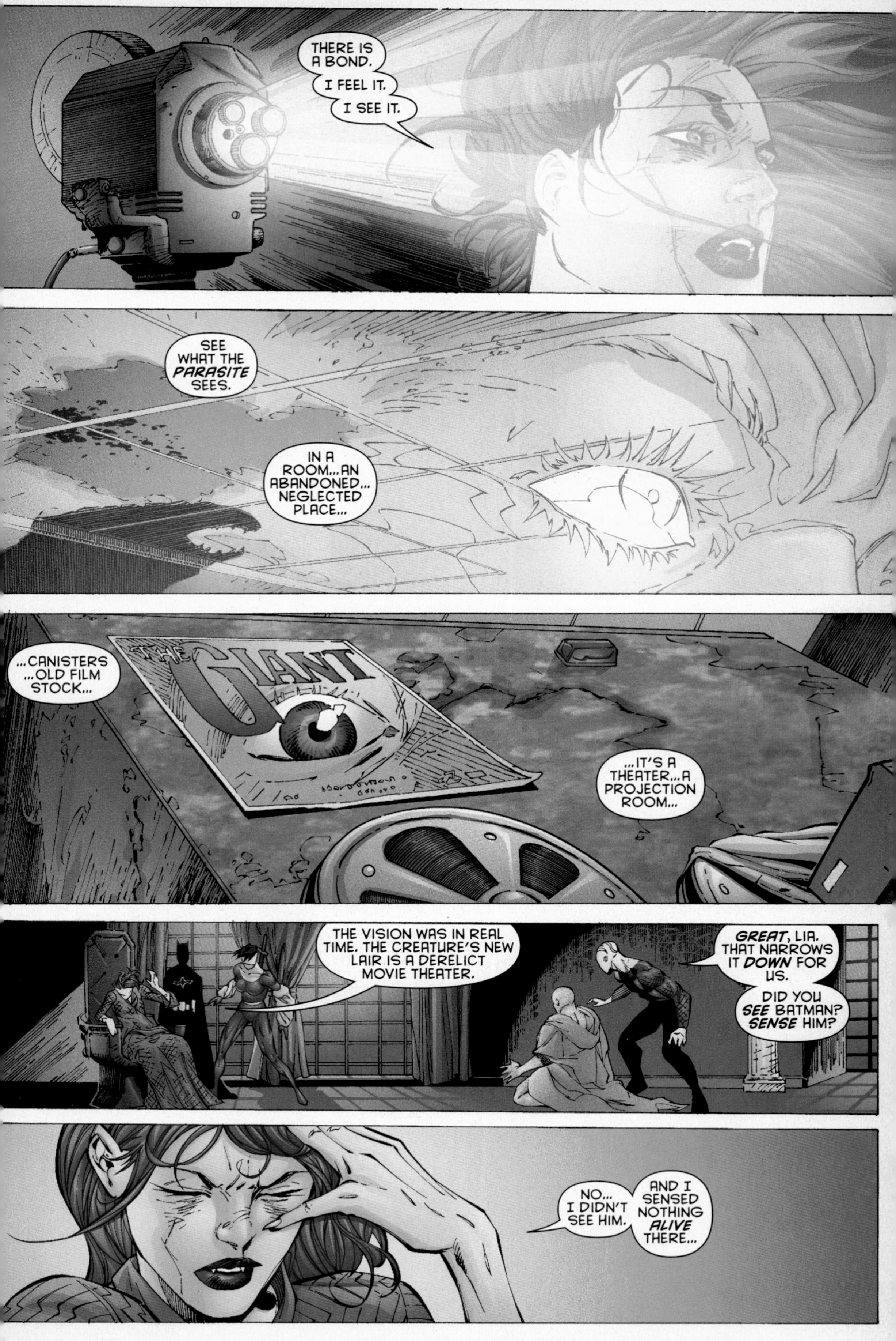
THERE IS A BOND.
I FEEL IT.
I SEE IT.
SEE WHAT THE PARASITE SEES.
IN A ROOM...AN ABANDONED... NEGLECTED PLACE...
...CANISTERS ...OLD FILM STOCK...
THE GIANT
...IT'S A THEATER...A PROJECTION ROOM...
THE VISION WAS IN REAL TIME. THE CREATURE'S NEW LAIR IS A DERELICT MOVIE THEATER.
GREAT, LIA. THAT NARROWS IT DOWN FOR US.
DID YOU SEE BATMAN? SENSE HIM?
NO... I DIDN'T SEE HIM.
AND I SENSED NOTHING ALIVE THERE...

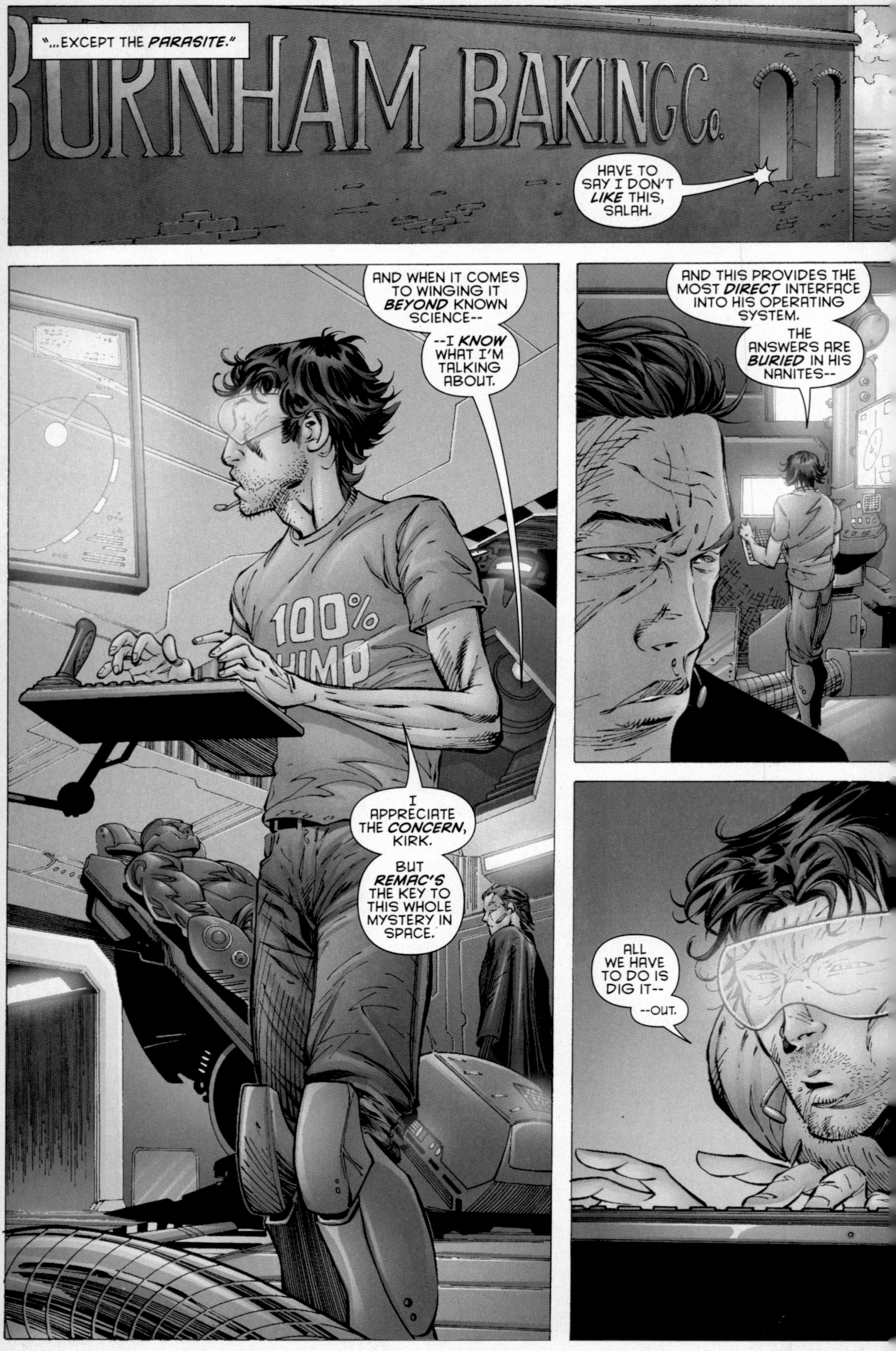
"...EXCEPT THE *PARASITE*."
BURNHAM BAKING Co.
HAVE TO SAY I DON'T *LIKE* THIS, SALAH.
AND WHEN IT COMES TO WINGING IT *BEYOND* KNOWN SCIENCE--
--I *KNOW* WHAT I'M TALKING ABOUT.
I APPRECIATE THE *CONCERN*, KIRK.
BUT *REMAC'S* THE KEY TO THIS WHOLE MYSTERY IN SPACE.
AND THIS PROVIDES THE MOST *DIRECT* INTERFACE INTO HIS OPERATING SYSTEM.
THE ANSWERS ARE *BURIED* IN HIS NANITES--
ALL WE HAVE TO DO IS DIG IT--
--OUT.

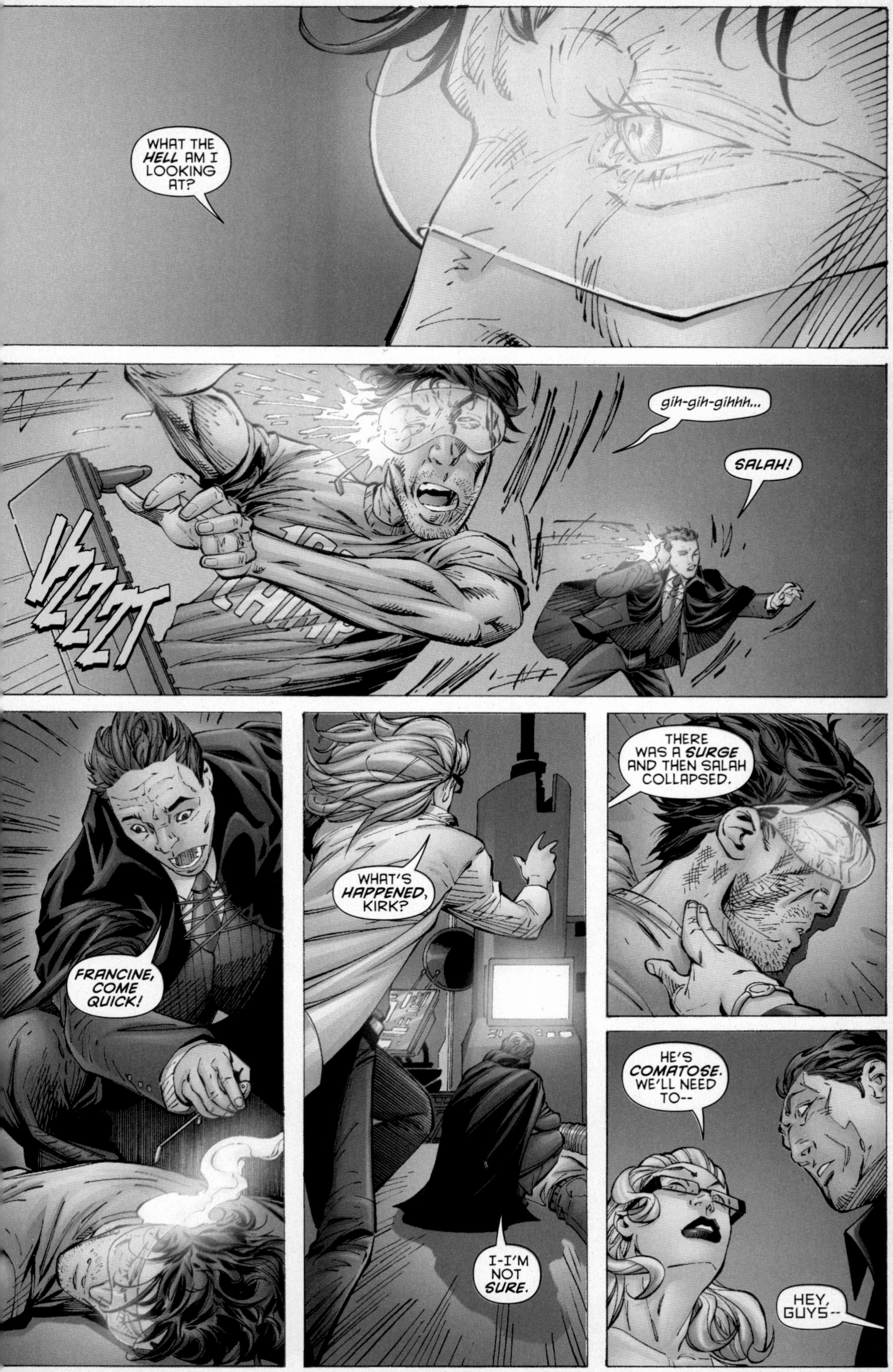
WHAT THE HELL AM I LOOKING AT?
gih-gih-gihhh...
SALAH!
VZZZT
FRANCINE, COME QUICK!
WHAT'S HAPPENED, KIRK?
I-I'M NOT SURE.
THERE WAS A SURGE AND THEN SALAH COLLAPSED.
HE'S COMATOSE. WE'LL NEED TO--
HEY, GUYS--

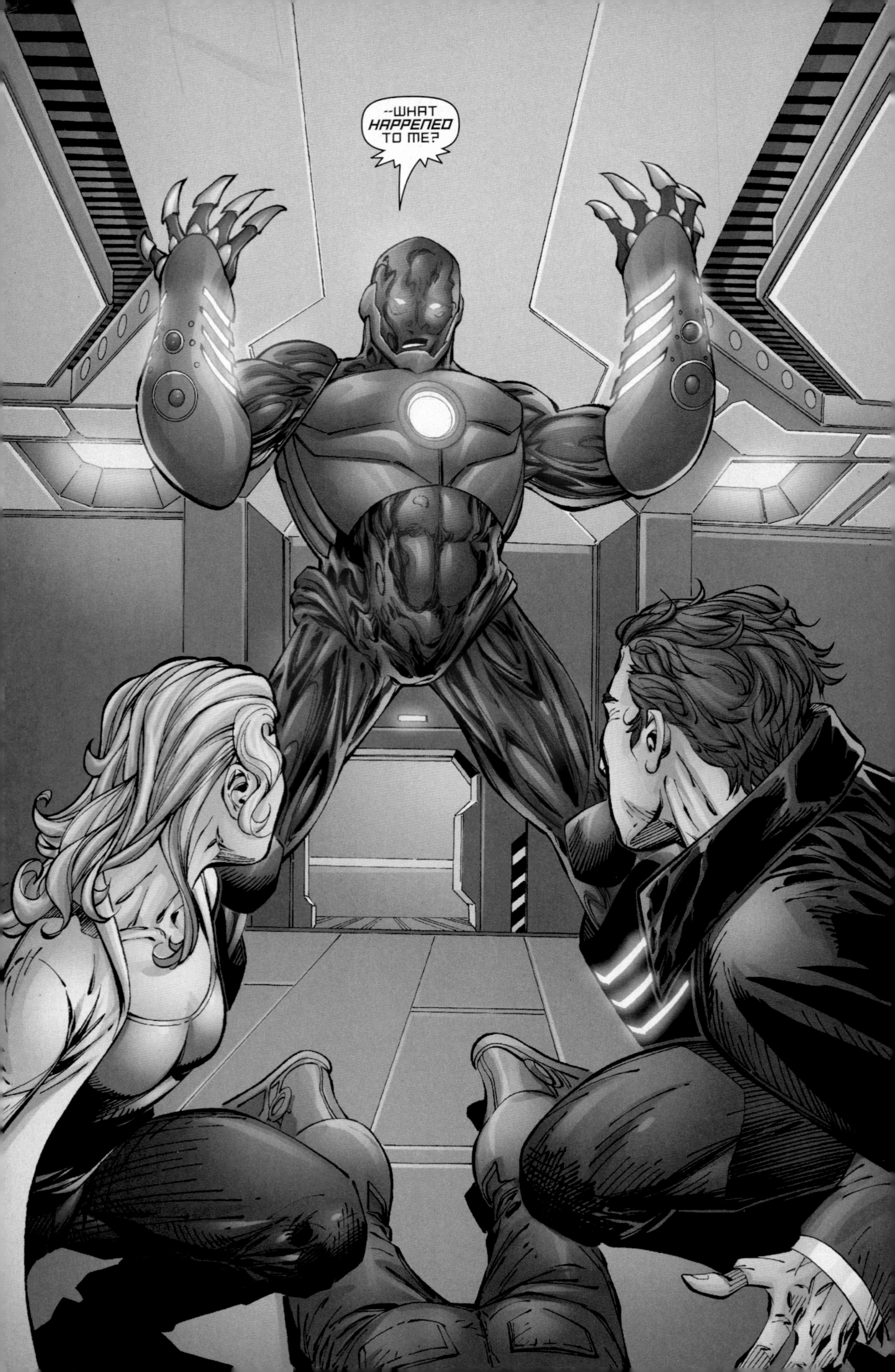
--WHAT HAPPENED TO ME?

# MORE CLASSIC TALES OF **THE DARK KNIGHT**

BATMAN: HUSH
VOLUME ONE

**JEPH LOEB
JIM LEE**

BATMAN: HUSH
VOLUME TWO

**JEPH LOEB
JIM LEE**

BATMAN:
THE LONG HALLOWEEN

**JEPH LOEB
TIM SALE**

BATMAN:
DARK VICTORY

**JEPH LOEB
TIM SALE**

BATMAN:
HAUNTED KNIGHT

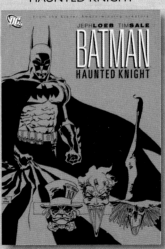

**JEPH LOEB
TIM SALE**

BATMAN:
YEAR 100

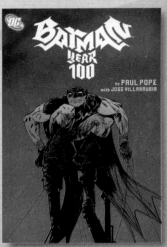

**PAUL POPE**